VALUE MIGRATION

VALUE MIGRATION

*How to Think Several
Moves Ahead of the Competition*

Adrian J. Slywotzky

CORPORATE DECISIONS, INC.

HARVARD BUSINESS SCHOOL PRESS

Boston, Massachusetts

VALUE MIGRATION^{SM} is a proprietary trademark of Corporate Decisions, Inc. and an application for registration of this trademark has been filed with the U.S. Patent & Trademark Office.

Printed in the United States of America
00 99 98 97 96   5 4 3 2

Library of Congress Cataloging-in-Publication Data

Slywotzky, Adrian J.
    Value migration : how to think several moves ahead of the competition / Adrian J. Slywotzky.
        p. cm.
    Includes index.
    ISBN 0-87584-632-7
    1. Corporations—Valuation.   I. Title.
    HG4028.V3S57   1995
    658.4'012—dc20   95-20178
                                                                CIP

The paper used in this publication meets the requirements of the American National Standard for Permanence of Paper for Printed Library Materials Z39.49-1984.

Photo credit: © Bill Miles Photography, Boston, MA.

CONTENTS

Preface

Value Migration describes an outside-in approach to strategy. It begins with the customer and works its way back. It requires thinking from the environment back into the company's capabilities and direction.

This approach originated in 1983, when my partners and I founded Corporate Decisions, Inc. At that time, the consulting field was dominated by an inside-out approach to strategy that focused on cost and total quality management. While these techniques—which persist today—are valuable and necessary, they are also self-limiting. We saw the need to provide a different perspective, one that would help managers and business leaders address the issue of sustained long-term value growth. Our mission required that we spend most of our time with our clients' customers. In looking for value growth, it became increasingly clear that the customer was the key. Developing a strategic understanding of how current and prospective customers change through time could serve as a compass that would point to the best direction for any company seeking to create value growth.

Toward the end of the 1980s, after we had had literally thousands of interactions with customers, we began to observe a recurring pattern across a number of industries. Our clients, the management teams of large, successful companies, found themselves increasingly frustrated in thinking about the future. They were beginning to see the emergence of new competitors that, although starting small, were winning away their most valuable customers. The old rules of success, dictated by market share and scale, were no longer valid. Value was migrating.

Our work for clients in many industries allowed us to develop the framework described in this book. I want to thank those clients who inspired us to look deeper into the phenomenon of Value Migration—to document it, study it, understand it. Their input, feedback, and questions made all the difference in transforming intriguing ideas into pragmatic ways of dealing with the opportunities and challenges of this new game. (The examples in this book come from industries and companies that have experienced, both as beneficiaries and victims, Value Migration. In several cases, we have studied the industries as part of our client work, but we used no private information in developing the examples.)

My partners, and the work they have done for our clients, have been the source of the ideas, insights, and methods explained in this book. Pivotal in the development of these ideas was the work of David Morrison in industries such as chemicals, computers, consumer products, financial services, health care, and telecommunications and Kevin Mundt in industries such as retailing, printing, packaging, and financial services. As founding partners of CDI, their insights helped form the basis for *Value Migration*. The work of the other partners at CDI in a variety of industries deepened our understanding and confirmed our early feeling that we were on to something unique and powerful: Kirk Grosel in pharmaceuticals and health care; John Kania in retailing, printing, and coffee; Fred Linthicum in computing, chemicals, and textiles; Ted Moser in textiles, printed products, consumer goods, and the automotive industry; and Bill Stevenson in retailing, chemicals, and financial services. I would like to thank them all for their continued contributions and support.

I would like to express special thanks to Professor Benson Shapiro of the Harvard Business School. Ben has been not only my best teacher, but also an extraordinary mentor and colleague. Our collaboration on articles and case studies over the past five years laid the groundwork for exploring many of the themes in this book.

Several people contributed significantly to turning these ideas into a book. I would like to thank Ann Hardt, CDI's director of marketing, for initiating the process that put me in touch with a number of editors who helped me shape my ideas and that ultimately led me to the Harvard Business School Press and my editor, Carol Franco. Carol's enthusiasm from the very beginning was a source of reinforcement and encouragement. Carol was extremely helpful in guiding our writing, focusing us on the central themes, and motivating us toward completion. Mark Fischetti, a freelance writer and editor, helped us articulate complex ideas more simply as well as challenging us to keep up the pace of the chapters.

Charlie Hoban was my invaluable collaborator on this project. Without Charlie's managerial and editorial skills and his constant contributions to developing the substance of the book, the project would not have reached completion. He led the internal research efforts, helped shape the structure, managed the rewriting and editing processes, and significantly improved the content of several sections. He maintained the momentum of the project, sheltered me from the storm, and simply made it all happen.

Finally, I would like to thank the staff at CDI who helped shape our ideas and research into a book. The team included John Davidson, Bill Lockhart, Rick Wise, Neil Houghton, John Turner, Colin Boyle, and Steve Glick. Steve's extraordinary editorial talent and thoughtfulness were especially appreciated. These people did the research for the examples of Value Migration used throughout the book. Their energy, insight, and persistence, prevented the project from concluding in 1998, after many billions of dollars of additional value would already have migrated.

PART I

Concepts

Chapter **1**

The Challenge of Value Migration

- What is my company worth today? What will it be worth five years from now?
- Is my business design obsolete? What should my next business design be?
- What five moves will capture the next cycle of value growth in my industry?

FROM 1984 TO 1994, IBM and DEC lost $55 billion in market value, while Microsoft, Intel, EDS, and Novell were gaining $80 billion.[1] The reallocation of value within the computing industry was rapid and dramatic.

During the same decade, the operating margin of Nucor, a steel minimill operator, was double that of the large integrated steelmakers. The $5 billion market value Nucor created exceeded that of U.S. Steel, a company whose revenue was twice as great as Nucor's. Over two decades, the integrated steel producers saw their value migrate to four very different business designs, one of which was Nucor's minimill model.

From 1983 to 1994, while the market value of many traditional department stores stagnated or declined, the value of five new retailing business designs grew by more than $100 billion.

Do these examples constitute a pattern of mismanagement on a vast scale? Hardly. They do, however, constitute a pattern that reflects *the increasing obsolescence of traditional business designs, a pattern of accelerating* VALUE MIGRATION℠ *away from increasingly outmoded*

3

business designs toward others that are better designed to maximize utility for customers and profit for the companies.

It is widely acknowledged that products go through cycles, from growth through obsolescence. It is not as well recognized that business designs also go through cycles and reach economic obsolescence. Customer priorities—the issues that are most important to them, including and going beyond the product or service offered—have a natural tendency to change; business designs tend to stay fixed. When the mechanism that matches the company's business design to the structure of customer priorities breaks down, Value Migration begins to occur.

Value Migration and Business Design

Value migrates from outmoded business designs to new ones that are better able to satisfy customers' most important priorities. A business design is the totality of how a company selects its customers, defines and differentiates its offerings, defines the tasks it will perform itself and those it will outsource, configures its resources, goes to market, creates utility for customers, and captures profit. It is the entire system for delivering utility to customers and earning a profit from that activity. Companies may offer products, they may offer technology, but that offering is embedded in a comprehensive system of activities and relationships that represents the company's business design.

Consider, for example, Nucor, a company prospering in the otherwise "unattractive" steel industry. Nucor's primary focus has been on producing non-flat rolled steel for construction applications. Its customers demand a minimum acceptable quality level and otherwise care about only one thing—*price*. The company built its entire business design around this central reality of its customers' priorities. The conventional explanation of Nucor's success is the use of low-cost technology and raw materials (electric ore furnaces that melt scrap steel). But this is only one element of its business design equation. The other critical components include *low-cost* (rural) and *flexible* (nonunion) labor and *low overhead* (a headquarters staff of 23 for a business with revenue of $3 billion). Through employing an explicit policy of reliance on external sources of technology, Nucor has also achieved a low-cost position in R&D and technical development. All in all, it employs a superb business design to serve a customer group whose decision-making system is dominated by price.

The migration of value can affect a specific division of a company, a whole company, or even a whole industry as customers make de facto choices about the business designs that best meet their needs. Value can migrate to other business designs within an industry or flow out of one industry and into another with designs better configured to satisfy customer priorities and make a profit. In the steel example, value flowed within the industry from the integrated steelmakers to alternative business designs like those of Nucor and the next-generation integrated mills in Japan and Korea. At the same time, value was flowing out of the entire steel industry as companies in other industries—plastic and aluminum—emerged with business designs that better satisfied the emerging priorities of specific customer groups such as canners and auto manufacturers.

Measuring the Value Migration Process

To understand the direction and magnitude of Value Migration, it is helpful to establish a set of metrics. *Market value* is a measure of the power of a business design to create and capture value. It is defined as the capitalization of a company (shares outstanding times stock price plus long-term debt) at any given time. Like all financial numbers, market value has its flaws: it is volatile, it is subject to the ups and downs of the stock market, it is affected by quarterly earnings-per-share changes and analysts' recommendations. But as the sum total of the analysis and opinion of thousands of investors and investment professionals, it is the best measure of a business design's economic power and future earning potential. The market value of a large, diverse company with multiple business designs is the aggregation of each individual design's ability to perform in the market.[2] Throughout this book, the market value of companies, groups of companies, and entire industries will be used as a pragmatic proxy for value creation and decline.

The success of a business design in creating value is independent of company size. Quite often, new, small firms introduce the most innovative and powerful business designs and capture most of their industry's value growth. The power of a business design, therefore, must be measured by the amount of *market value relative to the size of the company*. Taking revenue as a useful estimation of size, the ratio of market value to revenue allows us to compare the value creation power of business designs of different scales. For example:

	1994 Revenue*	1994 Market Value*	Market Value/Revenue
U.S. Steel	$6.1	$4.1	.7
Bethlehem	$4.8	$2.7	.6
Inland	$4.5	$2.3	.5
Nucor	$3.0	$5.0	1.7

*in billions

Thus, while all these companies manufacture steel, and U.S. Steel, Bethlehem, and Inland are much larger, Nucor's more powerful business design has succeeded in creating significant, sustained value growth.

If revenue is a measure of the mass of a business design, the market value/revenue ratio is an indicator of the profitability and momentum of that design. Is it capturing value? Is it losing value? At what rate? The ratio is a feedback mechanism that indicates how a design is valued relative to its competitors—and to investors' options in other industries.[3]

The ability to measure the relative power of business designs provides a diagnostic for understanding the direction and velocity of Value Migration. These metrics are also extremely useful in understanding how the economic power of a business design changes.

The Three Phases of Value Migration

A business design can exist in only one of three states with respect to Value Migration: *value inflow, stability,* or *value outflow*. These states describe its relative value-creation power, based on its ability to satisfy customer priorities better than competitors do and thus to earn superior returns.

VALUE INFLOW. In inflow, the initial phase, a company starts to absorb value from other parts of its industry because its business design proves superior in satisfying customers' priorities. Typically, a competitor that triggers a Value Migration shift employs a new business design responding to customer priorities that established competitors had failed to see or had neglected. Value flows into such designs because of their superior economics and the emerging recognition of their power to satisfy customers. Microsoft and EDS are among companies experiencing the value inflow phase.

STABILITY. The second phase, stability, is characterized by business designs that are well matched to customer priorities and by overall competitive equilibrium. This phase can vary in length, depending on the rate at which customer priorities change and new, more effective business designs emerge. During the stability phase, value remains in the business design, but expectations of relatively moderate future growth prevent new value from flowing to the company. Companies such as DuPont are in this phase.

VALUE OUTFLOW. In outflow, the third phase, value starts to move away from an organization's traditional activities toward business designs that more effectively meet evolving customer priorities. Although the value outflow may start slowly, it accelerates as a business design becomes increasingly obsolete. Companies like DEC and Bethlehem Steel have seen value flow out of their business designs.

As a business design passes through the three phases of Value Migration, the task of management changes. At each stage, managers must make dramatically different kinds of moves, and those moves determine winners and losers in the Value Migration process.

Value Migration and the Game of Business

Value Migration is not new. Value migrated away from Ford's vertically integrated, single-car-focused business design toward GM's price-laddered business design in the 1920s. It moved from grocery store chains to supermarkets in the 1930s, from fragmented merchandisers to national catalogue sales in the 1890s (Sears), and to national merchandise chains in the 1920s (Sears again). Business designs and customer priorities have been moving into and out of phase for decades, creating and destroying fortunes in the process.

In the 1990s, however, the rate of Value Migration has increased in many industries. The game of business has changed. Throughout the 1960s and 1970s, it was like football, with short bursts of intense activity called plays. If you executed the plays well, you gained ground, scoring profit. But you did a great deal of standing around and waiting, which created a manageable pace. Scale and market share were all-important, in most cases assuring profitability. Large-scale, large-market-share players like IBM, DEC, and U.S. Steel prospered.

Sometime in the 1980s, the game changed, the pace quickened. It was no longer football. It was basketball. Scale and market share were important, but they provided less protection than formerly. You had to be fast as well as big. You had to pay attention all the time or the other side would score on you—repeatedly. This change was signaled by a mid-1980s flurry of articles. Speed. Speed. Speed. That was what mattered. Consumer electronics and PC software firms were frequently cited as effective examples of organizations that focused on getting new products to market as quickly as possible. The fastest companies prospered.

Even as industry was learning and polishing its "basketball" skills, however, the game was being redefined. Between 1987 and 1993, the rules that determined success and profit changed in a radical and disquieting way. New players like Microsoft and TeleCommunications, Inc., succeeded by employing new, nonspeed-based skills such as identifying and owning the strategic control points in their industry. Mass and market share no longer offered the profitability and value protection they once provided. In fact, newcomers could use your mass against you, convincing customers that what you were good at, what you were big at, was increasingly irrelevant to their future priorities. In industry after industry, leaders stumbled. From steel to computing to air travel to retailing, much smaller newcomers with innovative business designs preempted most of their industry's value growth (see Figure 1-1).

Several factors are driving this decline of the giants:

1. Customers in many industries, becoming more sophisticated, are less apt to pay high prices simply to stay with a known brand if a less-costly, high-quality substitute is available.

FIGURE 1-1   TRADING PLACES

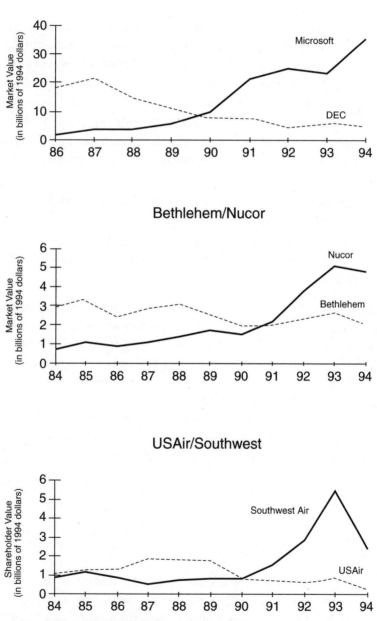

DEC/Microsoft

Bethlehem/Nucor

USAir/Southwest

SOURCE: CDI Value Growth Database.

2. The competitive circle has expanded. An increasing number of international and entrepreneurial competitors with innovative business designs can provide superior utility to customers.

3. Advances in technology, which have made it far easier to produce lower-cost substitutes for many manufactured goods and components, have created more cross-category competition than existed in the past (e.g., steel versus plastic versus aluminum).

4. Many businesses are becoming less scale intensive. Lower-cost information, extensive use of outsourcing, and a trend away from manufacturing intensity are all reducing barriers to entry.

5. Improved customer access to information has lowered switching costs.

6. New competitors have easier access to capital, removing the advantage of a large existing cash flow associated with an established position.

The decline of IBM's value was the symbolic event that signaled the transition to the new game. Unexpected by—and bitterly disappointing to—many investors, it didn't seem to make any sense. In 1983, many considered IBM the best-managed company in the world.[4] In 1987, it earned its peak profits as a corporation. By 1992, however, its market value had fallen by more than 70 percent from 1983—$70 billion of market value had been lost.

What was most disorienting to executives and investors was the growing disproportion between size and value.

	1994 Revenue*	1994 Shareholder Value*
IBM	$64	$43
Microsoft	$5	$36

*in billions

How could Microsoft, a company with $5 billion in revenue, be worth nearly as much as IBM, a company with *twelve times* as much revenue? While executives realized that the nature of competition was changing, they had difficulty articulating what the change was.

An in-depth and candid conversation with an extremely successful pharmaceutical executive during 1994 captures the point:

Just a few years ago I felt differently about the future. I knew what my three most important moves were. I knew precisely what we had to accomplish to grow the company's value. Restructure and fine-tune the sales force. Bring disciplined economic thinking to the marketing investment process. Create a genuine dialogue between marketing and R&D, and work to reduce R&D development time—by a lot.

Today I'm in a different predicament. I don't know what my top three moves are. There might be five moves that matter. Or one. I can sense that the rules have changed. But I can't put my finger on what they are. It feels awful.[5]

He was right. The rules have changed. The frequency and speed of Value Migration have turned the task of management into chess. Execution and speed are still important, but neither is adequate anymore. Managers must learn new rules for this new game. New questions must be asked: Speed toward what? Where will I be allowed to make a profit? Where will the value in the industry be? What *new* core competencies do I need? What do I *need* to be good at? What moves do I need to make to capture the next cycle of value growth?

Chess is a game of moves and countermoves. Assessing the differential power of each piece and each square on the board, the player conceives of and then executes a series of moves that creates a strategically advantageous position—for a while. Then, as the board changes, advantage has to be created again. It is a complex game. The manager must look at his or her situation—the board, the pieces, the competitor's pieces, the customer's pieces—and ask: What's my next move? What series of moves must I make to achieve and maintain value growth?

The new game of business has been so disorienting to executives and investors because it is different, founded on a new and fundamentally different set of assumptions about what is important:

From	*To*
Revenue	→ Profit
Share of Market	→ Share of Market Value
Product Power	→ Customer Power
Technology	→ Business Design

Such a shift is the departure point for understanding Value Migration. Different factors, requiring a different mind-set, are what count today. The mind-set must focus on understanding where the value in an industry resides today and where it will move in the future.

As customers' priorities change, value can shift away from activities—be they manufacturing, marketing, sales, or specific types of R&D; from products—say, buggy whips, slide rules, mainframes, or basic materials; from customer segments—such as regulated, profitless segments in home health care; and from entire business designs—for example, integrated broad product line manufacturers, traditional department stores, hub-and-spoke airlines, or proprietary computer systems. Activities, skills, and business designs that were once highly rewarded fade into economic irrelevance.

It's not that the value disappears, but that it moves—rapidly at times—toward new activities and skills and toward new business designs whose superiority in meeting customer priorities makes profit possible. In some cases, customers are the only beneficiaries of Value Migration because the industry's current business designs offer customers high utility but fail to recapture any of that utility in the form of pricing and profits. (Environmental remediation, for example, provides great utility to customers, but the industry's business designs have not succeeded in recapturing any significant level of profitability for shareholders.) While the Value Migration process creates huge economic vulnerability, it also opens large new spaces of opportunity.

A Strategic Perspective on the Customer

The first task of top management is to understand the direction and velocity of Value Migration in its industry. Without such understanding, diligent effort by thousands of excellent workers is misdirected. Even worse, thousands of jobs and billions of dollars of market value are placed at unnecessary risk. Enormous resources are invested without producing any returns, and opportunities for new value growth are lost.

To meet the challenge of Value Migration, managers must ask, Where in my industry will I be *allowed* to make a profit? How is that changing? What is driving the change? What can my organization do about it?

Beneath these questions lies a more fundamental inquiry: What is the changing pattern of what customers need, want, and are willing to pay for, and what business designs respond most effectively to this changing pattern? To answer these questions, managers must first create a moving picture of their customer—one that is strategic, accurate, and actionable.

Customers make choices based on their priorities. Those choices develop potential value for the businesses from which they buy. At any given time, the pattern of those choices allocates value to various business designs. As customers' priorities change and new designs present customers with new options, they make new choices. They reallocate value. These changing priorities, and the way in which they interact with new competitors' offerings, are what trigger, enable, or facilitate the Value Migration process.

One of the most powerful examples of Value Migration occurred in the computer industry, where value moved away from business designs built around proprietary mainframes and minicomputer systems to business designs built around workstations and PCs and finally to those built around the elements of computing functionality that customers most value—processor chips, operating systems, low-cost distribution, communications software (network software, groupware), and systems integration. What matters to customers, what makes them willing to pay a premium, shifted as their previous priorities were met, as they became more sophisticated, and as new priorities emerged or better ways of satisfying old priorities were developed. Customers' choices have redistributed value from outmoded business designs—those of IBM and DEC—to others that deliver more utility to customers and profit to shareholders—those of Intel, Microsoft, Novell, EDS, and others (see Figure 1-2).

Changing customer priorities, then, trigger the Value Migration process, creating opportunities for new business designs. Incumbents frequently ignore or overlook such opportunities, presenting significant openings for newcomers.

Understanding customer priorities requires understanding more than just customer needs. *Needs* refer to the benefits and features of products that customers would like to buy. Most market research focuses on needs. But what customers really want is the result of a complex decision-making system. They are influenced by a number of external factors—regulation, commoditization, the offerings of

FIGURE 1-2   COMPUTER INDUSTRY VALUE MIGRATION

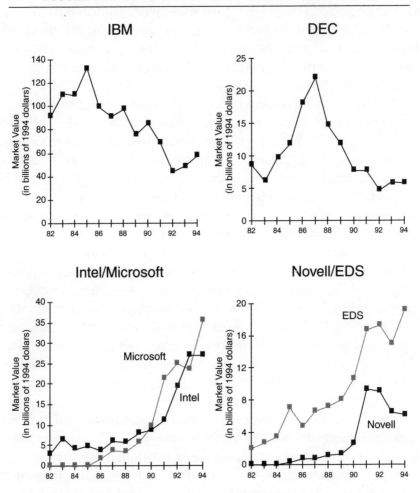

Within a decade, IBM and DEC lost $80 billion in value while new specialized business designs gained $80 billion.

SOURCE: CDI Value Growth Database.

new and existing suppliers, technology, and factor costs. These factors are processed through the refractory lens of a customer's system of decision making, presenting a set of clear, well-defined customer priorities. Figure 1-3 illustrates this effect. Understanding the decision-making system and resulting priorities constitutes a strategic understanding of the customer.

FIGURE 1-3   THE CUSTOMER'S DECISION-MAKING SYSTEM

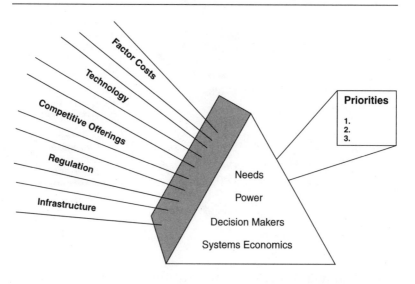

External forces have an impact on customer needs, economics, and decision making. What emerges are new customer priorities.

Analyzing customers' decision-making systems makes it possible to interpret what customers say they want. It also helps decipher what customers are not saying and to anticipate what they will say in the future. Needs analysis describes what *products* the customers want. Priorities analysis determines what *business design* creates the greatest utility for customers and profit for the provider (see Figure 1-4). For example, in the business forms market, customers describe their needs as high-quality products, quick-cycle delivery, and low price. Extensive market research reveals how well various suppliers meet these criteria. A priorities analysis, however, will reveal something completely different. It will show that the top priority for many large customers is to accomplish the transition from paper to electronic forms. The implications for the business designs of form suppliers are clear and profound.

In business-to-business settings, understanding a customer's decision system means knowing as much (or more) about the customer's business as its management does. It requires a level of relationship well beyond the traditional sales rep–purchasing agent,

FIGURE 1-4   THE MECHANISM OF VALUE MIGRATION

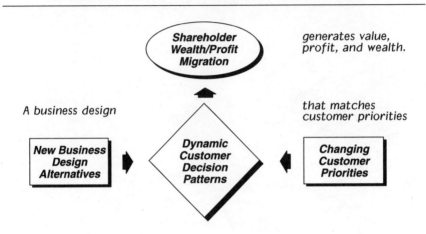

supplier-customer structure. It means understanding functionality, systems economics, customer power, and the customer's entire decision-making system. In a consumer setting, it is understanding the underlying behaviors, utilities, and functionalities that *create* the expressed needs.

These dynamic customer decision systems are usually distinct for discrete segments of the market. Understanding customers at the level of their decision-making system is difficult but worth the effort because it allows you to recognize customer priorities and how they change. Once you have achieved this level of understanding, you can anticipate Value Migration. By perceiving what underlies those priorities, what causes things to be important, you can formulate a customer priorities *trajectory*. Figure 1-5 illustrates the changing priorities of the steel industry's automotive customers, which created major opportunities for new, plastics-based business designs. A management team that has a clear and accurate picture of the unfolding trajectory of customer priorities enjoys substantial advantage in anticipating and preempting Value Migration by building the right business design to meet tomorrow's customer priorities.

Institutional Memory

When a company is established, it crafts its business design around its customers. In fact, customers are the focus of everything the

FIGURE 1-5   CHANGING CUSTOMER PRIORITIES

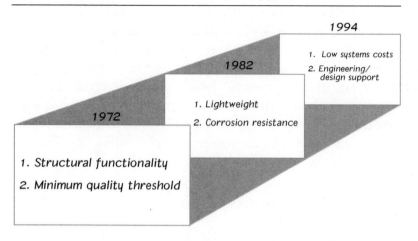

company does because mere survival depends on satisfying the initial customers' priorities. As an organization grows and becomes more successful in the value-inflow phase, however, that focus begins to blur. No longer is every customer critical to survival, and internal issues begin to compete effectively for management's time and attention. The tendency is for customers to move from center stage to the periphery as management turns its attention to fine-tuning its successful business design. Powerful norms, values, and behavior become established in the organization's mind-set and culture. In other words, *institutional memory* is built.

When a business design moves from stability to value outflow, institutional memory becomes an increasingly powerful barrier to detection of the outflow of value. Although customers begin defecting, opting for new business designs, warning signals from the marketplace rarely penetrate an organization's protective layers. And if they do, they are met with denial. "This is what has made us so successful" goes the insistent response. The organization's ability to move is lowest at precisely the moment when the need to move is greatest.

With a large market value, a company in the stability phase can ensure the financing required to move in new directions and acquire capabilities needed to thrive in a new environment. But after the transition to value outflow, market value shrinks, talent departs, cash flow diminishes, financing is more difficult to obtain, and competitors are likely to have staked out strong positions in the new areas of value growth. At this point, the company is caught in a powerful downward spiral. Large revenue streams have led to a large infrastructure that customers see as "cost-added," not value-added. When these costs and head count are removed, morale declines and the best performers in the organization leap to competitors with innovative business designs that offer the promise of significant value growth. Customers move. Talent moves. Value migrates away.

Learning to Play Business Chess

There are always winners and losers in the Value Migration process. At critical junctures, companies must make sharp transitions to a new, more effective business design or risk losing the value they've built. The historical record provides examples of companies that have identified key moves and made transitions effectively. In the 1950s, value migrated from radio networks to TV networks. NBC, the leader in radio, led the transition to network TV. Also in the 1950s, value migrated from tabulating to computing. IBM, the leader in tabulating systems, entered computing in 1953. By the end of the decade, it had achieved undisputed leadership in the new value space. In the 1930s, value flowed from chains of small grocery stores to chains of supermarkets, which were larger in scale, broader in product offering, and lower in cost. A&P made the move belatedly. Although the shift was traumatic and late, the company emerged at the other end of the transition process with its leadership position intact. More recently, as value flowed out of television manufacturing, Motorola switched to semiconductors and communications equipment. As commoditization threatened the long-distance telephone industry, AT&T invested in business designs that created significant new areas of value growth.

In each transition, the trauma of change was the trauma of changing *how* the company did business. For A&P, for IBM, for Motorola, it was not just a technology or format. It was how these companies organized themselves, how they configured their resources, and how they fashioned their approach to the customer.

The examples of companies that have successfully changed their business design in response to changing customer priorities demonstrate that Value Migration is not a process beyond your control. As a manager, as a fiduciary responsible for shareholder wealth, and as an investor, you have choices. In every industry, there is a limited set of key moves that allows you to take advantage of the next cycle of value growth. Every business design has a limited value creation lifecycle. Managers must act to create the next viable business design. IBM may have made such a move with its purchase of Lotus and its innovative Notes product. Nucor may have missed one as minimill saturation has threatened its unique position. The key questions are: Which move should I make? Which future business design element will be most important? Which future competitors do I have to worry about most? It is a complex game.

When you learn to play chess, you start by becoming acquainted with the pieces. You learn how to deploy them, how to capture them. Then you acquire some basic moves, simple techniques—openings, traps to look for, end-game moves. Next you learn the strategic values of the different squares and the importance of controlling the four central ones. You can finally play chess competently because you know the rules.

Learning to play well enough to win, however, involves learning patterns.[6] Winning is based on the ability to see and understand patterns quickly. Patterns allow the player to see moves in series, to look at the position of the pieces on the board and see strategic meaning. The player who grasps the most patterns has a tremendous advantage. In fact, chess grand masters can describe and use hundreds of discrete patterns with great facility.

One learns to play the game of business chess the same way. A set of basic rules must be understood. Part I of this book describes the basic rules of Value Migration and the workings of the new game of business. Equipped with that set of tools, you can play the game.

Playing the game well, however, requires that you become familiar with its patterns. You learn chess patterns by studying games played by others. Fortunately, as Value Migration has been experienced in industry after industry, many of its basic patterns are becoming clear. While complex, the interaction of customer priorities and business designs can be mapped and understood.

Part II describes seven basic patterns that every manager and investor should know. There are, of course, dozens of others. New ones emerge constantly as Value Migration affects new industries. However, the seven included here have proved to have wide applicability and are the beginnings of a basic vocabulary.

Part III is devoted to learning to play the game well on a day-to-day basis. It is about the specific actions that you can take to avoid value loss and to preempt the next cycle of value growth. The final chapter of the book focuses on the increasingly high-stakes nature of the decisions that determine future value growth. In most cases of Value Migration, five or fewer key strategic moves determined how value was redistributed in the next cycle of value growth in the industry. The chapter provides a way of thinking about these moves that can help your organization improve its odds of making the right decisions.

Chapter **2**

Not Technology— Business Design

- Is my company's value growth driven by technology or by its business design?
- What are the assumptions on which my business design is built?
- How long will my current business design retain its economic power?
- When will a new business design be needed to capture the next cycle of value growth?

VALUE MIGRATION DESCRIBES the flow of profit and shareholder wealth across the business chessboard. Value leaves economically obsolete business designs and flows to new business designs that more effectively create utility for the customer and capture value for the producer. The first step toward mastering patterns of Value Migration is to understand the interaction between customer priorities and business design.

For decades, the customer didn't matter. This sounds heretical, but it is true. If you invented the VAX, the customer would come to you. If you invented drugs like Mevacor or Tagamet, the customer would come to you. If you invented Lotus 1-2-3, the customer would come to you.

For those decades, technology was the major driver of value growth. The VAX created billions of dollars in market value for DEC. One product, Tagamet, turned SmithKline into a multibillion dollar pharmaceutical giant. 1-2-3 allowed Lotus to create $1 billion of value in a few short years. The Xerox copier created $11 billion of value growth. Polaroid's instant photography, $2 billion. These successes were all technology and product driven.

This force for value growth will, of course, continue. But technology alone is no longer the fundamental engine of value growth. One reason for this shift is that, in many industries, the rate of breakthrough technological innovation is slowing. The chemical industry offers a classic example. An MIT study that identified major innovations in the chemical industry on a global basis quantified the technology depletion phenomenon. The number of major innovations exceeded 40 in the two decades from 1930 to 1949. It fell to 20 in the 1950s and 1960s, and to only 3 in the 1970s and 1980s[1] (see Figure 2-1). The innovation curves for dyestuffs, steel, textiles, consumer products go even further back, but tell the same story.

The second reason is that rapid imitation limits the value creation cycle of *any* technological breakthrough. A technology can create and capture value only as long as it remains scarce. But the globalization of business and vastly improved capital and information flows now prevent virtually any technological breakthrough from being kept proprietary for long. As fast followers rapidly imitate and distribute breakthrough products, price and gross margins collapse.

FIGURE 2-1   MAJOR INNOVATIONS IN THE CHEMICAL INDUSTRY

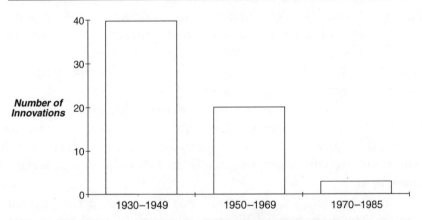

SOURCE: MIT Commission on Industrial Productivity working paper. "The Transformation of the U.S. Chemicals Industry," vol. 1 (Cambridge, Mass.: MIT, 1989).

Although technological innovations continue to create substantial utility for the customer, they often cannot return the cost of capital. In the computing industry, for example, DRAM memory chips dramatically increased computing utility for customers, but their rapid commoditization has substantially diminished value growth for producers.[2]

Consider Figure 2-2. The cases in the left-hand column were nearly pure technology plays. By contrast, those in the right-hand column were not fundamentally based on technology. They may have used varying degrees of process or product technology as part of their overall approach, but it was business design that drove value growth.

Firms with technologically similar product/service offerings can produce radically different value growth performances. Southwest

FIGURE 2-2   NOT TECHNOLOGY, BUSINESS DESIGN

Traditional Sources of Economic Discontinuity	New Sources of Economic Discontinuity
• The Xerox machine	• Federal Express – superior logistics and execution
• The VAX computer	• Nucor – low-cost steel production
• Medical breakthroughs	• Wal-Mart – low-cost distribution
• The VCR	• SouthWest Air – point-to-point system
• Lotus 1-2-3	• Intel – rapid product development

Products/technologies/ manufacturing prowess alone can create value growth.

Business designs that meet customers' most important priorities are necessary to create value growth.

Air and United Airlines use similar equipment to offer basic air transportation, but Southwest's ratio of market value to revenue (1.1) is more than triple United's (.3). Intel's chips are no better than AMD's, but Intel's market value has grown sixfold to more than $26 billion since 1984 (AMD's to only $2.4 billion). Nucor and Bethlehem both make steel, but Nucor's value has more than doubled since 1989 while Bethlehem's has declined. Even when companies' product/service offerings are technologically comparable, differences in business design can produce markedly different patterns of value growth.

Consider also the numerous instances in which a clear technological advantage has failed to drive value growth. Apple's Macintosh Operating System easily outperforms Microsoft's Windows, but Microsoft is the most powerful company in computing, while Apple struggles. German camera manufacturer Leica is the undisputed technological leader in photography, but it has been pushed into a tiny up-market niche by the technologically inferior Nikon and Canon. Sony's Betamax VCR, Xerox's personal computer, and Visicalc's spreadsheet program were all breakthrough technologies that failed to capture significant value for their creators.

The outstanding performance of technologically undistinguished companies and the disappointing record of some technological leaders point to one important observation: *Technology alone, not embedded in an effective business design, is no longer a viable approach to generating sustained value growth.*

Ask yourself these questions about the status of breakthrough product innovation in your industry:

1. Has a recent major technology breakthrough led to dramatic value growth?
2. Is another breakthrough likely in the next five years?
3. What are the odds that my company will own the breakthrough technology exclusively?
4. Will my company own it long enough to create significant value growth?

If your answers to these questions are positive, you are likely to be in an industry that is still in the highly productive phase of its technology innovation curve. You are lucky—and rare. Most companies and managers face a very different situation. For them, the crafting of a superior business design is critical to future value growth. Breakthrough technology is not going to save the day. We have entered the age of business design.

Constructing a Business Design

Constructing a business design requires making critical choices along a number of dimensions. If the business design is to succeed, its elements must be aligned with customers' most important priorities. Equally important, the elements must be tested for consistency with each other to ensure that the business design functions as a coherent, mutually reinforcing whole.

The foundation of a business design is a set of basic assumptions about customers and economics. Since these assumptions profoundly influence the design's overall strength and viability, the architect must examine and make them all explicit. A business design inconsistent with its basic assumptions will fail. A business design built on invalid assumptions will fail.

Building a profitable business design is challenging. But there is a set of questions that can help the architect select the most powerful elements.

Dimension	Key Questions
Fundamental Assumptions	How are customers changing? What are customers' priorities? What are the profit drivers for the business?

Once the foundation of the business design is made explicit, the next task is defining those elements that match customers' most important priorities. These are the choices that determine what the customer sees when choosing among business design alternatives.

Dimension	Key Questions
Customer Selection	Which customers do I want to serve? Which ones will drive value growth?

Dimension	Key Questions
Scope	What products/services do I want to sell? Which support activities do I want to perform in-house? Which ones do I want to subcontract or outsource?
Differentiation	What is my basis for differentiation, my unique value proposition? Why should the customer want to buy from me? Who are my key competitors? How convincing is my differentiation relative to theirs?
Value Recapture	How does the customer pay for the utility I provide? How are my shareholders compensated for the value I create for the customer?

Having established the core of the offering that will create utility for the chosen customers, you must define how your organization delivers that utility and the degree to which it can earn a profit while doing so.

Dimension	Key Questions
Purchasing System	How do I buy? Transactional or long-term relationship? Antagonistic or partnership?
Manufacturing/Operating System	How much do I manufacture versus subcontract? Are my manufacturing/service delivery economics based primarily on fixed or variable costs? Do I need state-of-the-art or ninetieth-percentile process technology?

Capital Intensity	Do I choose a capital-intensive, high-fixed-cost operating system? Or a less capital-intensive, flexible approach?
R&D/Product Development System	Internal or outsourced? Focused on process or product? Focused on astute project selection? Speed of development?
Organizational Configuration	Centralized or decentralized? Pyramid or network? Functional, business, or matrixed? Internal promotion or external hiring?
Go-to-Market Mechanism	Direct sales force? Low-cost distribution? Account management? Licensing? Hybrid?

In constructing a business design from the dimensions defined above, the architect must realize that some choices are more important than others. While fundamental assumptions form the foundation for all business designs, other elements may be more, or less, crucial, depending on the industry and the approach of the management team. For instance, if a business design has truly innovative customer selection and differentiation, it may be able to succeed with very traditional value-recapture mechanisms. In labor-intensive businesses, the importance of the organizational configuration and human resource policy may vastly outweigh that of R&D. Customers and investors will reward brilliant choices in the few key areas that really matter rather than a business design composed of safe choices across the board.

The Evolution of Business Designs

For decades, many successful industry leaders employed a single, dominant business design that represented their key choices and assumptions: integrated manufacturing, in-house R&D, direct sales force, broad product line, a command and control organizational hierarchy, and a value-recapture mechanism based on a per-unit price. For a number of important economic reasons, largely related to the genuine advantages of scale economies, this fundamental business design worked extremely well. Its long-running success, however, dulled the senses. It created a broadly pervasive notion that this was how business was done. The design's fundamental elements were considered "givens."

In the past decade and a half, many of these givens have been successfully challenged. "We must do R&D in-house." Successfully challenged by the steelmaker, Nucor. "We must use a direct sales force." Successfully challenged by Dell's mail-order PC business. "We must do our own computing in-house." Successfully challenged by the outsourcing business design of EDS. "We must do our own manufacturing." Successfully challenged by Nike and countless other companies. Every single dimension of a firm's business design involves choices, not givens. In the next decade, how these choices are made will determine the difference between value growth and stagnation or economic obsolescence.

To illustrate, consider two airlines—United and Southwest Air. Both deliver air travel. Both employ essentially the same technology. But they employ fundamentally different business designs.

- United's *scope* is national. It attempts to serve all the major metropolitan markets in the United States. Its key *value-recapture* mechanism is individual seat pricing managed by its computer reservation system. The core of its *manufacturing/operating system* is a hub-and-spoke network and a large, varied fleet of planes. Its *organizational configuration* is dominated by unionized labor.

- In contrast, Southwest Air's *scope* is regional. CEO Herb Kelleher chose to focus on a limited number of cities, which allows Southwest to dominate in selected markets rather than competing head-to-head across all markets. Its *value-recapture* mechanism is across-the-board low prices, which simplifies the purchasing process. Southwest employs a point-to-point *manufacturing/operating system* and maintains only a few types of aircraft, which reduces the complexity of maintenance and service. An important part of

Southwest's *organizational configuration* is low-cost, high-productivity non-union labor.

The business designs that these two companies have crafted resulted in sharply contrasting value growth performance. While United has had wildly volatile and disappointing profits in the past 15 years, Southwest has had consistently high levels of profitability. The relative power of these business designs is reflected in the fact that the market value/revenue ratio of United is .3 while Southwest's is 1.1.[3]

The way that different competitors make and implement business design choices determines who wins and who loses in the new game of business. Figure 2-3 illustrates the business design choices that the two airlines have made. The first level compares the critical elements of each competitor's business design. The second level makes explicit the key assumptions underlying the business design choices. This type of comparison will be used throughout this book

FIGURE 2-3   BUSINESS DESIGN COMPARISON

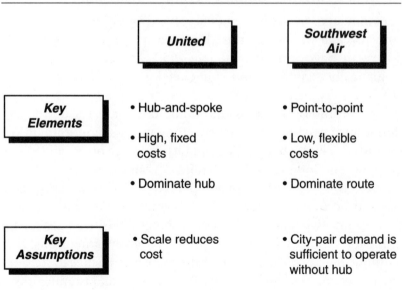

Same industry. Same technology.
Two radically different business designs.

to illustrate the sharply contrasting business designs used by various companies.

The Pioneers of Business Design

Although product and technology innovation was industry's primary value growth driver in the 1950s, 1960s, and 1970s, a few creative business designs produced huge shifts in value during that period. Some early examples—Toyota, McDonald's, and Carrefour—reflect extraordinary clarity of thought about the true nature of customer demand and the true economics of their businesses. The business design choices they made foreshadowed what would be required to win in the post-technology, post-scale-economies business environment—the landscape of the 1990s. A quick study of how these designs were constructed illustrates how new business designs can create sustained value growth.

Toyota Reinvents Manufacturing—and Selling

One of industry's most phenomenal value-growth stories was a result of the reversal of several time-honored assumptions in the auto industry. In Nagoya during the late 1950s and early 1960s, Toyota systematically examined and challenged a set of deeply ingrained and powerfully held convictions about the making and selling of cars. By rethinking these assumptions, the company developed a superior business design that met customers' most important priorities (substantially higher product quality at lower price) and created a three-decade-long record of significant value growth.

Toyota is widely perceived as a paragon of manufacturing excellence—an accurate but incomplete perspective. Toyota employs a highly innovative and economically potent business design that encompasses choices made along a number of key dimensions. Toyota's unique *manufacturing system,* innovative approaches to *scope* (use of outsourcers), *purchasing systems* (demands on and training of suppliers), and *go-to-market mechanism* (the dealer network) all combined to create a business design that met customer priorities effectively and generated enormous value for the company (see Figure 2-4).

FIGURE 2-4   TOYOTA VALUE GROWTH

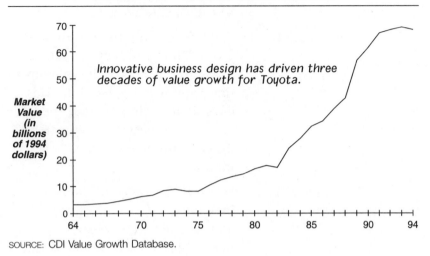

SOURCE: CDI Value Growth Database.

Taichi Ohno, Toyota's legendary head of manufacturing, and Shigeo Shingo, his industrial engineering consultant, started the new business design process by questioning the five key assumptions that defined the manufacturing dimension of the traditional automotive business design.[4] They were shocked by what they found.

Assumption	Ohno and Shingo's Challenge
1. Maximize machine utilization	Operations focused on maximizing utilization of capital. But capital was the least costly component of the operation. Labor was the most costly. (In fact, labor cost was five times as high as capital cost.) That was what should be optimized. They reconfigured their process to make certain that worker time, rather than machine time, was well used.

Assumption	Ohno and Shingo's Challenge
2. Setup times are fixed	Eight-hour setup times were a given. Ohno and Shingo found a Swiss firm that had reduced setup time from eight hours to four. This gave them their first clue. They initiated a process that ultimately drove setup time down to two minutes.
3. Build to inventory to get lower unit cost	When they examined their inventory, they found enormous accumulated costs, waste, and masked production problems. The imperative: minimize inventory.
4. Inspect at the end of the process	This practice prevented bad goods from being shipped to customers. But it also allowed bad goods to be produced. Economic logic dictated upstream inspection.
5. Maximize backward integration for maximum control	This premise assumed a firm could be excellent across an incredibly broad range of activities. Even the enormously talented would find this premise false. Ohno and Shingo developed a network of suppliers whose specialization created quality at far higher levels than Toyota could achieve on its own.

Less well-known than Toyota's extraordinary manufacturing innovations is the way in which it challenged the auto makers' basic assumptions about selling. Industry wisdom held that cyclicality of demand was beyond auto makers' control. The best they could do was maximize capacity utilization and adjust pricing to demand intensity in order to capture maximum value. But Toyota's commitment to "Understand the essential nature of customer demand" led it to reexamine this conventional perspective.[5] Determined to smooth the demand cycle, Toyota's sales staff took an initiative unmatched by any of their U.S. or European counterparts. Rather than wait in dealer showrooms, they called on customers in their homes. Like Toyota's manufacturing, its selling system was flexible. The lower the natural demand, the more intense the selling effort. The higher the natural demand, the less intense the selling effort. The result was that Toyota enjoyed much more stable overall demand and commensurately more consistent levels of sales and profitability.

Finally, the Toyota product development system also reversed the traditional R&D process of (1) invent and (2) sell. For Toyota, the approach was to (1) map what the customers want and (2) invent that. Toyota built a cumulative database on households that included information on their current and expected buying preferences. While other manufacturers conducted market research and focus groups, Toyota tapped into the knowledge of its existing customers to develop new products.

This capability proved extremely useful in the development and launch of Toyota's Lexus line of luxury cars in the 1980s. By understanding the priorities of customers who had bought its cars (before trading up), Toyota was able to design the Lexus to provide the right features at the right price point. It then targeted individual customers as Lexus candidates. Toyota was able to extend its value recapture by converting a Toyota customer into a Lexus customer.

Toyota was a pioneer in the discipline of building a customer-driven business design (see Figure 2-5). Its financial success was, in turn, driven by a superior insight into how profit was generated. For most companies in the 1960s and 1970s, technology, market share, and scale economies were the drivers of success. Toyota had neither technology, nor scale, nor market share. Competing through innovative business design was its only option. It is not surprising that Toyota's key outcome variables (revenue, market share, profit, cash, and market value) have behaved so consistently for three decades. Value has migrated to Toyota's business design, and continues to migrate in that direction as competitors abroad (and even in Japan) struggle to keep the distance between themselves and Toyota from growing.

FIGURE 2-5   BUSINESS DESIGN COMPARISON

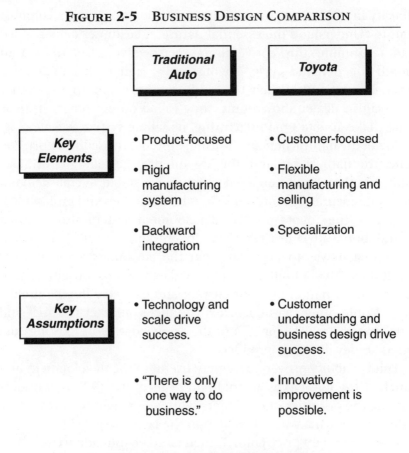

	Traditional Auto	**Toyota**
Key Elements	• Product-focused	• Customer-focused
	• Rigid manufacturing system	• Flexible manufacturing and selling
	• Backward integration	• Specialization
Key Assumptions	• Technology and scale drive success.	• Customer understanding and business design drive success.
	• "There is only one way to do business."	• Innovative improvement is possible.

Toyota challenged traditional auto manufacturing assumptions and created a more customer–matched business design.

McDonald's Redefines the Franchise

While Toyota revolutionized the automotive industry, McDonald's initiated an equally radical business design in food service. Both efforts began in the mid-1950s. Both were built on a foundation of penetrating insight about the customer and the economics of the business. Both explicitly challenged and reversed industry assumptions to create a more potent business design. Both triggered a migration of value away from competitors whose business designs were characterized by poor customer performance and economics.

In 1954, Ray Kroc was selling multimixer machines, primarily to corner drugstores and soda fountains. The demographic shift toward the suburbs, however, began to erode his previously profitable position with urban restaurants. He saw value migrating inexorably away from his business.

In experiencing this shift first hand, Kroc came upon an opportunity to create a whole new value space. When he made a sales call to the McDonald brothers' restaurants in California, he saw that their combination of speedy service and a 15¢ hamburger could be the foundation of a successful new business design. Kroc presciently realized that the key to unlocking this value was perfecting the McDonald's approach and franchising it to hundreds of eager entrepreneurs.

Kroc acquired the franchising rights to McDonald's, and became the architect of a heretical business design. The idea of franchising fast-food restaurants was not unique. Franchise chains were already expanding rapidly. But most chain owners were primarily interested in selling the original franchise license or supplies. They didn't focus very much on the success of the individual stores. As a result, the franchisees were not given a meaningful advantage over their competition, and, indeed, were often hurt by poor-quality restaurants in the same franchise. Consumers were not consistently well served by the industry's existing business designs.

Kroc took a different approach. His most basic assumption was that he had two key customers: the end-consumers *and* the franchisees. The success of his business design would depend on the loyalty and growth of *both* groups.[6]

To create value for the end-consumers, he focused first on *scope*. McDonald's would offer a menu of 10 items, all at low prices. Kroc's limited scope not only catered to the priorities of a nation hungry for decent quality, low-cost food but also created value for the franchisees, which could reap enormous economic advantages by concentrating on a small number of products.

But Kroc's most dramatic business design innovation was his revolutionary *manufacturing/operations system*. McDonald's improved every aspect of the food preparation process, from potato farming to the packaging of the hamburgers, in order to improve the franchisee's profitability:

> The McDonald brothers had not given [Kroc] a secret recipe for
> hamburgers, milk shakes, and french fries. He possessed no
> patents, no technological breakthrough, and no new product.
> Kroc was not handed a Xerox or a Polaroid. Managers of other
> restaurants knew that their food, when properly prepared, was
> more or less competitive with McDonald's. . . . While there
> were many reasons why McDonald's would wind up dominating
> an industry where no one had a special advantage, its competi-
> tors agreed on only one thing: McDonald's took more seriously
> the task of building a uniform operating system.[7]

In order to build a successful *operating system* for the fast-food chain,
equipment and kitchens were redesigned. The entire system was
carefully optimized as if it were a large factory.

Supporting McDonald's operating system was its innovative
approach to purchasing. For example, in its constant search for quality, McDonald's traced the many problems of inconsistency in french
fry quality to variations in the temperature at which farmers stored
their potatoes. Working closely with the farmers and suppliers,
McDonald's managed not only to obtain superior supplies at a
reduced cost, but to transform the businesses from which it was
buying.

Kroc also extended innovation to the area of *human resources and
organizational configuration.* Managers took an intensive course at
Hamburger University, were given a book on the best way to prepare
a hamburger, were supported by field consultants, and were given
only one franchise at a time—to ensure that every McDonald's customer was served a high-quality meal efficiently and consistently.

McDonald's is a powerful example of an internally consistent
business design based on several daring and insightful assumptions.
With human resource policies that redefined what it meant to be a
franchisee, innovative supply agreements, a lasting and meaningful
differentiation based on quality and value, McDonald's created an
integrated system that has proven difficult for competitors to imitate.
The value growth of this business design has continued for 30 years—
creating $24 billion in market value.

McDonald's success has not been due to the invention of new
technologies, but rather the invention and continuous improvement
of its business design. It is an outstanding example of building tre-

mendous economic power through astute and innovative forms of vertical relationships (downstream through franchisees, upstream through suppliers). It is a business design that many locational businesses in the 1990s have yet to understand and fully exploit.

Carrefour Redefines Distribution

When French entrepreneurs Marcel Fournier and Denis Defforey opened the first Carrefour hypermarket—a huge store that carried everything from groceries to clothes—in a Paris suburb in 1963, they had an idea that would revolutionize the French and later European distribution systems in the next 30 years. By 1993, Carrefour was an international chain of hypermarket stores generating $21.2 billion in annual sales and a market capitalization of roughly $10 billion. Again, it was not technology that created this value. It was the creation of a novel, customer-matched, cost-effective business design.

The distribution system that dominated France up until the mid-1960s was a highly fragmented system of *petits commerçants* (small shopkeepers). Every town or neighborhood had its own *charcuterie* (butcher shop), *boulangerie* (bakery), and other specialty stores. Personal relationships often developed between the shop owner and the customer. The stores were owned by families and usually were passed down from generation to generation.

While these shops were considered by many in France to be an inseparable part of the national heritage, they were highly inefficient and inconvenient both for the customer and the distributor. With the emergence of dual-parent working families, customers no longer had the time or the desire to visit several stores in order to do the daily shopping. Large distributors of consumer products did not want to service thousands of tiny stores.

The development of the hypermarket by Fournier and Defforey created a new value proposition that better met customers' existing needs. Their business design was simple but effective. Instead of enormously time-consuming multistop shopping, Carrefour offered "everything under one roof." This broad *scope* enabled the customer to buy bread, meat, cheese, car tires, and children's clothing—all with a broad selection of competitive offerings—at the same location. Carrefour stores were enormous, averaging 100,000 square feet by

1993, compared to an average of less than 5,000 square feet for traditional stores. Instead of constructing stores downtown, Carrefour built them on the edge of town, providing easy access for customers with cars as well as distributors.

In the 1970s and 1980s, Carrefour improved its business design to expand its scope dramatically. Today, it offers credit cards, insurance, discounted gas, and banking and travel services. By 1993, Carrefour, one of many hypermarket chains in France (Le Clerc, Casino, and Hyper-U are others), had opened 114 stores in France, accounting for 11 million square feet of retail space. *Petits commerçants* were unable to compete on price or on product selection. The customer priority upon which they had been founded—a personal relationship with the customer—no longer sufficed. Value migrated rapidly toward the hypermarkets as the *petit commerçant* business design became obsolete.

As with Toyota and McDonald's, the early hypermarkets were an anomaly. They were ahead of their time: a triumph of business design during the age of product and technology, and the foreshadowing of a process that would not reach critical mass until three decades later.

The Age of Business Design

Toyota, McDonald's, and Carrefour proved that business design can be as powerful as technology in creating and capturing value. Constant business-design improvement created sustained profit and value growth—even in the absence of patents and proprietary technology. But the success of these pioneers during the 1960s and 1970s did not catalyze widespread experimentation with new designs. Only gradually did players in a broad range of industries begin to realize the tremendous economic power of reversing traditional assumptions and systematically building a business design from customer priorities up. But by the mid- to late 1980s, there was an unquestionable increase in the level of business design innovation. Although we have no way of measuring the overall rate, the increasingly frequent introduction of new business designs, and the dramatic value growth they have created, has been difficult to ignore.

The discipline of business design innovation began to gain momentum in the 1980s. A number of inventors created powerful business designs that captured enormous amounts of value. The achievements of Merck, Nordstrom, The Home Depot, Federal Express, Microsoft, and TCI signaled a rising tide of business design innovation (see Figure 2-6).

Today, we are entering an increasingly productive phase of the business-design innovation cycle. The repertoire of successful business designs to be studied, customized, and improved upon is growing rapidly. In the age of business design, success depends on the speed and skill with which competitors understand these designs and improve and adapt them to their particular customers.

Assessing a business design's value-creating power requires a detailed understanding of how well that design meets customers' most important priorities—both today and in the projectable future. An equally important task is evaluating the ability of the business design to capture profit. Business design evaluation does not use the same metrics as a traditional company profile. It requires answering the following questions:

- What are the customer and economic assumptions on which the business design is built?
- Are those assumptions still valid? What might change them?
- What are customers' most important priorities? How are they changing?

FIGURE 2-6   THE TSUNAMI OF BUSINESS DESIGN

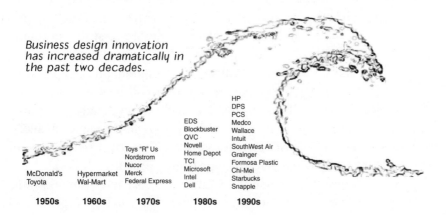

Business design innovation has increased dramatically in the past two decades.

1950s	1960s	1970s	1980s	1990s
McDonald's	Hypermarket	Toys "R" Us	EDS	HP
Toyota	Wal-Mart	Nordstrom	Blockbuster	DPS
		Nucor	QVC	PCS
		Merck	Novell	Medco
		Federal Express	Home Depot	Wallace
			TCI	Intuit
			Microsoft	SouthWest Air
			Intel	Grainger
			Dell	Formosa Plastic
				Chi-Mei
				Starbucks
				Snapple

- What elements of the business design are matched to the customers' most important priorities? How well are they served? What priorities are not well served?

- How does the business design compare to competitors'? What differentiates it? Does the customer care about that differentiation?

- Are competitors' business designs based on the same assumptions as yours?

- How internally consistent is the business design? Are there elements that do not support the meeting of customer priorities?

- How cost effective is the business design?

- Can the business design recapture value? How sustainable and defensible is that recapture mechanism?

- How long will the business design be sustainable? What changes in customer priorities will require changes in it?

- What alternative designs are already being employed that meet the next cycle of customer priorities?

These questions are the crux of strategy in the age of business design. They are uncomfortable when they are asked for the first time. Learning how to answer them faster and better than your competitors will allow you to anticipate, recognize, and respond to Value Migration in your industry.

Although the age of business design has only recently begun, it has already generated significant results. First, it has enabled tremendous value growth. Second, it has created a rich set of models and templates for future architects of business design to study, emulate, modify, and improve. Third, it has challenged many firmly entrenched assumptions, including the unstated but deeply held conviction that a particular business design will be viable forever.

In fact, business designs have a well-defined cycle of value growth, stability, and obsolescence. Technologies become obsolete. So do business designs. They represent the third of three important cycles: the product lifecycle, the customer priorities lifecycle, and the business design lifecycle. Great value is lost when breakpoints in the cycle are not detected, and when the different phases of the cycle are not managed according to their strategic, tactical, and organizational requirements.

The next chapter explores the dynamics of the business design cycle, its manifestations in terms of value creation and capture, and the management requirements for effective decision making in all its phases.

Chapter 3

The Three Phases of Value Migration

- Where is my business design in its lifecycle?
- How should my decision making change as my business design moves through its lifecycle?
- When will I have to develop my next business design?

JASON FROMM HAD JUST RETURNED FROM AN INDUSTRY ANALYSTS' MEETING IN NEW YORK CITY. He had forgotten how frigid the Big Apple could be in February. He was glad to be back at his firm in Mountain View, California, and he was very glad to be in the software business.

Fromm stumbled over a few empty boxes strewn about the executive suite. He smiled in satisfaction. Here he was, standing in the gleaming new headquarters of Advantage Software, a company he had started only three years ago. Although it was almost evening, his employees were busily unpacking. They were as eager as he was to finish the move and get on with the work. A year earlier Advantage employed 180 people; the payroll was now 300. Fromm planned to hire another 200 during the first three quarters of 1986.

Several people came over to ask him how the meeting had gone. They were more than curious. Most employees owned stock in the company.

"Within 10 minutes, I had them eating out of my hand," Fromm grinned as he walked into his new office. His boast was backed with performance. Advantage Software had gone public in 1985 at a stock price of $20 per share. This January, just six months after the IPO, the stock had hit $27. The company's market value was six times as great as its total revenue.

Advantage's stock continued to climb throughout 1986. Top talent came knocking on the company's door. Employees created great products, even in the face of impossible deadlines. Customers loved the company's line of sophisticated yet easy-to-use word processing programs. They provided all the utility customers could dream of, and they were easy to buy—shrink-wrapped and available in retail computer outlets and catalog warehouses nationwide. Value was migrating to software companies with Advantage's business design. It provided just what customers wanted.

Each copy of Advantage's flagship product sold for $495, yet cost no more than $20 to manufacture. The resulting profits drove the stock to $70 by 1988. The company grew to 1,200 people.

Advantage's stock remained above $70 as the January 1989 calendar was hung. This puzzled some observers, however. To them, Advantage's shrink-wrapped software had become something of a commodity. Several other companies were producing similar products and selling them at similar—or lower—prices. Competition was intensifying and market demand was leveling off.

At a Boston Computer Society conference in March, Fromm told a packed house about a wonderful future of dramatically increased productivity in the software development process. He boasted about the enormous volume Advantage was shipping every quarter. He finished to thunderous applause.

But Fromm's speech didn't change the facts. Advantage's business design was maturing rapidly. This time when Fromm returned to Mountain View, he was greeted with three resignation letters. Each was from a star employee; each person was joining a different startup software company. Two of these startups were working on communications software rather than personal productivity tools. Fromm was mystified. Why would they risk joining fledgling businesses instead of staying with an emerging software giant?

The next morning Fromm came out of a finance meeting more puzzled, and perhaps even slightly anxious. (As the company's leader, he was caught between facing the facts and exuding confidence, between caution and inspiring optimism in employees.) Revenue and profits were well below projections. But, they *were* still growing. The company's market value was only slightly higher than its revenue. Fromm shrugged off his concern as he met the builders who would finish the company's newest headquarters before year's end.

Once in the new facility, Advantage had even greater capacity to develop refined versions of its products. Its marketing team expanded advertising campaigns to promote the firm's brand-name recognition.

The company's competitors, however, were slashing prices. Their word processing programs now sold for $349, even $299. Spreadsheet prices had dropped below $200. Despite Advantage's reputation, customers began to realize that giving up a few features was worth $100 a copy. The startups were hitting their production stride, too, offering creative new products that captured the customers' imagination.

Advantage's stock, after reaching a high of $90, had drifted down to $80. Though shareholders remained upbeat, Fromm knew he had to address the erosion. He decided to hold an off-site management retreat early in 1990. At one session, Advantage's CFO—an inveterate straight shooter—predicted in sobering tones that prices would continue to fall drastically. He said Advantage needed to cut its prices or it would lose market share. His projections caused an uproar. They violated the company's upbeat culture. Employees dubbed him "Dr. Doom."

But market prices for word processing software continued to fall. Advantage's profit margins shrank from 30 percent to 5 percent. Revenue growth stalled. The stock dropped to $50. (The ratio of market value to revenue fell well below one to one). Defections mounted. By the end of 1991, Advantage was consistently missing its product launch dates.

Shrink-wrapped software, Advantage's only type of product, would take a beating in the next two years. Some vendors sold word processing programs for $99. Others began to offer integrated "suites" containing a word processing program, spreadsheet, graphics software, and database program in a single package for $495. Customers threw away their incompatible programs. Meanwhile, the communications software firms, no longer startups, were experiencing rapid profit growth on high-margin electronic mail, communications, and networking software. Fromm envied his competitors' more robust, broad-based business designs.

In 1993, Fromm gave more speeches than ever—most of them in-house to boost employee morale. Advantage had just announced its third round of layoffs.

The "merger" announcement came out in *The Wall Street Journal* in March 1994. Portland Software would buy Advantage for $17 a share. The *Journal* noted that the offer was $3 below Advantage's IPO price nine years earlier. Yet it was a 30 percent premium over current market prices. Many industry analysts and Advantage employees wondered why Portland wanted Advantage in the first place.

The Three Phases of Value Migration

Advantage Software is a fictional company, but a similar triumph and demise unfolded at several very real software firms. Their business designs shared the basic elements of Advantage's:

Dimension	Advantage's Design
Differentiation	"Best of Breed," ease of use, loyal installed base
Scope	Single product
Value Recapture	Stream of revenue from frequent upgrades
Go-to-Market Mechanism	Indirect distribution channels (retail, mail order)

These business designs went through distinct phases as value migrated. Historically, the migration of value into and then out of a business design has taken much more than a decade, but in the future the cycle is likely to accelerate.

A business design can be in one of three phases with respect to Value Migration: Value can be flowing in, value can be stable, or value can be flowing out. In the inflow phase, an aggressive company starts to capture value from other parts of the industry because its business design is superior in meeting new customer priorities. Advantage entered the market with a new business design built around shrink-wrapped software. It gave customers exactly what they wanted—an inexpensive, primary utility. No longer did users have to rely on the hardware maker's captive software, which often was cumbersome and incompatible with other machines.

In the stability phase, business designs are well matched to the priorities of a broad base of customers. Though the number of competitors is increasing, most are profitable. As value in the software market was migrating from hardware-based companies to independent software developers, Advantage captured that value flow and rose with the tide from 1983 to 1987. But the uniqueness of the company's business design was eroding. Several competitors offered similar products embedded in similar business designs.

In the outflow phase, value starts to migrate toward new business designs that more effectively meet evolving customer priorities. The once-mainstream business design loses relevance for more and more customers. No longer able to satisfy customers' most important priorities, companies often cut prices to retain market share. The destructive cycle that follows drives profits and value out of the business design.

Fromm and his management team failed to recognize that customers placed no premium on Advantage's *specific* word-processing package. Any one would do. Better yet, an integrated bundle of all the basic personal productivity programs would make their lives simpler. Competitors that sensed this shift in customer priorities offered suites. Advantage did not. Value flowed out of business designs built around single, shrink-wrapped products and into those built around suites.

As customer priorities relating to personal productivity were being satisfied, group productivity emerged as the critical new priority. The communications revolution was on. It required the creation of a fundamentally new business built around communications software.

Dimension	**"Communications" Design**
Differentiation	Speed, performance, ease of use, multiplatform, capable of customization
Scope	Enterprisewide communications infrastructure

Dimension	"Communications" Design
Value Recapture	Product and upgrades, plus initial customization and ongoing service
Go-to-Market Mechanism	Combination of direct and indirect (value-added resellers)

Advantage's business design had become obsolete. It no longer matched customer priorities. Customers were not willing to pay enough for the utility that Advantage provided to allow it to make a profit. While revenues remained high, they no longer created any value for shareholders.

As a business design moves through these three phases, its ability to generate profit rises and falls as well. A business design's profit curve is a fundamental driver of its value curve. Figure 3-1 illustrates the cycle. After an early subsidy period characterized by operating losses, operating profit grows rapidly. As the business design matures into stability, profit growth slows. As the design becomes obsolete and enters value outflow, profit plummets. Finally, most business designs that are part of a corporate portfolio tend to be subsidized at the end of their lifecycle, destroying value until they are shut down or replaced.

Managing the Business Design Lifecycle

To remain competitive, a company must understand its business design's ability to capture value in the inflow phase, its sustainability in the stability phase, and its vulnerability in the outflow phase. This understanding allows companies to answer the question, What's my next move? Executives who can identify the phases of both their own and their competitors' business designs will be able to anticipate Value Migration, protect existing value, and capture future value. Executives who are not sensitive to transitions from one phase to another will miss opportunities. Worse yet, they will fail to see threats that destroy the value their current business design has created.

The three phases may seem clear on paper, but companies find them hard to discern when they are immersed in their own markets and competitive battles. Fromm did not see Advantage Software's

FIGURE 3-1   BUSINESS DESIGN PROFIT CURVE

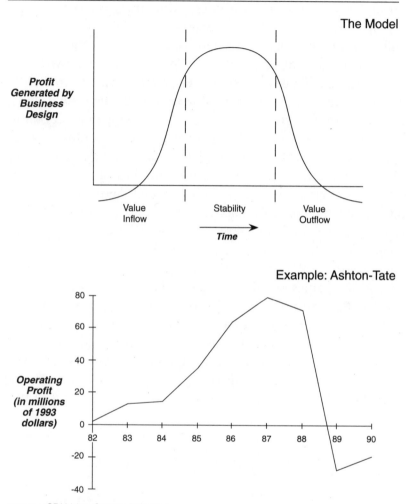

The Model

Profit
Generated by
Business
Design

Value   Stability   Value
Inflow   Outflow

Time

Example: Ashton-Tate

Operating
Profit
(in millions
of 1993
dollars)

SOURCE: CDI Value Growth Database.

progression through the business design lifecycle until it was too late. Only through a systematic mapping of the Value Migration status of each business design can management anticipate transitions and respond effectively.

Mapping Value Migration

A useful metric for evaluating a business design within the three phases of Value Migration is the ratio of market value to revenue.

Because this metric represents a combination of current mass (revenue) and future expected earnings momentum (market value), it can help provide a signal of increasing or declining business design vitality. When the market value/revenue ratio is high, investors expect the business design to achieve significant profit growth. Companies with a high market value/revenue ratio (usually greater than 2.0) are typically experiencing value inflow. In the stability phase, this ratio is usually between 0.8 and 2.0, indicating that expectations for future profit growth have been tempered. In outflow, the ratio drops below 0.8 as the business design's ability to generate profit declines. This ratio is, therefore, a useful indicator of the power of a business design at any given point in time.[1] Figure 3-2 provides a model that can be used to map the three phases of Value Migration and summarizes the characteristics of each phase.

This three-phase model can be used to describe Value Migration among business designs at different levels: between industries, between companies within a single industry, and within a single company. For example, value is flowing out of the steel industry and into the plastics industry as players such as GE Plastics develop business designs that meet the priorities of certain customers more effectively than the integrated steel mills. Within the computer industry, value is flowing out of DEC's business designs and into Microsoft's. Within a single company, value is flowing out of IBM's

FIGURE 3-2   THE THREE STAGES OF VALUE MIGRATION

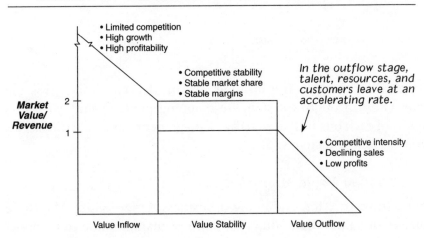

mainframe-based business design into IBM's systems integration business design. In all cases, value is migrating to and from business designs as customers make choices among alternatives in the marketplace (see Figure 3-3).

WHERE IS MY INDUSTRY? Mapping Value Migration at the industry level is a useful first step because it creates a context in which to evaluate individual business designs. It helps to calibrate what you can and should expect from a business design within the industry. Positioning industries is straightforward because the evidence is everywhere. In 1995, the telecommunications industry is in the inflow phase. The strong value growth and high market value/revenue ratio of a broad range of telecommunications companies suggest that the industry's business designs will continue to create and capture value. Other indicators support this view: growth in the number of companies and their employment, increased venture capital and IPO activity, and strong industrywide profit growth. The same metrics and indicators reflect the Value Migration phase of other industries. The chemical industry is in the stability phase; the defense industry is in the outflow phase. These positions are often the result of large societal, economic, and technological shifts. The ascendance of the telecommunications industry has been driven by revolutionary technology accompanied by customer-matched business designs; the decline of the defense industry, by policy and peace.

An industry in the inflow stage provides numerous opportunities for capturing value. Many companies have business designs whose value is growing. A stable industry offers value growth opportunities to those companies that improve operational efficiencies while continuing to serve customer priorities. Some business designs succeed; some fail. An industry in the outflow stage has dwindling opportunities for capturing value. A company enjoying strong value growth here is an exception. Companies in these industries must reduce costs, restructure, find an isolated niche, or withdraw. Map your industry. Understand the overall Value Migration context for your business design(s). Then go on to answer the next question.

WHERE IS MY BUSINESS DESIGN? Having established the context of Value Migration for your industry, you know what to expect

FIGURE 3-3   VALUE FLOW: LEVELS OF ANALYSIS

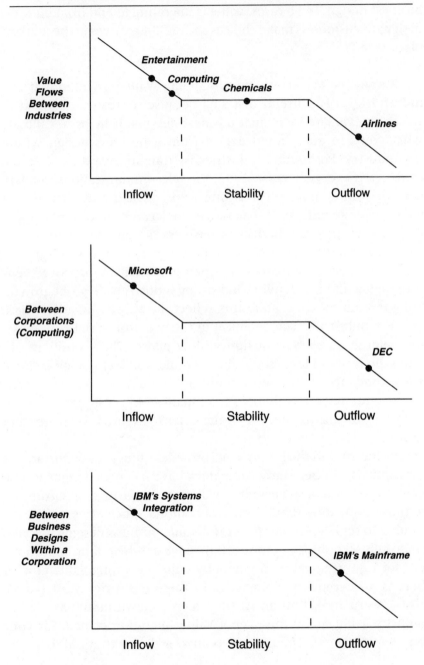

when examining the position of specific business designs. Positioning business designs in phases can be complex. Ideally, each business design would be valued separately by investors. In reality, individual business designs are sometimes stand-alone companies and sometimes but one of many business designs within a much larger company.

Single-design companies. In companies that engage in only one type of business, or are dominated by one business unit, information on the value of a business design is usually plentiful. The market value/revenue ratio of these companies is a fair assessment of their business design. Nucor, Bethlehem Steel, and USAir are companies that have essentially a single business design. In other cases, it is the *predominant* business design that is being valued by the market. For example, IBM has a number of different operating units, each with its own business design, but for many years the market valuation of the corporation was driven by its integrated business design built around mainframe computers. Figure 3-4 illustrates the Value Migration status of a number of publicly traded companies whose valuation is based primarily on one business design.

Multiple-design companies. For companies that have multiple designs that need to be disaggregated for fair evaluation, the process

FIGURE 3-4   VALUE MIGRATION STATUS, 1994

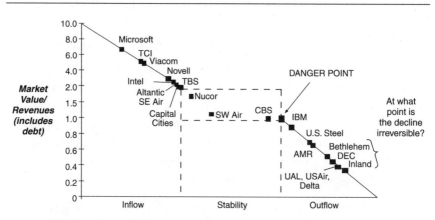

SOURCE: CDI Value Growth Database.

is more complex. There is no easily defined index such as market value/revenues. Only in rare cases are investors able to value business designs separately.[2] While easy metrics are hard to find, one bellwether indicates the strength of any business design—the customer, the creator of value. Following the customer will show you where the value is. Customers vote on business designs every day.

Customer behavior can highlight business designs that are significantly superior (value inflow), roughly equivalent (stability), or dangerously inadequate (outflow) in meeting customer priorities. Watching customer behavior over time allows you to recognize the Value Migration phase of the business designs among which customers are choosing.

As an exercise, compare business designs at opposite ends of the three-phase continuum. Auto makers have been leaving Big Steel and going to plastics makers. Why? Montgomery Ward's parking lot is empty while The Home Depot's has traffic jams. Why? Frequent fliers are leaving United for Southwest Air. Why? Customer behavior shows you where a business design is positioned. It also highlights those designs that are stronger (Are they threats? Should you emulate them?) and those that are weaker (Are there lessons to be learned? Pitfalls to be avoided?).

Small companies usually have only one business design. Large companies often have several. Each design must be evaluated to determine which customers the company is winning and losing, and which markets it can preempt. Identifying the phase of a business design is not necessarily difficult—if you are objective. Each phase has unique organizational, structural, and managerial challenges.

Decision Making in the Business Design Lifecycle

Knowing which Value Migration phase your business design is in enables you to maximize your organization's value growth. Not knowing can lead to unexpected collapse. What Fromm at Advantage Software felt, but was unable to recognize, was that the three phases of the lifecycle were very different. As a business design moves through its value cycle, management objectives change. The new game of business challenges management to:

1. construct a business design that will create and capture value,

2. maximize the ability of that design to perform during Phase I,

3. adjust investment intensity as the design moves to Phase II,

4. optimize the profitability and sustainability of the stability phase,

5. identify the requirements of the next generation design before competitors do, and

6. manage creatively the transition to the new business design as value begins to flow out of the obsolete one.

PHASE I. There is a confluence of potent elements in Phase I: excitement, confidence, a spirit of conquest. There is also strong management, the ability to attract top talent, and an advantaged strategic position in the industry. The business, the leadership, and the organization all seem to be blessed.

It is easy to get caught up in the euphoria of Phase I. Managing the value inflow effectively depends on stepping back and performing a rational, systematic analysis. Management should focus on answering the following questions:

- How large and how long will this inflow be? What can we do to accelerate or sustain it?

- Are we well positioned to maximize the amount of value we can secure?

- What other organizations are benefiting from this flow? What are their strategies?

- What will signal that this phase is ending?

Answering these questions allows management not only to take full advantage of a well-crafted, customer-matched business design, but also to prepare for the transition to the stability phase.

In Advantage's case, Phase I lasted only a few years. In the past, many companies have enjoyed longer periods of value inflow. For NBC, the era lasted from 1955 to 1975; for IBM, from 1953 to 1983. Today, with international competition, short product lifecycles, and knowledgeable customers, it is unlikely that any firm will enjoy a lengthy inflow phase.

TRANSITION FROM PHASE I TO PHASE II. Phase changes are difficult to recognize because they are usually subtle. In physics, transitions between physical states (vapor to water, water to ice) are easy to see because they occur at sharply defined temperatures. In Value Migration, phase transitions are easy to miss. There are no sharp transition points. Often there isn't even a definition of the next phase. Examples of good detection are rare. Examples of timely response are even rarer.

Transitions between phases are the times of greatest vulnerability for a company. They also present the greatest opportunities for new value growth. For young companies, analyzing the business design often means analyzing the company. In these cases it is important to assess the position of the business frequently; there is no portfolio to provide a buffer should you miss a transition, or decide to retrench too late. Advantage Software fell victim to just such a missed transition.

Recognizing the inflection point between Phase I and Phase II can be exceedingly difficult. As the unambiguously positive performance data of Phase I give way to more qualified results in Phase II, a tug of war between optimism and fact clouds clear vision. There is a modulation of the growth rate, a softening of price, an increase in head-to-head competition for key accounts. Even after several quarters of mixed results, explanations centering on "seasons," "industry cycles," and "special circumstances" creep into management debates. Margins decline, same store sales stagnate, job applications slow, and interest from the investment community dwindles. While all these factors indicate that the company has slipped out of Phase I, management retains the heady confidence that came with dramatic value inflow. CEOs, CFOs, and even board members allow capital spending and headcounts to rise steadily.

If all other indicators fail to show that a Phase I business design is shifting into Phase II, revisit the customer. In Phase I, customers have a clear, simple priority and are hungry for all you can produce. But the first time their priorities appear to be changing, or the first time they have a new option from a competitor, your business design may well be entering the transition into Phase II.

The transition point to Phase II is a critical moment in a business design's lifecycle. Decisions at that moment affect the longevity and profitability of the stability phase that follows. Answering the following questions will enable management to make the right moves to maximize value growth and ensure value protection:

- What adjustments to the basic business design are necessary for it to continue to capture value (keeping it in Phase I)?
- How much capacity, in human and capital asset terms, will be required to sustain profitability as growth slows?
- With which customers has the design established the strongest franchise? Which customers are most likely to defect?

PHASE II. There is a curious mixture of elements in Phase II business designs that impedes clear thinking about economics. Volume is high. Revenue is growing. Yet profit might not be growing as quickly. Customers are generally satisfied with their choices. There is strong repeat business (or at least a one-for-one replacement in the customer base), and the company focuses on superior execution of those activities that have led to success in the past. This phase might be termed "the comfort zone."

The same factors that have shortened the inflow phase of business design lifecycles have also shortened the stability phase. Lotus had only a few years before it was forced to reinvent itself to survive. Dell's time in the stability zone lasted only a few years before the company had to make significant modifications to its business design. If you're in the stability zone, you're probably already under attack from new business designs.

Management faces different challenges in the stability phase. Answers to new questions become important. The first set of questions focuses on optimizing the existing business design.

- What process optimizations can improve the profitability of the existing design?
- How should capital budgeting decisions change? What adjustments should be made to our hurdle rate?

The second set of questions focuses management's attention on the end of the stability phase and the need to respond while there is still time to capture the next wave of Value Migration.

- What might upset the apple cart? Which competitors are trying to do so? Should *we* do so?
- What are *customers telling us* that indicates value might begin to migrate elsewhere?
- What should we do now to stay ahead of the tide once value begins to migrate?

TRANSITION FROM PHASE II TO PHASE III. As a business design moves from stability to value outflow (from Phase II to Phase III), institutional memory limits an organization's ability to detect and respond to the need for change. The organization's inward focus impairs its ability to pick up signals from customers and competing business designs. Only when changes in customer behavior are reflected in the quarterly financial statements does the organization begin to see that it is no longer in stability. By then it is usually too late.

It is easy to miss the inflection point between stability and value outflow (see Figure 3-5). Institutional memory stands in the way of seeing these movements clearly. Like Fromm at Advantage Software, managers tend to "stay the course." They forget to define their competitors by focusing on new customer desires, and they respond to upstart companies just as Fromm did—by refusing to consider them serious competitors.

FIGURE 3-5   VALUE FLOW OVER TIME

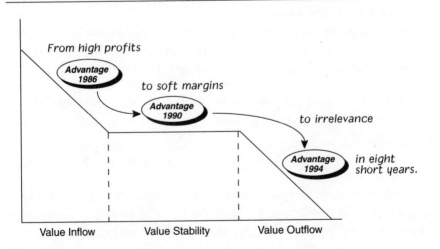

Instead of creating new business designs better matched to changing customer priorities and expectations, executives often believe that they can reverse the flow of red ink by cutting costs or improving efficiency, even when they have no new utility to offer to customers.

PHASE III. As in the inflow phase, there are clear elements at work here. Performance and market confidence begin to erode. Inside the company, denial and defensiveness reign as managers try to protect "their people." Executives face difficult decisions: Cut back or continue to invest in businesses that are likely never to provide a return above the cost of capital.

Across every industry, there are companies that could not move quickly or effectively enough to protect their value, much less achieve value growth. Like Advantage Software, most were not able to recognize what was happening to their previously successful business design until it was too late.

Protecting value once outflow has begun depends upon confronting the obsolescence of the business design head-on. Once denial is overcome, answering these questions will help management craft the right moves:

- How basic is the threat posed by this migration?
- How can we protect value in the business? If we can't, how fast can we get out?
- What investments in new business designs can we make to capture the value that is flowing away?

As a business design moves through its lifecycle, the challenges facing management change. A rigid decision-making agenda is a dangerous limitation. Focusing on the metrics of Value Migration can spur managers to look forward and confront the new issues critical to the future of their organizations.

Managing the Wild Card: External Events

Business designs are inexorably pulled from Phase I to Phases II and III by changing customer priorities and the availability of new business designs. This natural progression, however, can be interrupted. Unexpected external events can suddenly make a business design jump from one phase to another. Innovation, regulation, trade restrictions, aggressive pricing, hyperinflation, even war can cause value to migrate into or out of a particular business design. The invention of the videocassette recorder created new revenue streams for Hollywood studios, pushing some of them that were well into Phase II back into Phase I. Events can also catapult a business design from initial anonymity to runaway Phase I growth. For example, the 1973 oil embargo boosted the sales of compact cars and catalyzed the ascent of the Japanese auto makers.

External shocks can have profound effects on the success or failure of your business design. An effective response to such shocks depends on a thorough understanding of your business designs and those of your competitors as well as the effect of the shocks on your customers' priorities. Early comprehension of the implications of the shocks (while your competitors are still considering their options) often allows you to mitigate their damage or capitalize on the opportunites they may offer.

Keeping Phase in Focus

It is easy to forget that the relevance of your business design to customers is constantly changing. The challenges of daily operations and the success of your current design frequently absorb your attention. The inevitability of Value Migration (it *is* happening to your organization as you read this) suggests that ongoing Value Migration analysis should be a top managerial priority.

Central to this analysis is an assessment of your design relative to those of competitors. It is those competitive designs that are challenging yours in the mind of the customer. Having a clear and complete competitive field of vision enables you to know your competitors and to anticipate the phase shifts that will limit the value-creation and value-protection power of your business design. The next chapter demonstrates how to establish an appropriately broad competitive field of vision.

Chapter **4**

Defining the Competitive Field

From Tunnel Vision to Radar Screen

- Which competitors will be the most important ones in my industry five years from now?

- Are their business designs similar to mine or completely different?

- Which emerging business designs have the combination of superior customer performance and superior economics that will cause value to migrate away from my business design?

VALUE MIGRATION is triggered when a critical mass of customers chooses one business design over those of its competitors. The process can be swift and dramatic, as the advantaged business design gains revenue, profit, market value, and, ultimately, industry leadership.

It is new competitors, rather than entrenched incumbents, that typically set off new waves of Value Migration. Unencumbered by institutional memory, new entrants and nontraditional players are often most sensitive to emerging customer priorities and most able to craft business designs to meet them.

This competition places incumbents in an intensely uncomfortable position. Maintaining leadership depends on the ability to identify competing designs, assess their utility to the customer, and respond effectively. To stay ahead of Value Migration, established players must constantly evaluate competing business designs and decide which ones really matter.

In the past, most companies had to know three to six competitors very well. Coke had to know Pepsi. GM had to know Ford and Chrysler. U.S. Steel had to know Bethlehem, National, J&L, Inland, Republic, and Armco. Siemens had to know GE and Westinghouse. But today, 30–50 companies may be your competitors. It is no longer sufficient to benchmark your strategy against those of similar firms. You are now competing with companies that have very different business designs from yours, companies that you would have trouble describing as "in your business."

Discovering new competitors is even more important than keeping an eye on old ones. Why? As noted above, it is the business designs of the newcomers, the renegades, the fringe players that typically create and capture the next cycle of value growth.

From Tunnel Vision . . .

To an outsider who can dispassionately observe a particular industry, identifying the nontraditional players that may dominate the industry in the next decade can be simple. But if your own industry is the one you are trying to analyze, vision is often distorted by past patterns of success and the industry norms that have defined the competitive field—in short, by "industry-think." Industry-think is a powerful force that grows stronger over time. You see the same companies every year at industry trade shows. You belong to the same industry associations. You begin to think the same way. Furthermore, industry analysts, government statistics, and the financial markets constantly try to classify your company and group it with similar-looking competitors. And as traditionally defined industries mature, established competitors focus their efforts on operational benchmarking and the incremental optimization of traditional business designs. All these events and processes create a sense of structure and security where there should be none. Ultimately, they lead to tunnel vision: an intense focus on a relevant but incomplete set of competitors.

. . . to Radar Screen

What is needed in place of tunnel vision is a radar screen that is formed by a scan of the marketplace with a single question in mind: Who is best positioned to serve and move ahead of changing customer priorities? Rather than defining competitors as "those companies that do the same things I do," this radar screen defines the competitive field of vision as those business designs that customers can choose from in satisfying their priorities.

The difficulty is creating a mechanism for identifying those competitors. Where do they come from? What do they look like? How do you know which ones to take seriously? Often, by the time your accounting system highlights customers' migrating away, it is too late to react. However, there is a logic and structure to the process by which new business designs enter a competitive field. By familiarizing yourself with the conditions that create opportunities for new entrants, you can gain a critical advantage in detecting and tracking them—before they gain critical mass.

The Expanding Competitive Field

The new competitive business designs that trigger Value Migration are many and varied. Sometimes they are new companies that satisfy a specific customer priority better than all incumbents. Other times the new competitors are effective at reaching customers that are underserved by existing business designs. In yet other cases, the new competitor is a company that was once a supplier or a customer but is now participating in a different part of the value chain. Even traditional competitors can create a new design to respond to customer priorities in new ways. In all these cases, the traditional field of vision—focusing on the companies that look like yours, that Wall Street analysts put in your "industry group"—is too narrow to see the new designs coming.

This chapter will examine four different cases in which the traditional field of vision was too narrow: retailing, business publishing, financial services, and home entertainment. The common denominator in all these examples is the crippling institutional memory and strong industry-think of traditional competitors. In each case there is also a change in the customer base, because of either the emergence of a new segment or the changing priorities of existing customers. In the financial services industry, external shocks played an important role in triggering Value Migration by making new business designs economically more attractive and competitive. In home entertainment, seemingly distant business designs have combined to form immediate, potent threats to incumbents.

Entry Focused on the Changing Customer

The customer drives the entire Value Migration process. However, it is important to realize that there are specific types of interaction between the customer base and new business designs, that can dramatically alter an established player's competitive environment. For instance, an incumbent's existing customer base may grow more sophisticated or develop new priorities. Or, an incumbent may have simply ignored an entire geographic, demographic, or behavioral segment. Either dynamic can create opportunities for entry by innovative business designs. The result is a dramatic expansion of the competitive field.

The ability of an incumbent to detect and track these new entrants depends in large measure on its understanding of the interaction between the customer base and new business designs. The evolution of the retail industry in the past 15 years demonstrates the peril of ceding a close rapport with the customer base to nontraditional business designs.

RETAILING. The companies that dominated the retailing industry in the period following World War II failed to maintain a broad competitive field of vision. Because they lost touch with both the composition and the evolution of American consumers, they gave away massive value growth and leadership of the industry to competitors they barely would have identified as being in the same business only 10 years earlier.

For most of the postwar era, the retail world was led by two traditional groups. Department stores like Macy's, Marshall Fields, and May's dominated the high-end segment. Mass merchandisers like Sears, Montgomery Ward, and JC Penney concentrated on selling a variety of middle-market brands. These major players hardly noticed the highly fragmented collection of small hardware stores, specialty shops, and boutiques that were consumers' only other options.

During the 1980s, however, industry dominance desensitized the retail giants to a number of trends that began to affect the way consumers shopped.

1. While GDP growth remained steady, the benefits of that growth were spread unevenly. Large numbers of people saw their incomes stagnate or decline in real terms, and became extremely price-conscious consumers.

2. Across the income spectrum, time was becoming an increasingly precious commodity. As women entered the workforce, many households had, for the first time, no one regularly able to devote large blocks of time to shopping for basics. As work became more demanding and people of all ages struggled to do their jobs, commute, see their families, and enjoy themselves, the time available for shopping declined significantly.

3. Many Americans began to place greater value on their own sense of individuality, distancing their personal lives from what they perceived as "anonymous" institutions such as government or giant companies. These consumers were gravitating to stores and merchandise that had personality, flair, and a more distinctive image.

These changes in the customer base created an opportunity for new business designs to expand dramatically the competitive field in the retail industry. Although some of the dominant retailers captured these customer trends in surveys and market research, none responded by reinventing its basic business design.

It was the much smaller business-design innovators that seized the opportunity created by the shifting customer base. Specialty stores, such as The Gap and The Limited, realized that consumers with a strong sense of individualism would pay premium prices at a boutique with a distinctive, consistent image. Specialty stores departed sharply from traditional department stores on the dimension of scope, focusing on apparel and "editing" their collections to fit into 10,000-square-foot stores. They also pioneered new mechanisms of value recapture by developing private label brands. The result was a powerful new business design that helped consumers quickly, easily, and confidently choose a reasonably priced, fashionable wardrobe; it also succeeded in creating more than $4 billion in market value.

An even more potent new business design that inserted itself between the department stores and their customers was the "Super Store" or "Category Killer." Competitors—such as The Home Depot, Toys "R" Us, and Circuit City—offered cost-conscious, time-pressed consumers better prices, greater service expertise, and a virtual guarantee that they would leave the store with a product they wanted. Like the specialty stores, these new entrants innovated on the dimension of scope. Unlike the specialty stores, they opted for enormous breadth and depth within a particular merchandise category. Another distinguishing characteristic of the superstore business design was highly efficient purchasing operations, which won concessions because of their tremendous volume. Customers have flocked to superstores, and the investment community has followed as this new business design had created more than $60 billion in market value by 1994.

Both specialty stores and superstores entered, won customers and profits, and broadened the competitive field in retailing by capitalizing on a change in customer priorities. However, another business design became the largest value creator in the industry by exploiting a second oversight by the incumbents: the existence of an entirely unserved customer group.

Wal-Mart realized that, although retailing competition was fierce in many major metropolitan areas, there were tens of millions of consumers in less populous, more rural "C" and "D" counties across the United States who were still buying most of their staples at general stores. By building huge 100,000-square-foot stores in these areas, Wal-Mart was able to offer customers both increased selection and lower prices for a broad range of nationally branded staples. This critical customer-selection strategy combined with an aggressive rollout plan has fueled Wal-Mart's sustained, large-scale growth. Other key dimensions of its business design have included innovative organizational configuration through employee stock-ownership plans and other measures, as well as superior purchasing and operational capabilities. By 1994, the combination of these elements had created more than $70 billion in market value.

If the traditional department stores had recognized that fault lines in the customer base could create opportunities for new business designs, they might have detected and responded to the new entrants more quickly. With their size and resource advantages, they might have blocked the newcomers or, better yet, staked out the new value space for themselves. But by failing to maintain intimate touch with the customer base, they allowed the new entrants to slip through the outermost concentric circles of the radar screen undetected. By the time the incumbents realized the magnitude of the threat, the new business designs had become powerful and entrenched.

The success of innovators makes it tempting for incumbents to focus on analyzing, benchmarking, and imitating them. But the retail world is changing so steadily that these new designs may already be outmoded. Retailers must predict how their customers' priorities will change again and how new business designs might satisfy them. Who are the faint lights on the perimeter of the radar screen today? (See Figure 4-1.)

Executives at the traditional retailers, notably Sears, have begun to make significant changes. Had the incumbents looked at their radar screen 10 or 15 years earlier, fewer department stores would be bankrupt and fewer mass merchandisers would be stagnant. But even as many business designs in the industry slide toward outflow, value growth opportunities remain. A retailer with a strong customer franchise could certainly start its own shopping network, emulate and improve on several other new retailing business models, and, most important, invest to develop the next-generation business designs in several retailing categories.

BUSINESS PUBLISHING. A second example of expansion of the competitive field driven by customer evolution occurred in business publishing. For years, the business reader had a selection of basic news and features from *Forbes, Fortune, Business Week,* and *The Wall Street Journal.* All the business designs of these traditional competitors included in-house reporting staffs, distribution through newsstands and subscription, and value recapture from circulation and advertising.

In the 1980s, core business readers became more demanding. Their most important priorities evolved from basic coverage of events

FIGURE 4-1   FROM TUNNEL VISION TO RADAR SCREEN:
RETAILING

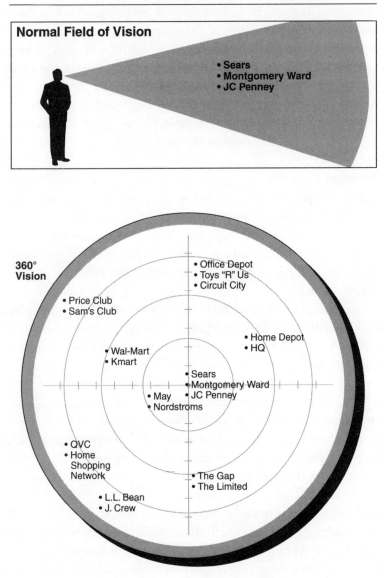

*The Value Migration perspective expands the field
of vision to include seven business designs that are
encroaching on the department store inner circle.*

in the business world to increased analysis, depth, and substance. One business design that responded, capturing significant value growth, was *The Economist*. Its approach to customer selection was unabashedly elitist, targeting affluent decision makers and advisers in business, politics, and finance. *The Economist* also deployed a distinctive value recapture mechanism, pricing its weekly offering at $3.50 (newsstand) and $2.00 (subscription), well above traditional business magazines. Premium pricing reinforced its highbrow image, and also enabled it to cover all costs through circulation revenues alone, a feat rarely achieved in the industry. These new approaches, plus substantial advertising revenues, combined to generate enviable profitability.

Other entrants that seized on the increasing sophistication of the customer base included investment newsletters, clipping or summary services, and on-line databases. These players have rethought almost every dimension of the traditional business-magazine design, from outsourced reporting to per-page value capture.

As the established customer base of business readers was growing more sophisticated, another dynamic was creating opportunity for further expansion of the competitive field: The general public was dramatically increasing its interest in business.

One player well established in mainstream journalism that began to compete in earnest for business readers was the *New York Times*. In the late 1980s and again in 1995, the *Times* upgraded the depth, analysis, and commentary of its daily business section. Springboarding off the paper's strong existing franchise with affluent, literate households, the revamped Business Day section quickly became a viable alternative to *The Wall Street Journal*.

In the 1990s, a series of economic, technological, and behavioral trends combined to create a third shift in the priorities of business readers. Downsizing at large companies, cheaper access to information technology, and a renewed interest in personal lifestyle were making many Americans abandon traditional employment patterns to become entrepreneurs or work out of their homes. Although these information-age workers were highly skilled, they wanted basic business and personal finance advice. How-to publications like *Inc.*, *Success*, and a raft of others met this priority, offering material that was less analytical but more prescriptive (see Figure 4-2).

FIGURE 4-2   RADAR SCREEN: PUBLISHING

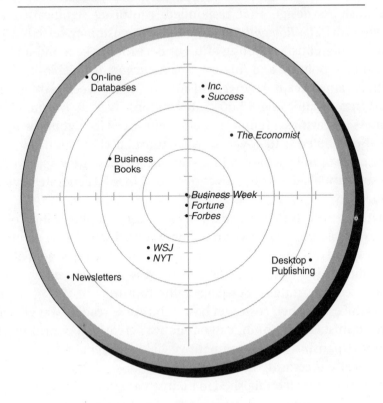

*Competition for readers' hours is continually
expanding to new business designs.*

Unlike retailing, the business publishing industry lacks clear losers that were displaced from industry dominance by new business designs. But what has been the opportunity cost of a limited competitive field of vision? What new value-growth possibilities have mainstream business magazines missed?

Entry Catalyzed by External Shocks

The growth of Wal-Mart from a nontraditional competitor to the world's largest retailer within 30 years illustrates the way in which a poorly examined customer base allows new business designs to enter the competitive field.

But perhaps the most dramatic market opportunities for new business designs are created by external shocks. As discussed in the previous chapter, external shocks include large-scale political, macroeconomic, technological, and regulatory changes. These phenomena can abruptly upset the business chessboard, recasting both customer priorities and the economic viability of different business designs. For instance, the OPEC embargo and consequent rise in the price of gasoline immediately elevated fuel efficiency in the hierarchy of customer priorities. The Airline Deregulation Act of 1978 had a less direct impact on the priorities of air travelers, but dramatically affected the range of business designs that airlines could deploy.

External shocks can be very difficult to predict. What is not difficult to predict, however, is that shocks will create significant opportunities for new business designs. So while all organizations may not be able to afford the luxury of trying to predict the exact nature and timing of external shocks, there is no established competitor that can afford *not* to expand its competitive field of vision once a shock has occurred. In the wake of a significant external shock, the most important question becomes: What new business designs may be taking advantage of the situation to encroach on the incumbent's customer franchise?

FINANCIAL SERVICES. A vivid example of how external shocks can rapidly widen the competitive field occurred in the financial services industry. Between the late 1970s and the late 1980s, a series of market shocks dramatically altered the financial priorities of American households. If the incumbent commercial banks had fully comprehended the effects of these shocks sooner, they might have protected their positions more effectively or even taken advantage of the new opportunities to grow their value. But, as in retailing, strong institutional memory slowed the ability of the industry leaders to expand their competitive field of vision.

From the 1950s into the 1970s, the priorities of the vast majority of American savers remained largely unchanged. Heads of households who had lived through the depression and World War II valued easy access to funds and rock-solid security. They wanted a secure financial future. For most, the key to reaching that goal was dutifully setting aside some fraction of income for savings. In comparison, maximizing the performance of those saved assets received little attention.

Offering basic savings accounts, commercial banks built a business design that matched these dominant customer priorities. Their scope was limited, consisting of a federally mandated level of return (the interest rate on savings accounts) linked to a guarantee of security from the Federal Deposit Insurance Corporation. Commercial banks kept most aspects of their operational system, such as accounting and statement processing, in-house. The dominant go-to-market mechanism was the local branch office, which fostered customer loyalty.

By the late 1970s, however, the external shock of inflation radically altered customer priorities. By 1979, inflation was running rampant at 13 percent. Bank savings rates were set by law at 5.25 percent, and the public suddenly realized how much it was losing with savings accounts. Americans' traditional priorities of security and convenient access to savings were displaced by the need to protect the value of capital.

As a result, many people withdrew their money from local bank accounts and placed it in money market funds. Run by money managers such as Fidelity Research and Management Co. and investment banks such as Merrill Lynch, these vehicles offered savers returns that rose with inflation, with minimal associated risk. Elements of the underlying business design included an operations system that outsourced selected back-office tasks and a go-to-market mechanism that used direct mail or tele-sellers instead of the downtown branches of commercial banks. In 1979, there were $10 billion invested nationally in money market funds. By 1982, the total had grown to $250 billion.

Shortly after commercial banks began to offer money market funds to compete with these new designs, another external shock changed customer perspectives. By the mid-1980s, Wall Street's longest postwar bull market was under way. Just as the shock of inflation caused households to prioritize wealth protection over liquidity and security, so the rising market drove customer priorities a step further: from wealth protection to growth. The key priority became optimizing returns. Savers became investors.

Some people went directly to brokers that had retail operations— Dean Witter, Shearson, and Merrill Lynch. These business designs expanded scope dramatically, offering a full spectrum of risk and return plus the advice and guidance that many individual investors required. Brokerage houses depended heavily on the effectiveness of their dominant go-to-market mechanism, the direct sales force. Where commercial banks' value recapture device had been the spread between interest charged on loans and interest paid to depositors, brokerages relied on commissions paid by the customer.

Others turned to mutual funds. These players modified brokerage houses' scope by offering a smaller number of investment opportunities while relieving the customer of the responsibility of picking individual stocks. Research and development became an important component of this business design. The operations system outsourced many noncore tasks to statement processors and transfer agents.

A third market-related shock that reshuffled customer priorities once again and created opportunity for new entrants was the stock market crash of October 19, 1987. Stung for the first time by capital losses, many investors reevaluated their financial priorities, placing renewed emphasis on security. Large insurance companies responded with a business design whose scope emphasized safety and solidity. Many of them began to offer annuities and similar products. The go-to-market mechanism of these players piggybacked off the existing customer relationships in their core insurance business.

In 1975, the financial services market consisted of four distinct categories. Competitors within each could get away with tunnel vision. But not today. In 1995, the radar screen shows four types of competitors, each raiding the others' domain, all competing for the same customer. "I used to track six banks," a local banker notes. "Today I have to track over 100 different financial services firms who are competing for my customers' accounts. Measuring where the money is going is getting tougher. Parsing through the data is getting harder and harder. It gives me a headache."

Although Wall Street and the government might still draw some distinctions among commercial banks, investment banks, insurance companies, and mutual fund companies, customers do not. They are looking for the option—in terms of risk and return, the portfolio of savings and investment choices, the level of service and information—that best matches their priorities. These ever-expanding choices have created a more educated, sophisticated, and demanding customer base. Customers now make the risk-return trade-offs themselves, choosing among products and distribution channels.

As the number of options available to the customer has exploded, new business designs have arisen to meet customers' latest priorities—advice and evaluation. Financial consultants now help customers sort through their options. As their numbers have grown, they have become an important influence on how the players are perceived. In crafting their business designs, companies must choose whether to work with these advisers, or compete with them. The same phenomenon is under way in the health care field; employers hire expert consultants to untangle the web of health plan options and choose the best ones.

As financial services players formulate business designs to be effective in the newly expanded competitive field, yet another new competitor is emerging. If insurance companies seemed like strange competitors to the commercial banks, Microsoft must seem completely foreign. By attempting to acquire the personal finance software company Intuit in 1994, Microsoft clearly signaled its intention to enter the field of financial services (see Figure 4-3). Microsoft CEO Bill Gates has publicly described his vision of an electronic transaction system that will compete head to head with existing checks and credit and debit cards.

The importance of the attempted Microsoft/Intuit combination transcends the world of financial services. It vividly illustrates how two business designs that, when taken alone, are of little significance to a given competitive field can become a direct and powerful competitor if combined. This pattern of two or more business designs working as a system is vital to understanding the Value Migration in one of today's most dynamic areas: the convergence of television, entertainment, and telecommunications.

Systems of Business Designs as a Competitive Entity

Business designs rarely exist in isolation. Relationships between buyers and suppliers, manufacturers and distributors, outsourcers and subcontractors create complex interdependence in all industries. For instance, in the computing industry, the value-added-reseller business design is a stand-alone design that also serves as a go-to-market mechanism in the business designs of many computer manufactur-

FIGURE 4-3   RADAR SCREEN: COMMERCIAL BANKS

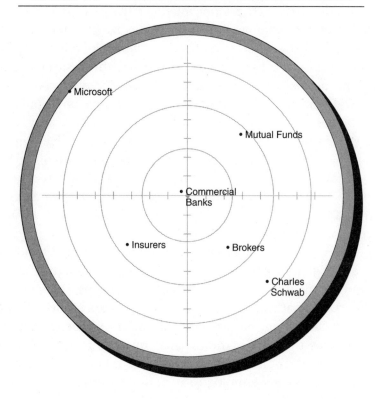

*The real threat comes from unconventional players
outside the traditional banking boundary.*

ers. How two or more business designs are combined often affects
the ability of each to create and capture value. On a stand-alone
basis, many business designs offer little competitive threat. But combined with other business designs, they create substantial utility for
customers and capture value for each of the constituent parts.

The formation of systems of interlocking business designs can
have a decisive impact on the competitive field. When combined
with complementary business designs, previously obscure competitors can emerge to fundamentally reshape an industry. This
effect is particularly evident in the home entertainment industry,
where systems of business designs have created substantial value
growth.

HOME ENTERTAINMENT. Television networks rose to great heights in the 1950s. The value of the networks grew rapidly as branded products companies began to realize the power of this national advertising vehicle. With the exception of a few tiny independent stations in a handful of major cities, the customer had no compelling home "video entertainment" alternative to ABC, CBS, and NBC. Even outside the home there was only one option: the movie theater.

In the early 1970s, engineers at Ampex and Sony began to develop the videocassette recorder (VCR). Sony's launch of the Betamax was the first attempt at commercializing this new technology. Then in 1976, through a brilliant series of licensing arrangements, Matsushita established VHS as the home video standard. It rapidly replaced Sony's struggling Beta format.

Even as video cassette recorders began to penetrate households, the threat to network television was limited. Although customers had acquired an alternative conduit for video signals, there was very little entertainment content to fill the new pipeline. Matsushita was able to earn handsome returns, but its early revenue, profitability, and value growth came at the expense of 8mm movie equipment and still cameras, not network television. As a home entertainment business design, VCR technology and manufacturing excellence was incomplete.

What eventually enabled the VCR manufacturer business design to threaten network television stations was the easy access to content—in the form of the video-rental-store business design. Combined, these two designs triggered the first major wave of Value Migration in home entertainment.

As VCR penetration continued to rise, video store chains such as Blockbuster expanded at a rapid rate, increasing the number of new stores by 50 percent annually. By the early 1990s, there was a video store in every moderately sized town in America, and in many young, affluent households video rentals consumed 20 percent of prime time market share (4 hours out of 22; two movie rentals a week). This new business design system forced its way into the competitive field and commanded a high-profit, high-value position.

Even as they wired VCRs to their own TV sets, network executives failed to expand their competitive field of vision. They defined their business based on the activities they engaged in—programming, broadcasting, selling advertising—rather than the activities their customers engaged in—video entertainment. The executives saw television as an exclusive carrier, not a black box that could serve as a screen for any source of home video entertainment.

Institutional memory also limited the network leaders' ability to recognize the implications of another emerging system of business designs: cable television. As with home video, the penetration of the conduit into millions of American homes failed to raise the networks' guard. Once again, it was only the emergence of new video content that made the competitive threat apparent. But by then, the two business designs had combined, triggering a second major wave of Value Migration.

Cable TV began as a way to deliver better viewing quality to areas with poor reception. Regulators granted local monopolies. Although thousands of entrepreneurs flocked to the field, the networks saw cable as only one thing: infrastructure. The cable operators were in the business of wiring homes. That wasn't a threat to network market share. On the contrary, it would bring network programming to more viewers. But the networks missed two key points when they looked at cable. First, the physical cable created tremendous new signal capacity. Second, the ability to control what signals were sent down the line meant that, for the first time, viewers could be charged for each program. Networks found this a difficult concept to grasp. After all, their business design, built around a single value recapture mechanism (advertising), had enjoyed decades of success.

With the emergence of specialized programmers such as Home Box Office, MTV, CNN, and ESPN, the new business design system was complete. Viewers could watch a feature film instead of the usual (and often lower-quality) network movie. Sports fans could count on watching their favorite teams, not just what was being shown in the networks' regional broadcast area. No longer were busy people restricted to the news at 6 and 11 to catch up on current events.

As with home video, the combination of conduit and content eventually created a business design that siphoned substantial value away from the networks. And the cable TV business design created its own virtuous circle: More capacity stimulated more programming; more programming convinced more customers to pay for the capacity, even if they received the three networks, an independent station, and public broadcasting for free.

Alone, the cable system business design only could deliver high-quality signals for the networks. Alone, the programmers were left fighting for limited network air time. Together, these two business designs created utility for customers, captured value for both contributors, and hastened the slide of the networks into value outflow.

As happens in many industries when the competitive field begins to expand, early revenues to the neophytes were small. In 1985, the advertising revenue of *all* cable channels combined was less than $700 million. *Each* network had a revenue base in the $3-billion range. But as customers began to vote with their dollars and their remote controls, the opposite trajectories of the competing business designs became clear.

Not only did the networks fail to detect the emergence of the initial cable TV business design, they also missed the emergence of a second generation of cable competitors. Entrepreneurs like Ted Turner packaged a variety of cable programming to create a hybrid alternative, which included specialized regional coverage. If you couldn't find the basketball game you wanted to see on ABC or ESPN, you could probably find it on the Turner Broadcasting System channel in Atlanta. If you didn't like the movie selection on HBO, TBS had one you could watch. Even colorized classics. Other entrepreneurs took the concept further. In the 1980s, the number of independent TV stations rose from 500 to 1,000. Rupert Murdoch and Barry Diller decided to sign them up, creating a fourth network—Fox.

By 1993, cable operators were generating $7 billion in revenue for the programming producers. Half came from advertising, half from subscriber fees. In areas with high cable penetration, such as Hartford, Connecticut, the market share of the three networks fell from 95 percent to less than 50 percent. Adjusting for video cassette and video game penetration, the true market share was below 40 percent. Fox had achieved more than 6 percent share nationally, and was growing.

In the mid-1990s, the radar screen in the home video entertainment industry is thick with competing business designs (see Figure 4-4). It has expanded beyond the original networks to include several new networks (Fox, Time Warner, UPN, and nationwide PBS), 30

FIGURE 4-4   RADAR SCREEN: NETWORKS

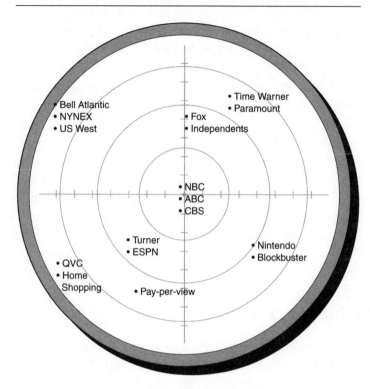

*Several radically different types of business
designs are competing for customer viewing hours.*

sizable cable channels, 10 major video store chains such as Blockbuster, and two major video game companies—Nintendo and Sega.
The common denominator is not the activities in which these companies engage—they still have quite different business designs. It is
the competition for share of the viewer's attention.

These erstwhile renegades are now facing the next cycle of value
flow. Home shopping channels are the fastest growing segment of
the cable industry. Although the home shopping business design
today may be incomplete (just like that of the early VCR), that will
change in the next few years.

The former regional Bell operating companies are also entering
the field. In partnership with creative agencies, they are developing

a business design system to deliver video programming over phone lines. At the same time, cable operators are telling long-distance carriers such as Sprint and MCI to side-step local phone companies, which charge high fees for access to individual homes, and use cable TV lines instead to reach customers.

The home video entertainment companies must expand their competitive field of vision even further to consider the penetration of computers into the home. The most basic definition of customers' video options would be based on the number of recreational hours a day a person sits in front of a cathode ray tube. In this view, computer games, educational software, and the looming giant—CD-ROM—will cut into classical television hours. These applications, plus services like home shopping, could be combined in a new system of business designs that may even redefine the competitive field beyond home video entertainment to home video usage.

Establishing Your Own Radar Screen

Though uncomfortable, expanding your competitive field of vision is one of the most efficient ways to uncover signals about the major new value-growth opportunities in your industry. At a minimum, you must continually examine the competitive field for defensive purposes. But you can also use the analysis to structure a sound offense—to identify new business designs that have the potential, in current or modified forms, to create significant new profit growth.

If you can push aside the effects of institutional memory, denial, and tunnel vision, you will clearly visualize the entire competitive field. You will see new competitors approaching your customers soon enough to be able to respond to them effectively, or to preempt them completely. You will be able to exploit the new opportunities presented on your radar screen.

Reaching this point does not have to be difficult. There are two exercises you and your colleagues can perform to improve your ability to evaluate the changing nature of your competitor set.

First, initiate a dialogue or debate within your management team on the questions, "What is our competitive field?" and "What should it be?" Simply initiating the dialogue has a powerful liberating effect. It highlights and challenges the basic assumptions of institutional memory. It forces an orientation toward customers and away from traditional competitors. It also forces a search for early warning signals about change, often a fertile source of ideas about future customer behavior.

To catalyze the discussion, ask these questions:

- What are your customers' most important priorities today? What will they be in 1999?
- How are changes in the customer base creating opportunities for new business designs?
- How did the last external shock alter the competitive field? Who is positioned to capitalize on the next one?
- What minor competitors could become immediate threats when combined with another business design?
- Do any of the new business designs that have already forced their way into your market represent powerful new growth opportunities?
- Should you invest in them? Copy them? Can you?
- What will happen if you decide not to?

When you work through these questions, you might find that your competitive field is stable and will remain so. That would be extraordinary. Consider yourself fortunate. Even in this case, however, you should reexamine your assumptions about what your customers want and where they can get it. Spend time with your customers, and prospective new ones, to understand what *they* think their options are. Then ask yourself: Is there an opportunity to initiate change so you can lead customers into the future? Is there a way for you to initiate Value Migration—in your company's direction?

As a second exercise, take a piece of paper and draw four concentric circles—a makeshift radar screen. Place your own business model in the center. Fill the inner circle with the names of your direct competitors. In the next circle, put in the names of your indirect competitors. In the third circle, write down your "remote" competitors (the ones that "sort of" compete with your business design).

In the outer circle, stretch your imagination. Include the truly remote, and ostensibly insignificant, competitors. Several of your customers—or most valued prospects—have already decided to go with companies in this circle.

Once you've done this, draw a fifth circle. Include in it names of companies that are not yet competitors, but might become ones soon.

This is a difficult exercise to do in a way that really reshapes how you think. Three tactics can help:

1. Reverse the denial impulse ("They don't compete with us.") in favor of the inclusion impulse ("If customers or prospects consider them an option, they're a competitor.").

2. Work the radar-screen exercise with a friend or colleague who is outside your company and industry.

3. Do a preparatory exercise by using a different company and industry. Try computing, airlines, printing, fast foods, beer . . . or an industry that parallels yours, say, chemical engineering if you are an electrical engineering firm. Often, by starting the thought process in the context of other industries, your team can progress rapidly because there is more objectivity. Then apply what you have learned to your own radar screen.

Moving from tunnel vision to radar screen and maintaining a broad competitive field of vision is one of the most important first steps to mastering the new chess game of business. Only by understanding the circumstances that consistently create opportunity for new business designs, and by systematically tracking those that matter, can you position your organization to emerge as a beneficiary, not a casualty, of the next cycle of Value Migration.

PART II

Seven Patterns Every Manager Should Know

Introduction:
Recognizing Strategic Patterns

Part I of this book described how Value Migration works. It defined the mechanisms of cause and effect that define the timing, scope, and magnitude of migration. It also presented a set of tools for analyzing and describing Value Migration in any industry (see Figure II-1). But merely knowing the basic elements and parameters of Value Migration does not make one a proficient player of the game of business chess. As in chess, with its thousands of possible combinations of pieces and positions, achieving success in the new game of business hinges on the ability to *apply* these analytical tools with the high order of skill that comes from studying and mastering numerous patterns.

To play chess well you need to learn patterns. By examining patterns, you see how specific positions can lead to specific outcomes. By then looking several moves ahead and envisioning the implications of your current position, you can identify and focus on the most important pieces and positions—the linchpins of your strategy. One way of learning to recognize the patterns on the chess board is by studying the games of others.

In business chess, of course, there are no pieces, no squares, no boundaries on a board. But the principles of chess hold—moves and countermoves, cause and effect, the unfolding game with strategic advantage created, lost, then created again—and the same method of learning them applies. Learning a Value Migration pattern means

FIGURE II-1   CAPTURING VALUE GROWTH

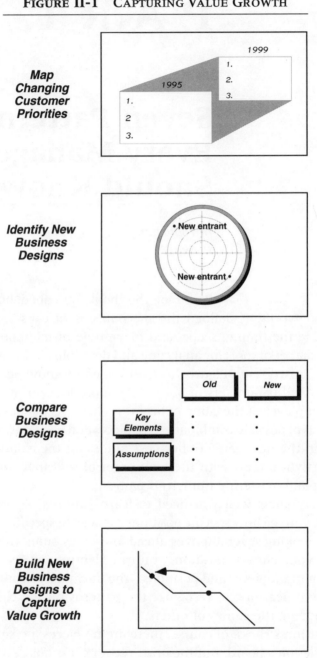

Map Changing Customer Priorities

Identify New Business Designs

Compare Business Designs

Build New Business Designs to Capture Value Growth

learning those cause-and-effect relationships and recognizing the conditions and circumstances that lead to specific outcomes. In each case of Value Migration, the interaction of changing customer priorities and business-design alternatives creates a flow of value. The ways each of these elements interacts with the others to create a specific outcome define a Value Migration pattern.

Part II of this book describes seven Value Migration patterns that have unfolded and continue to unfold within and across major industries, affecting business designs of all types. Each chapter analyzes a fundamental pattern and challenges you to apply it to a real-world situation by making choices based on limited information at critical junctures in time.

As you read the stories, keep in mind the following questions designed to help you recognize cause and effect, identify relationships among the elements, and anticipate the outcome of the pattern.

Patterns in Changing Customer Priorities

- Who is the customer? Is the set of decision makers and influencers changing?
- How are customer priorities changing? What are expectations for performance? For cost?
- What new customer groups or segments are becoming more important? How different are the priorities of various segments within the market?
- How are customers evolving? Are they growing more powerful? More sophisticated? More capable? How are their economics changing?
- How do external shocks affect customer priorities? What new priorities emerge from these shocks?

Patterns in Business Design Alternatives

- How do alternative business designs differ? What business design dimensions are most important in determining which designs succeed and which fail? Which elements are critical to meeting customers' priorities?
- Where do the new business designs come from? Entrepreneurs on the attack? Established companies in different

industries? Companies that participate in other parts of the value chain?

■ What characteristics of the incumbents' business designs affect their ability to respond to Value Migration? Economic structure? Managerial behavior? Impetus to change?

■ How do external shocks affect the economic attractiveness of each business design?

Patterns in Value Migration

■ How do new alternative business designs match with customer priorities? How do they displace the incumbents?

■ How much additional utility is created for the customer? How much of that utility is captured as profits by the providers?

■ How is value reallocated among business designs? What is the rate and magnitude of the value flow? Is there new value growth or merely reallocation of existing value?

The answers to these questions define a Value Migration pattern.

Chapter **5**

Multidirectional Migration

From Steel to Materials

- Is my business design flexible enough to serve different customer segments effectively?

- Are my customers' priorities changing in ways to which I can respond?

- Is my business experiencing multidirectional Value Migration, with value flowing away from my business design to *several* different types of new business designs simultaneously?

NEXT TIME YOU GO FOR A DRIVE, look at your car. It probably contains a good deal of plastic, not just in the interior, but in the engine, the fenders, even some body panels. Say you stop at the store to pick up some beer and soda. The cans are made of aluminum. It's likely the refrigerator you'll put them in is made with both plastic and aluminum. If your apartment or office building is reasonably new, there's a good chance that the steel used in it came from Japan, or an American minimill.

In 1960, all these products were made of steel, and all the steel came from huge integrated steel mills. Eight American companies—U.S. Steel, Bethlehem, National, Republic, Armco, Jones & Laughlin, Inland, and Youngstown Sheet & Tube—dominated the U.S. steel market and had an estimated total market value of $55 billion.[1] By

1993, the market value of the survivors had fallen to an estimated $13 billion. Industry employment, which had peaked at 450,000 in the 1970s, had fallen to 135,000.

The steel story illustrates two fundamental mechanisms that cause value to migrate from some business designs within and across many industries. First, customers turned to steel suppliers with new business designs that integrated steelmakers thought were only on the fringe of their market. Second, customers turned to business designs that were built around materials that performed better than steel. This substitution enabled a whole new set of competitors to siphon off the value that had been created by the steel industry (see Figure 5-1).

The lessons of Value Migration in the steel industry apply to any company that serves several customer groups, each evolving in a different direction. The experience of the U.S. integrated steel companies is especially relevant to any large, established competitor that adds capacity in big increments that are expensive, permanent, and nonconvertible. Chemicals, autos, aluminum, printing, even retailing and banking face similar situations. Executives in these industries still have important moves available to them. In the next few years, those moves will have major implications for their companies' future value growth.

FIGURE 5-1   MULTIDIRECTIONAL MIGRATION

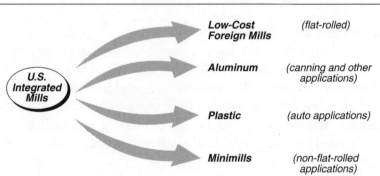

In steel, value migrated away from the integrated mill model to four new business designs better matched to customer priorities.

The Integrated Steelmaking Business Design

In the 1950s and 1960s, the integrated business designs of the major U.S. steel companies generated tremendous value growth. Following the depression and World War II, steel-hungry industries such as autos, construction, appliance manufacturing, and canning were shifting into a powerful expansion mode. The business design of the U.S. mills was perfectly tailored to meet the rising demand. Through vertical integration, the mills achieved extremely low unit costs at high utilization rates. Because their customers depended on steel for growth and had no alternatives to domestic supplies, the integrated mills had all the power.

The U.S. Integrated Steel Mill Business Design

Fundamental Assumptions	There are no significant substitutes for steel.
	American customers want American-made steel.
	The blast furnace/basic oxygen furnace method is the only way to produce large volumes of high-quality steel economically.
Business Design Elements	**Integrated Steelmakers' Choice**
Customer Selection	Broad line, serving multiple customer groups with varied needs and priorities
Scope	Full product line
	Full vertical integration
Manufacturing System	Blast/ basic oxygen furnace
	High fixed cost, low incremental cost
Capital Intensity	High

Business Design Elements	Integrated Steelmakers' Choice
R&D	In-house
Organizational Configuration	Unionized labor
	High overhead/fixed costs

The success of the integrated business design encouraged a dangerous mind-set, perhaps most apparent at the Duquesne Club, the venerable institution in Pittsburgh where steelmakers met for lunch and dinner. They talked about capacity utilization, the adoption of new furnace technology, and the number of cars being produced. Rarely was there mention of a nontraditional competitor.

By the mid-1960s, the business design of the integrated mills was generating tremendous revenue, cash flow, and market value. Year after year of buoyant demand created high utilization rates, profitable growth, and entrenched institutional memory that conditioned how steel makers thought, what competitive threats they saw, and what customer signals they heard. They would have found it difficult to understand someone like Ken Burns.

Burns learned about the power of institutional memory the hard way. In his early thirties, he was a rising star at U.S. Steel. He was called a financial genius. He was also ambitious. At a meeting early in 1966, he announced that he was going to spend his vacation visiting several Japanese steel mills. Eyebrows rose. Disapproval radiated from every person in the room. Burns didn't understand the negative reaction of his colleagues. After all, the Japanese had built some of the world's finest steel mills. He wanted to become the best executive in the business, and felt that understanding the competition was a key step in that process. Burns went anyway.

He was overwhelmed by what he saw. For instance, Nippon Kokan's No. 1 blast furnace had significantly greater annual capacity than U.S. Steel's largest one. The scale of the furnace, the improved basic oxygen process, and the efficient straight-line configuration of the raw-materials handling systems were eye-openers.

The purpose of Nippon Kokan's production innovations was to dramatically improve the economics of the highly efficient U.S. integrated mill model. Burns knew he was looking at the next-generation integrated steel business design. Although he could not see the actual numbers for the plant, he knew to within 5 percent how much lower its costs must be. But the impressive cost position of the current system was not what really worried Burns. It was how much better the Japanese design would be in the future.

When Burns returned to Pittsburgh, he approached U.S. Steel's leaders. He talked passionately about what the Japanese were doing, and what their future cost position would be. They were building the next generation integrated mill business design. But no one listened. The value of the U.S. market that Japan's mills had captured was tiny. Besides, strong lobbying in Washington would severely restrict the imports of foreign steel.

Although the integrated producers dismissed the Japanese mills, their customers in the construction industry did not. Big contracting and engineering firms—which were busy building roads and entire cities in addition to dwellings—bought as much steel as the Japanese mills could export.

Thanks to heavy tariffs on higher-quality steel, which eliminated the Japanese price advantage, the U.S. integrated mills maintained a firm hold on automotive customers. While core customers were well protected, peripheral ones (such as small equipment manufacturers) were not. When salesmen representing Japanese steel products offered acceptable quality at lower prices, these customers responded with orders.

Given the high costs of transporting steel, how were the Japanese able to offer low prices? The key to their next-generation integrated mill business design was a ruthless and systematic attack on every cost component in the value chain. They optimized upstream in the steelmaking process, then downstream in a perfectly prioritized sequence of cost improvements. Transportation costs were driven down first (large-scale shipping). Then ore (new sources in Australia). Then coal (new sources in Brazil). Then larger blast furnaces. Then basic oxygen furnaces (300 tons per heat scale). Finally, continuous casting, a new production process that eliminated a major process step—ingot making—significantly reducing costs.

Business Design
U.S. Integrated Mills vs. Japanese Integrated Mills

	U.S. Integrated Mills	Japanese Integrated Mills
Fundamental Assumptions	American customers want American-made steel.	Quality product at low prices will gain customers and market share.
		The U.S. integrated design can be improved at every step of the value chain.
Manufacturing/ Operating System	Scale economies Low ratio of continuous casting	Massive scale economies Straight-line configuration Plants situated on deepwater harbors Rapid adoption of continuous casting
Organizational Configuration	Trade union	Company union

Although creating the new business design had been costly, it was beginning to generate substantial returns for Japanese mills. The upgraded production processes gave them a 30 percent cost advantage over their U.S. counterparts—more than enough to offset transportation costs. This cost advantage might not have been apparent to U.S. steel executives, but they couldn't miss volume. By 1971, Japanese production (94 million tons) was fast approaching total U.S. production (110 million tons).

Many of Japan's moves were too capital intensive for the U.S. integrated steel companies to follow. But the continuous casting move made enormous economic sense for all players (casting saved up to $40 on a ton of product that cost $300). Acutely aware of the economic implications, the Japanese mills aggressively converted their capacity to continuous casting. By 1974, the portion of steel made in Japan by continuous casting was 30 percent. In the United States, it was only 7 percent.

At the same time, construction companies found that U.S. minimills were offering very competitive prices on low-end bar steel for reinforcing concrete (rebar). Minimills could offer low prices because their business design had several distinct advantages. Rather than smelting iron ore in basic oxygen furnaces, they collected inexpensive scrap and melted it in electric arc furnaces. Their plants were located in rural areas, where labor costs were 30–40 percent lower than in the urban production centers of the integrated mills. Their overhead was low. They were located close to major construction areas so builders and wholesalers could order products with shorter lead times and get faster delivery, a significant advantage in a booming construction market. The minimills also began to produce joists—higher-value products that allowed them to recapture significantly more value per ton of steel produced.

Business Design
U.S. Integrated Mills vs. Minimills

	U.S. Integrated Mills	Minimills
Fundamental Assumptions	The fully integrated, basic oxygen furnace method is the only way to produce high-quality steel economically.	Steel can be made economically in smaller quantities.
Customer Selection	Broad line, serving multiple segments of customers	Focus on construction in regional markets
Scope	Full product line	Low-end construction products (rebar)

	U.S. Integrated Mills	Minimills
Manufacturing/ Operating System	Blast furnace/ basic oxygen furnace	Electric arc furnace
	Iron ore as raw material	Scrap steel as raw material
R&D/Product Development	In-house	Cooperative (piggyback on equipment man-ufacturers, uni-versities)
Organizational Configuration	Unionized labor	Nonunionized labor
	High overhead	Incentive-based compensation
		Bare-bones over-head

Still, the integrated steel companies did not take the minimills very seriously. In the mid-1970s, minimills produced only a few million tons of steel per year. Leading publicly held minimills had an aggregate market value of $280 million by the end of 1975, less than 1 percent of the integrated mills' estimated total market value of $35 billion.

At least one minimill should have attracted the attention of the large steelmakers. Based in Charlotte, North Carolina, an innovative minimill named Nucor was growing rapidly under its hard-driving CEO, Kenneth Iverson. By the early 1970s, Nucor was producing steel joists in Darlington, South Carolina, Norfolk, Nebraska, and Jewett, Texas. More plants were planned.

As buyers of low-end structural steel discovered the minimill alternative, the canning industry also found new suppliers: compa-nies with business designs built around alternative materials. For years, beer and soda can manufacturers had been nagged by produc-tion problems with steel. Ease of manufacture, not price, dominated their purchase decisions. Reject rates in canning plants were persistently high because tin-plated steel was not an easily formable material. Furthermore, its weight added substantially to transportation costs.

Can manufacturers also realized that steel limited the appeal of their product to end-users. It was easy to open a steel can in a kitchen, but people at picnics, parties, football games, beaches, and offices had to scrounge around for a can opener. Beverage marketers knew that a "pop top" can would add to the utility of their product, but steel was unlikely to develop the formability needed to satisfy this unmet need.

Aluminum, however, was light and easy to bend. Exploiting this advantage, aluminum manufacturers launched a highly focused campaign against steel. A key factor in their business design was astute customer selection. Aluminum makers did not disperse their efforts over a broad range of applications but concentrated all their resources on knocking steel out of the beer can market. Early experiments in making aluminum cans succeeded, and pop tops became possible. By the late 1960s, 20 percent of beer cans were made of aluminum, and the Value Migration from the integrated steel manufacturers' business design to the aluminum-based business design was accelerating. By 1973, 50 percent of beer cans were aluminum. The aluminum players next trained their sights on soft drinks and quickly captured 20 percent of that market.

It all seemed a bit bothersome to Big Steel. They were losing the can market, but what could they do? Steel was steel. They couldn't change its properties, could they? The minimills—well, they were just too small to worry about. Besides, demand from the auto makers was higher than ever. In fact, many steel executives had just had their best production year yet.

But the integrated steel companies' reliance on a few familiar metrics—capacity utilization and tons produced—dulled their sensitivity to other, more disturbing numbers. By 1973, Japanese mills, U.S. minimills, and aluminum producers had displaced 20 million tons of steel from the integrated mills.

When the oil shock of 1973 jarred the industrial world, the integrated steel companies' insularity led to another critical error. While executives lamented the increased price of oil, they passed most of the added cost along to their consumers and assumed that foreign producers would do the same. The embargo even provided integrated steel companies a measure of reassurance: Since the Japanese mills were totally dependent on foreign sources of energy, the shock would force them to raise prices even more and they would lose proportionate market share. What these executives did not imagine in their leather chairs at the Duquesne Club was the incredible galvanizing effect that the embargo had on the Japanese mills. Cutting energy consumption furiously to remain competitive, the Japanese mills emerged from the crisis leaner and more formidable than ever.

It is 1974. As the CEO of Nucor or U.S. Steel, this is the situation you see.

- Although still less than U.S. total annual steel production (137 million tons), Japanese total annual steel production is increasing rapidly (111 million tons).
- Japanese mills produce 30 percent of their steel by continuous casting versus 7 percent for their U.S. counterparts.
- Aluminum has taken 50 percent of the beer can market and 20 percent of the soda can market. So far, the penetration curve for soda has mirrored that in beer but with a three-year lag.
- The market value of the leading U.S. integrated mills ($35 billion) is still more than a hundred times greater than that of the publicly traded minimills ($280 million).

What is your next move? How might rising oil prices alter your customers' priorities? Is the loss of the canning market a case of inevitable and irreversible materials substitution, or should you invest to counter aluminum's penetration? Should you imitate the business models of the Japanese mills and the minimills? Could you?

Different Customers, Different Priorities

By the late 1970s, the U.S. integrated mills had finally been jolted from their unchallenged dominance. As the trend toward aluminum substitution in canning became undeniable, several mills made a countermove. Together with Crown Cork & Seal, a metal and glass packager, they attempted to develop a lower-cost way of making cans from steel.

It was an excellent initiative to protect the market value of steel in can making, but too little too late. In 1978, Miller Beer made a major comparison of aluminum and steel on criteria of cost and ease of can manufacturing. The following year it switched to aluminum. By the late 1970s aluminum had the dominant share of the beer market and more than half of the soda market. The window of opportunity for a successful countermove had closed on steel.

The oil shock provided another opportunity to respond proactively to changing customer needs—this time in the automotive segment. Rising gasoline prices were beginning to create intense consumer demand for fuel-efficient vehicles.

This fundamental change in consumer priorities was detected immediately by plastics manufacturers. GE Plastics, Dow Chemical, and Borg-Warner focused their R&D efforts on making major advances in impact, heat, and solvent resistance. At the same time, engineers set to work determining which of the tough, light compounds were best suited to different uses such as auto bumpers, home appliances, and computer cabinets. By the end of the decade, plastics had become increasingly competitive with steel in many of these markets, and the plastics makers came knocking on Detroit's doors.

It was not the purchasing agents, but the design engineers who let them in. Auto designers appreciated plastic's light weight, rust resistance, and capacity to reduce both number of pieces in an assembly and factory retooling costs. Of course, plastic had serious disadvantages. It was not as recyclable as steel. It took longer to cast a plastic part than to stamp a steel one. Detroit lacked machining expertise. Nevertheless, improved gas mileage was an urgent priority, and plastics provided a way to reduce body weight and increase fuel efficiency.

Eventually, more auto makers began to realize the viability of the plastics option. The technical department at a major auto supplier noted that "progress in raw material technology will allow substitution of less expensive plastics for metal, especially in the engine area." When such views were articulated, steelmakers expressed skepticism, even disbelief. Big Steel's reluctance to take the plastics challenge seriously was reinforced by the difficulty of measuring the threat. It was simple to calculate the number of beer cans made of aluminum and compute the penetration rate. It was harder to quantify plastic's penetration into a bewildering array of auto applications. In 1975, only 4 percent of an average car's weight was plastic, and much of that was compounds, such as nylon for interiors, that did not compete with steel.

Three quantification steps were feasible, however. First, it was possible to identify engineering plastics that, unlike nylon, did compete with steel. Second, it was possible to calculate the equivalent weight of steel displaced in a car and therefore lost market share. Third, armed with this information, steelmakers could identify specific applications being attacked. Oldsmobile was making fenders and fascia with plastic; Chevy was making hoods and rear quarter panels. In addition to taking these steps, a steel executive could simply read *Modern Plastics* instead of *Iron Age*. In 1982, the journal reported that "Dow's ABS resins sales to the automotive market . . . are running more than 2 1/2 times ahead of what they were in 1980."[2]

To Big Steel executives who had witnessed aluminum's rapid conquest of the canning market, the gravity of the plastics threat should have been apparent. Just as lightweight, formable aluminum improved the customer utility of canned beverages, so did lightweight, functional plastics promise to improve the end-user appeal of automobiles. In two key applications, value was migrating to more potent business designs built around alternative materials (see Figure 5-2).

It is 1984. As the CEO of Nucor or U.S. Steel, this is the situation you see.

- Japanese total annual steel production (97 million tons) has surpassed U.S. total annual steel production (77 million tons). 95 percent of Japanese-produced steel is continuous cast versus 40 percent of U.S.-produced steel.
- Aluminum has displaced 95 percent of all steel in beer cans and 70 percent in soda cans.
- Plastics have displaced 15 percent of the steel in auto applications.
- Aggregate value of leading publicly traded minimills (now $1 billion) has been growing at a compound annual rate

FIGURE 5-2   RADAR SCREEN: U.S. STEEL

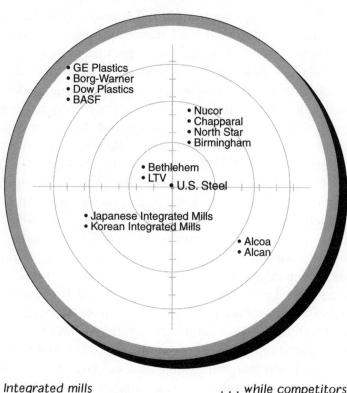

Integrated mills
focused on each other. . .

. . . while competitors
flew in from all sides.

of 15 percent for the past decade while that of leading
integrated mills (now $15 billion) has been declining by
9 percent annually.

■ Together, the Japanese mills, aluminum suppliers, and U.S.
minimills have displaced 35 million tons of steel from the
integrated mills.

What is your next move? What are the economic and market
share implications of the Japanese advantage in continuous casting?
What are the minimills' free cash flows and growth trajectories?
What do these metrics imply about their ability to capture more
customers and more value in an industry where the competitive
boundaries are being redrawn?

Obsolescence versus Redesign

By the mid-1980s, the migration of value away from the business design of the U.S. integrated steel manufacturers was increasingly clear. Competing business designs were gaining mass and momentum. (In 1985, the shareholder value of Nucor, at $1 billion, nearly matched the shareholder value of Bethlehem Steel, one of the largest integrated mills.) It was perhaps the last opportunity to decelerate value outflow from the integrated design that had enjoyed such a long period of value inflow and stability. Without a counterattack, the integrated model risked slipping down the value outflow slope.

But what options were available to the integrated mills? They could reduce capacity, cutting back to an efficient core. They could increase their continuous casting ratio, which was only 40 percent. They could focus R&D on improving steel's functionality along dimensions important to the automotive market. They could build a minimill; they might even buy into the plastics business.

The integrated giants were not the only firms at a crossroads in the mid-1980s: Minimills were too. Their business design had worked extremely well in the 1970s and early 1980s. However, the price of scrap had risen sharply (up 70 percent since 1983), and there were now at least a dozen minimills strategically placed across the country. It was time to start worrying about saturation. Nucor's Iverson was the first to see it—and to change his business design before it was too late. He was unwilling to try to hang on to past success the way the integrated manufacturers had.

Much of Nucor's strategic planning took place at Phil's Deli, in the mall across the street from its offices. One might imagine that a conversation like the following took place between Iverson and divisional manager Keith Busse in 1988.

> IVERSON: Keith, do you think our competitors will stop building minimills in the next few years?
>
> BUSSE: No way. They know how much money we're making.
>
> IVERSON: Meanwhile, will scrap supply go down?
>
> BUSSE: Sure. Which means scrap prices will go up—a lot.
>
> IVERSON: Right. So, now what do we do? It will take people five years to recognize it, but our business model is dead.

Iverson took a sip of his coffee, and continued.

IVERSON: Another question concerns the rebar buyers. Fifteen years ago there was one minimill—ours. The market was an empty space. Today there are 16 minimills, going on 20. How much room is left for growth?

BUSSE: Not much.

IVERSON: How much room for *profit* growth?

BUSSE: Even less.

IVERSON: There's probably $200 million of operating profit in this regional, minimill rebar game. Hell, we have half of it already. What we have here is not a formula for value growth. What we have is a formula for disaster.

Iverson flipped over his napkin and drew a simple curve. The sketch was not very complicated, but the message was very clear (see Figure 5-3).

Iverson's metric (minimill penetration of regional rebar markets) was not one that anyone tracked. But it was one of the most critical variables for the minimill business design. His picture was the essence of what mattered: The opportunity for revenue growth in rebar would be a fraction of what it had been. And the market would be

FIGURE 5-3   IVERSON'S NAPKIN

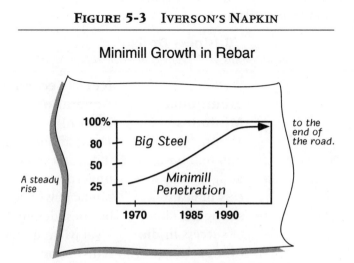

contested by an increasing number of regional minimills, driving down prices and profitability.

Expected scrap prices painted an equally bleak picture on the cost side of the equation. Across the country, stockpiles of scrap were being exhausted. At the same time, the stream of new scrap from industrial processes was diminishing as quality initiatives and lean production techniques cut down waste in heavy manufacturing. Overall, scrap supply was growing far less than scrap demand, causing upward pressure on prices and cutting further into minimill margins. To Iverson, these two trends were the writing on the wall: The minimill model that had been hugely successful for years had reached the end of its economic life.

What strategic moves would best counter the dual threat of rebar market saturation and rising price of a critical raw material? To give Nucor access to a new revenue stream, Iverson took a high-risk, but necessary, gamble on thin-strip continuous casting at a new plant in Crawfordsville, Indiana. The process would enable Nucor to produce up-market flat-rolled steel for use in construction, appliance, auto, and other manufacturing applications. By entering the upper end of the market, Nucor would pose a direct threat to Big Steel's core business. To lessen his company's dependence on scrap, Iverson built an iron carbide plant in Trinidad. He would ship cheap iron ore there from Brazil. Natural gas-fired reactors would produce iron carbide (a substitute for scrap), which would be loaded onto barges bound for New Orleans. This was, again, a risky but necessary change in Nucor's business design.

Business Design
Traditional Minimills vs. Nucor Second-Generation Minimill

	Traditional Minimills	**Nucor Second-Generation Minimill**
Fundamental Assumptions	The traditional minimill business design's past success indicates strong likelihood of success in the future.	The traditional minimills' past success has undermined the economic power of the business design. Survival will require reinvention.

Customer Selection	Regional construction customers	Regional construction customers, plus auto and other industrial manufacturers
Scope	Low-end construction products (rebar)	Expanded product line, including up-market products (flat-rolled)
Manufacturing/ Operating System	Scrap as raw material	Scrap substitute as raw material

Iverson's two initiatives fundamentally altered Nucor's business design, moving it from the precipice of value outflow back to the value inflow phase (see Figure 5-4). The traditional minimill model could not compete with Nucor's updated design.

Another person who recognized the predicament of traditional minimills was Carl Pfeiffer, president of Quanex, a minimill

FIGURE 5-4   BUSINESS DESIGN REINVENTION

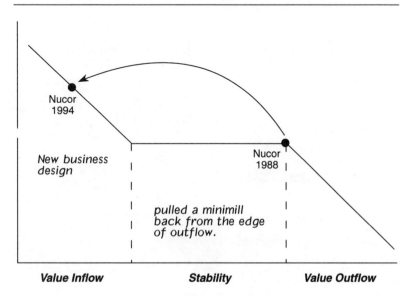

with plants in Jackson, Mississippi, and Fort Smith, Arkansas. Pfeiffer began to develop a different second-generation business model. From steel, he expanded into aluminum as well as other materials such as graphite composites and ceramics. "We were a specialty steel company," he said in the early 1990s. "We are becoming a specialty metals company. And we will be a specialty materials company."[3]

As these two minimill competitors were adjusting their business designs, so were some important customers. The auto industry was struggling to respond to the continually improving performance of Japan's auto makers. In November 1994, Toyota announced that it intended to be profitable at an exchange rate of 80 yen to the dollar. To keep pace, the U.S. auto companies heavily outsourced to the so-called Tier One suppliers, major subcontractors who provided automakers not only with components, but also large systems and subassemblies. The auto makers also needed global suppliers to support global platforms and global purchasing of materials and components. The priorities of Ford, GM, and Chrysler changed dramatically (see Figure 5-5).

The Tier One suppliers scrambled to accommodate the emerging priorities of the OEMs. By adding hundreds of engineers, they shifted from merely building parts to contributing to the design phase, optimizing manufacturing efficiency. They made acquisitions to develop

FIGURE 5-5   CHANGING CUSTOMER PRIORITIES

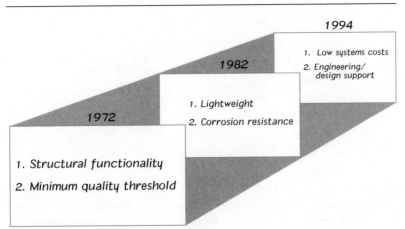

1994

1. Low systems costs
2. Engineering/
   design support

1982

1. Lightweight
2. Corrosion resistance

1972

1. Structural functionality
2. Minimum quality threshold

a global infrastructure. They were working hard to support the most radical new business design in the North American automotive industry since GM's Alfred Sloan defeated Henry Ford's Model-T with a multiproduct business model in the 1920s.

It is 1995. As the president of GE Plastics, the CEO of U.S. Steel, or the CEO of Nucor, this is the situation you see.

- The power in the relationship between the steel industry and its most important customer, the automobile industry, is shifting. In the 1960s, the steel supplier owned the capacity and therefore the power. In the 1990s, auto makers have several materials options (steel, plastic, aluminum, and composites) *and* several supplier options (integrated mills and now minimills, which have started offering flat-rolled steel).
- The identity of the customer is changing. Heretofore the OEMs (Ford, GM, Chrysler) were the decision makers. Now decisions are made by a combination of OEMs and Tier One suppliers.

What is your next move? Does the crowding of the high end of the market threaten your business design? Where should you invest your company's free cash to profit from the cyclical upturn of the mid-1990s?

Epilogue

Iverson has entered this situation with a business design that has significant advantages. His six years' effort to build thin-strip, continuous-casting capability has succeeded. He now sells flat rolled steel. His cost is dramatically lower than that of the integrated mills from both the United States and Japan.

The other advantaged business design belongs to GE. Jack Welch's plastics division is on the cutting edge of engineering solutions. In a buyer-supplier relationship dominated by product—like that between the steel and auto industries of the 1960s—sales reps talk to purchasing agents. But in the solutions world of the 1990s, engi-

neers talk to engineers to solve problems, and CEOs talk to CEOs
to create long-term partnerships. The age of CEO marketing has
begun, and Jack Welch is the consummate CEO marketer. He calls
upon automotive CEOs regularly—not only to sell plastics, but also
to forge long-term design and supply partnerships.

Welch has a powerful platform from which to operate. GE Plastics' sales of $1.5 billion to the auto industry have given him the
scale to develop a 100-person engineering solutions group. Unlike
traditional materials suppliers who enter clients' design processes
after specs are set, GE Plastics works with clients early enough to
define what the best specs should be.

Business Design
First-Generation Plastics vs. GE Plastics Engineering Solutions

	Plastics/Other Materials Manufacturers	GE Plastics
Fundamental Assumptions	Value proposition based on superior value per pound of product	Value proposition based on superior systems economics
Scope	Product	Solution
Manufacturing/ Operating System	Product engineers develop applications.	Product engineers develop applications. Engineering solutions teams help set specifications and implement solutions with customer.
Go-to-Market Mechanism	Mid-level selling	Senior-level selling

A comparison of metrics testifies to the power of the Nucor and
GE business designs (and to the relative weakness of that of the
integrated mills).

Competitor	1994 Revenue*	1994 Market Value*	Market Value/Revenue
Bethlehem	$4.3	$2.6	0.6
U.S. Steel	$5.7	$4.7	0.8
Nucor	$2.3	$5.1	2.2
GE Plastics	$5.0	$7.5**	1.5

*in billions
**valuation derived by applying industry multiples

By the mid-1990s, the companies that dominated the U.S. steel industry since its inception have contracted to a fraction of their former size. Big Steel's financial performance has improved, thanks to a cyclical upturn. However, it seems clear that companies using the integrated-steel-mill business design have fallen into the value outflow phase. Now what are their options?

Armed with an understanding of the Value Migration in their industry and a willingness to allocate capital among various business designs within their corporate portfolio, these companies could still flourish. The cash flow generated by the recent upturn could be invested in new business designs that offer the opportunity for value growth. Some of the integrated producers are doing just that. U.S. Steel recently announced an alliance with Nucor. And LTV announced plans to break ground for a new minimill late in 1995. These are good moves, but they come 10–15 years too late.

Yet, the companies that don't divorce their identities from the fundamental assumptions of the integrated model risk falling into what one industry analyst has termed "the death spiral."[4] If they invest in incremental improvements to integrated production that will never return the cost of capital, these companies' ability to return to a path of value growth will be extremely limited.

Lessons Learned: Patterns

After a long period of value inflow and stability, the integrated business design of Big Steel lost value to four new business designs: foreign mills, U.S. minimills, aluminum producers, and plastics producers. Each migration, in and of itself, was initially modest, but in combination the four became dangerously large. This pattern is increasing in frequency in the 1990s as more big companies age, and as more new companies from more countries compete in the same product and service markets.

Each wave of Value Migration was triggered by the interaction of customer priorities and a new business design. For example, Nucor was keenly aware of the price sensitivity and regional presence of rebar customers. To create utility for these customers, Nucor built an entirely new business design, altering the scope, manufacturing system, capital intensity, and organizational configuration of traditional steelmakers. Plastics makers realized that the external shock of the oil crisis would increase the importance of fuel efficiency to end-users. In response, they created a business design that carefully targeted the most responsive decision makers within a customer's organization (design engineers), and focused resources on developing customer-relevant applications. As auto customers' priorities evolved to include design assistance, GE Plastics innovated further, widening the scope of its offerings to include extensive engineering support (see Figure 5-6).

Nucor's success highlights a related lesson. Because its output was small, and because it wanted to avoid attracting the full attention of the large players, it confined itself to a low-end niche. Big Steel believed there were barriers between the low-end and the high-end niches. So by the time it responded, it faced a formidable competitor.

FIGURE 5-6   MULTIDIRECTIONAL MIGRATION

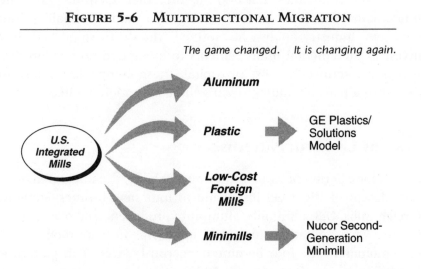

Nucor had reached critical mass and had established enough credibility to challenge the incumbents on a broad spectrum of products.

Replaying the Game

The steel story is rich in strategic moves and countermoves. And as is often the case in business chess matches, moves not taken proved as critical as moves taken. An analysis of the game focusing only on facts knowable at the time reveals both critical errors and key covering moves that could have protected significant value.

Strategic errors by the U.S. integrated mills included the slow adoption of continuous casting, fighting aluminum in beer and soda too late, not fighting plastics in automotive early enough, and not establishing a minimill division. For the minimills, a strategic error was not to begin working earlier to develop an alternative to scrap.

There were several important value growth moves that the big mills could have made.

1. *Start a minimill.* Better yet, start a minimill network, with a plant in five or six regions of the country. U.S. Steel and LTV have recently embarked on minimill initiatives. But these moves would have been much more effective 15 years ago. In the 1970s, a major steel mill like Bethlehem could have raised oceans more capital than little Nucor, and built a half-dozen small, $500-million facilities that would have preempted Nucor and other minimills from making strong inroads in specific market segments. (This move was not possible in Japan, by the way. There simply wasn't enough scrap to supply a minimill economically.)

2. *Change capital budgets.* Simultaneously reduce capacity in some product lines and enhance it in others. Move from five million tons of capacity to four million (and save the costs associated with capital maintenance), and increase the less-expensive continuous-casting portion of production from 20 percent to 80 percent. This would create a smaller but more economically powerful configuration.

3. *Redirect R&D to find new solutions to customer problems.* This would have required foresight in the 1960s, when can makers began to turn to aluminum. By 1976, steelmakers had lost half of this market. However, if they had learned from the Value Migration that had occurred in canning, Big Steel could have created the functionalities the car makers required, and limited the flow of value to plastics manufacturers. Steelmakers are doing this today—15 years later. If the rate of plastics penetration had been diminished, GE, Dow, and Borg-Warner would have altered their expectations for easy money in the auto industry, and reduced the growth role plastics assumed in their portfolios.

These moves would have had several important consequences. First, minimill growth would have been stunted. Second, the value decay of the integrated mills would have been slowed. A higher continuous-casting ratio or a lower capacity base would have extended Big Steel's ability to earn returns by more than a decade. Third, steel's loss of share in the automotive market would have been decelerated, creating better capacity utilization and significantly higher profitability.

If integrated mills had pursued some or all of these options, they might now have three different business designs: a downsized integrated mill, minimills, and materials solutions. These might have been different divisions or subsidiaries. The integrated mill organization would constantly search for ways to reduce its capacity and improve its cost position. Each minimill would seek rapid growth within its region to achieve a leadership position. The materials-solutions business model would provide maximum growth, offering automotive, machinery, and white goods manufacturers a "sophisticated steels" alternative to emerging aluminum and plastics offerings, which would offer "lower systems cost" in addition to materials functionality.

Application to Other Industries

The pattern of parallel value outflow has played itself out in several industries, and is currently under way in others, even some not oriented toward manufacturing. In each case, there are different sets of customers with different priorities and different purchasing options. And in each case, the companies that supply these alternatives define the competitive field. For instance, in retailing it was not the traditional rivalries among Sears, JC Penney, and Montgomery Ward that defined the relevant competitive boundaries, but new business designs such as specialty stores, superstores, and full-line discounters. In home entertainment, the greatest threat to the networks is not one another, but nontraditional competitors such as ESPN, Blockbuster Video, and alliances between content providers and regional Bell operating companies.

The American automobile industry failed to see a rising competitor that could leap from the low end to the high end as Nucor had. Japan entered the U.S. car market at the low end—with subcompacts in the 1960s. Detroit had little interest in this low-profit market. Slowly, without confronting the majors, Toyota and Nissan built a strong franchise, and big profits. Since 1986, they have rapidly pushed up into the luxury high end. Toyota's Lexus, Nissan's Infiniti, and Honda's Acura have displaced a large portion of the market from both U.S. and European makers.

In numerous industries, the strategic errors made in the steel game are being repeated. The incumbents are not taking advantage of the moves that are available to protect or create value. Which of these errors are being repeated in your industry? Which value growth moves are not being made?

Chapter **6**

Migration to a No-Profit Industry

Airlines

- Will my business design create utility for the customer *and* recapture value for my company?
- How is the composition of the industry's customer base changing? Is my business design well matched to the most important priorities of the high-growth segments?
- Can my business design move beyond its existing customer base and geographic scope and still earn a profit?

THE U.S. AIRLINE INDUSTRY lost more money in the early 1990s than it has earned since Kitty Hawk. Its very viability seems in doubt. Although the bleeding has been greatest in the major carriers, few smaller airlines fare any better. In 1992, the year that the industry lost a record $4 billion, only one major carrier, Southwest Airlines, earned a profit. Where has the value gone? Can any airline prosper?

In the past two decades airline companies have made 15–20 strategic moves and countermoves. Many were errors. They did not create value growth, but rather contributed to a pattern of large-scale value destruction. The Value Migration pattern in the airline industry was initiated by an external event in 1978: deregulation.

Unlike many external events, however, every airline CEO knew this one was coming.

The airline tragedy unfolds in three acts. It reveals a crucial message: A successful business design must meet customer priorities, but it must do so at a profit, and it must generate that profit in a sustainable way. There is no law that says there must be profit in an industry. An entire industry can become and remain profitless.

And yet, truly innovative business designs can recapture value even in an industry as embattled as airlines. One of the regional players became the only company to create lasting value for a decade after deregulation. Finally, in the 1990s, two other business designs emerged that offered some hope for value recapture (see Figure 6-1).

External events occur all the time in business, so any executive can learn from the airline story. The reaction of both the big and small carriers to deregulation also holds lessons for an industry that is largely unprofitable, or about to become so. Managers in industries where the chief product or service is turning into a terminal commodity—especially if the majors have high fixed costs and limited flexibility—can also learn from the airline pattern.

FIGURE 6-1   AIRLINE VALUE MIGRATION

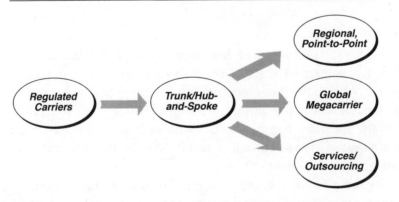

Airlines evolved into a profitless industry following deregulation, with only three pockets of profitability created by innovative business designs.

Act I: Impending Deregulation

Prior to 1978, there were three types of airline companies: trunk carriers that operated nationally, regionals that covered a portion of the country, and intrastate airlines that did not cross state lines. *Inter*state travel was highly regulated by the federal Civil Aeronautics Board (CAB). Trunk and regional carriers were limited in the fares and routes they could offer on this kind of flight. The CAB did not regulate *intra*state travel, however. The trunks, regionals, and small intrastate airlines all could compete freely in intrastate markets.

Business customers had a fairly comfortable and convenient time flying. But high ticket prices left air travel out of reach of most leisure consumers. Regulation limited price competition. At the same time, a few intrastate airlines, like Southwest in Texas, were selling seats at much lower prices. Congress was in a mood to deregulate.

The national carriers had reason to be concerned. Even though there were 290 airlines in operation, only 11 enjoyed trunk status (largest to smallest): United, American, Delta, Eastern, TWA, Western, Pan Am, Continental, Braniff, Northwest, and National. They accounted for an 87 percent market share of the domestic revenue-passenger miles (RPMs).[1] The domestic operating revenues for these carriers had grown from less than $10 billion in 1960 to $30 billion in 1978.

Despite this remarkable growth and their size, the majors had not achieved commensurate profits. Although the CAB's fare structure targeted a generous 12 percent rate of return on equity, the industry achieved only about a 7 percent return.

With no ability to compete on price, airlines had but one way to differentiate themselves: service. They spent to create "amenities" that might influence customer choice. But because revenues were generally fixed, competition in service simply increased the airlines' cost positions. It raised the ante for playing the game, which lowered the profitability for all trunk carriers.

In contrast, customer desire for lower fares directly affected competition on intrastate routes. Several small airlines—Southwest, PSA in California, and Air Florida—used a streamlined, low-cost business design and passed the savings on to consumers. For its Dallas-to-Houston flight, Southwest charged prices that were sharply lower than the CAB fare formula dictated. At those prices, air travel began to compete with driving (or trains or buses). Leisure travelers, who had a few hundred miles to cover, saved many hours. Small-business owners, who were more price-sensitive than corporate executives, found local airlines to be a much better option. Southwest created significant utility for new customer groups and had a business design that allowed it to recapture value.

As the airline deregulation bill moved through Congress in 1978, there was an air of anxiety but also hope in the industry. Competition would be good. Airlines would no longer be constrained in how much they could earn or how they might compete. Consumers would benefit as competition would offer better choice, better service, and better prices.

It is 1978. As CEO of American Airlines (a trunk carrier), CEO of Piedmont (a regional carrier), or CEO of Southwest (an intrastate carrier), this is the situation you see.

- Despite regulation, competition has reduced industry profitability.
- Customers in intrastate markets have responded to lower prices. Customers in regulated markets have responded to better service.
- With large fixed investments in equipment, your incentive is to maximize the utilization of that equipment.
- Deregulation creates new opportunities and new threats as previously monopolized routes are opened to competition.

What is your next move? How will deregulation affect customer priorities? Which customer segments will matter the most? Which business designs, previously prevented from being competitive, might lead the Value Migration process? Where should your strategic priorities lie: driving down costs, investing to build a larger airline, or focusing on select routes where you can dominate and be profitable?

Act II: The Rise and Fall of People Express

Competitive intensity quickly gained momentum after President Carter signed deregulation into law. Although the act left route assignments under the CAB's control until 1981, by late 1979, the CAB was allowing carriers to serve virtually any market. Competitors fought each other for the most attractive routes. To reduce costs and maximize the traffic moving through the system, the airlines tried to concentrate traffic along longer feeder routes that connected to their big-city hubs.

By using bigger planes across longer routes, this hub-and-spoke business design did cut costs. The largest carriers saved 4–5 percent of their operating costs.[2] But the majors still had an overall high-cost position, one that could be exploited by smaller competitors, with lower-cost positions, competing on price. Large scale did not assure low cost.

Southwest Airlines was the clear leader of this low-cost business design. Originally established in 1971 in Dallas to make local runs to Houston, it had expanded to other Texas cities. Its formula of low fares and no frills on short flights was a smashing success. CEO Herb Kelleher's planes were filled to capacity. Southwest was one of the few profitable carriers in the country. Planes were turned around in about 20 minutes, versus one hour for the majors at the congested hubs. That gave Southwest more flights and more passengers per plane per day. It also enabled Southwest to add more frequent flights between the cities, a convenient service, which attracted business travelers who were more interested in catching a plane at the last minute—at a low price—than wider seats or free drinks. Lower prices were possible because of the lower cost structure of the business design. The design matched what customers wanted extremely well (see Figure 6-2).

Kelleher also developed work rules that were far more flexible and cost-effective than the ones imposed on the majors by their unions. Southwest pilots flew nearly twice as many hours as pilots for the majors, at the same or lower salaries. Southwest had a more than 25 percent cost advantage over the hub-and-spoke operators. Before 1979 ended, Kelleher was already flying outside of Texas, thanks to deregulation. But he didn't stray too far from home.

On a national scale, the intensified route competition had serious consequences. United Airlines, the leader, gave up service between 123 city pairs by 1980, most of them short-haul direct flights. The other trunk carriers followed. It left spaces for competitors to grow, and to test new business designs.

FIGURE 6-2   BUSINESS DESIGN COMPARISON

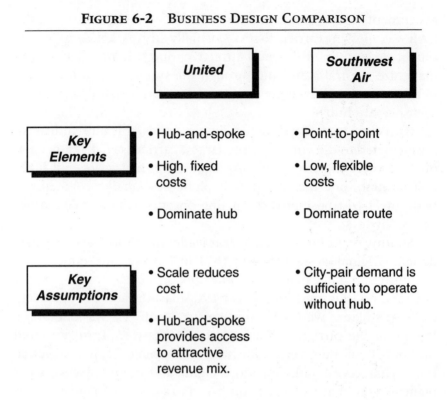

	United	Southwest Air
Key Elements	• Hub-and-spoke • High, fixed costs • Dominate hub	• Point-to-point • Low, flexible costs • Dominate route
Key Assumptions	• Scale reduces cost. • Hub-and-spoke provides access to attractive revenue mix.	• City-pair demand is sufficient to operate without hub.

At the same time, the airlines fought aggressively to win a position in those markets they perceived as structurally attractive. Seven different carriers entered the transcontinental marketplace, sparking a price war. Charter operator World Airways dropped fares to $99 on a New York-to-L.A. flight. American matched. No airline could operate that route profitably at such a low price. Consumers loved the fare wars; for the carriers, they were wars of financial attrition. The doubling of jet fuel prices in 1979 and 1980 pushed the major airlines deeper into financial difficulty.

All the publicity about prices should have made airline executives take notice. While American Airlines employees were tearing $99 boarding passes at gates crowded with first-time vacation fliers at New York's LaGuardia airport, company executives in Dallas continued to apply the same high-cost design to the same customer: the business traveler. The former trunk carriers didn't notice the inconsistency in their business design. An American Airlines sales-training manual stated that "American's basic sales policy is to sell the highest priced product that the customer is willing to buy." Tourists and other low-price seekers, who increasingly defined the new market, were seen as little more than seat fillers.

The majors had two options: lower costs or increase revenues. They tried to do both. American Airlines pressured its unions for more favorable "market rate" labor contracts. But vigorous expansion aimed at increasing revenue actually caused an increase in costs, and further locked the airlines into the hub-and-spoke system.

Meanwhile, more and more newcomers chipped away at the major's spokes. One new business design in particular—the no-frills carrier—met the priorities of the millions of new customers who had been previously priced out of the market.

The senior executive who led the way was Donald Burr. After being named president of Texas International Airlines in Dallas, he departed in the midst of a heated debate with his longtime friend and boss Frank Lorenzo. Burr was an entrepreneur who questioned the underlying assumptions that most managers took for granted. He proposed a more extreme version of Southwest's business design, which he would apply to the bustling East Coast, the most lucrative market in the nation. Burr convinced several key employees to defect from Texas International and set up shop with him at Newark Airport in New Jersey, only 14 miles from the huge New York City market. The new airline was called People Express.

Burr tailored his business design to the priorities of vacationers and price-sensitive business travelers. For them, an airline trip was only a commodity, a way of getting from one place to another.

In setting air fares, Burr looked as closely at the cost of taking a bus or a train or driving as he did at fares of the other airlines. After all, that's what customers did. By adopting the customer's point of view, Burr was taking the most accurate approach to analyzing the direction in which value could migrate.

Establishing low fares was one thing. Creating a business design that would be profitable at those fares was another. Burr believed there were no economies of scale in the airline business. A small airline, if properly designed, could have a lower cost position than the majors.

Burr's business design built on and went beyond the innovations developed by Southwest. His employees would also be nonunion. They would be paid less than industry norms, but would be given inexpensive stock options as incentives. The top executives would earn less than $50,000 a year. Employees would be cross-trained—to check baggage one day, to be flight attendant the next, boosting productivity. Tickets would be paid for in-flight, eliminating expensive counter operations. There would be no first-class, creating more seats. Tickets would not be distributed through travel agents, cutting out expensive commissions. No food would be served on board.

The inaugural flight of People Express was a $23 trip from Newark to Buffalo, New York, on April 30, 1981. When 39-year-old Burr boarded it, he panicked because only a few seats were filled. The media, however, marveled at People's amazingly low fares, and soon the Newark terminal was jammed. While American Airlines employees were still tearing up $99 boarding passes at LaGuardia, People's staff was collecting thousands of $23 and $35 fares, and tearing up the competition. Giddy weekenders would hop on a plane and ask, "Where are we going?" They didn't care, as long as it was cheap.

By 1983, People Express achieved an average load factor (the proportion of seats filled by paying customers) of 73.5 percent. The major carriers' load factors ranged from 53 to 65 percent. By 1985, People Express was one of the fastest growing companies in U.S. history, with revenues of $1 billion. American Airlines' passenger revenues were $5 billion.

United Airlines briefly attempted to mimic the upstart business design. A few months after People's introduction, United initiated a service called Friendship Express, which sought to match People's prices across a large number of markets. Despite management's intentions, United's high cost structure prevented success. Friendship Express was abandoned, and the effort was quickly forgotten.[3] No other major airline sought to copy People's business design.

Unfortunately Burr lost sight of his own model: Southwest Air. Southwest was expanding—at a controlled, well-managed rate. Kelleher would add one key city and serve it well, gradually beating out competitors and streamlining operations. Only then would he move into another market. People Express expanded much more rapidly. The dramatic growth left the company without an adequate computer system to handle the high traffic. Flights were severely delayed; the crowded terminals had become huge hassles. Customers wanted cheap prices, but they had a quality threshold. Blinded by his meteoric rise, however, Burr was convinced he could confront the majors on their own turf. In the summer of 1984, he expanded into the primary markets of United and American.

Now Burr drew the full wrath of the jumbo competitors. They undercut People's prices. Most aggressive was American Airlines. By the start of 1985, American developed a new schedule of low-priced fares. Although it had a raft of restrictions, American blitzed the public with ads saying American's new fares were cheaper than People's. The strategy was smart; because the lowest fares were available only to passengers who purchased them 30 days in advance, American could preserve its core market of business travelers, who made decisions with less lead time and would therefore continue to pay full fare.

Burr hurt his own cost position by purchasing expensive Boeing planes without considering which routes would allow those investments to pay for themselves. He also negotiated a leveraged buyout of Frontier Airlines, a very troubled carrier in Denver.

The final blow came in 1985, from Burr's mother. She booked a cheap flight for the Thanksgiving weekend on American. Burr later told the *New York Times Magazine*, "American had convinced the public that People Express was not in fact cheaper. Even my own mother fell for it."[4] Faced with competitive reality, burdened with debt and a bankrupt Frontier subsidiary, Burr merged his troubles with those of a most unlikely partner: Frank Lorenzo, CEO of Texas Air.

By the mid-1980s, most of the airlines spawned by deregulation had either failed or had merged into the larger carriers. Weak national competitors succumbed too. Texas Air had acquired Continental and Eastern. The majors had succeeded in outlasting their new rivals, but the battles had cost them dearly. They had driven profitability out of the industry.

Looking down from 30,000 feet, airline executives saw an uncertain competitive landscape. Although many of the new businesses were defeated, their rapid rise and fall left many questions unanswered. Only a person in denial could ignore that the People Express experiment had uncovered a very significant and large-scale new customer group.

It is 1988. You are the CEO of American Airlines. Or the CEO of Southwest. This is the situation you see.

- The fare wars have hurt overall profitability, but since the demise of People Express, profitability has improved.

- Airlines with strong union labor forces face increased pressure to return many of the concessions won earlier in the decade.

- Customers are increasingly price-sensitive as: (1) leisure travelers have become a greater portion of total passengers and (2) the market has been exposed to the commodity nature of the product.

- The hub-and-spoke business design has reached saturation as most markets are now well served by major competitors.

- The economics of pricing decisions have led competitors to match cut-rate fares rather than lose a share of traffic.

What is your next move? What insights did People Express give us about our customers? Are their priorities different? Who will now serve the low-budget customer? Who can make a profit doing so? What distinguishes Southwest from People's? Is its position sustainable? What should our company's strategic priorities be in the next five years? What's our next business design?

Act III: Toward Zero Profits

When external changes expand the number of possible business designs, radical new competitors may appear that capture previously unserved customer segments. In such times, it is important to remain flexible, to look to the edge of the radar screen, and to be ready to imitate new business designs quickly. People Express was a clear sign that a different business design was now possible.

However, the major airlines were not flexible enough to respond effectively. While the hub-and-spoke executives invented complicated yield management systems to optimize the revenue mix, many saw American's heavily discounted, advance-purchase fares as nothing more than a necessary evil. They did not see the potential of the enormous, latent customer group represented by Burr's mother, and relatives of their own managers, who were flying to and fro on Super Savers in a way they had never flown before. They were a voice that could have been heard.

Even when new competitors fail, there are often parts of their business designs worth emulating. People Express failed as a company because Burr grew it too fast. But his business design had recaptured great value by moving into unoccupied space—the price-sensitive market, an enormous vein of gold that had never before been tapped by the airline industry. In 1982, the Air Transport Association reported that 52 percent of air travelers were on a business trip. By 1991, the portion of business travelers had slipped to 46 percent, even as total passenger miles had grown by 75 percent. The inflow of a new type of customer was enormous. And the warning was clear: The future of the high-service, high-cost design was bleak. The primary concern of a growing majority of customers was cost, not service (see Figure 6-3).

Nevertheless, the majors forged ahead with the same business design, investing in new routes and equipment. In 1984, using the added cash flow from hard-won labor concessions, American Airlines placed a $1.3-billion order for planes from Boeing, the largest order in history. Other carriers followed, adding expensive debt to their

FIGURE 6-3   THE CHANGING CUSTOMER

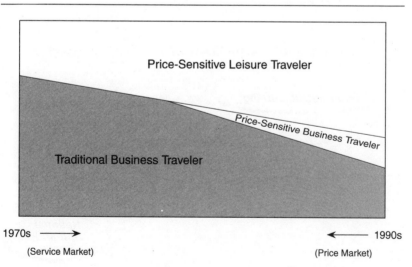

The massive inflow of price–sensitive travelers transformed air travel into a price–dominated commodity market.

balance sheets. Even though the aging majors needed to replace worn-out planes, demand was not growing enough to warrant this expense. Although passenger traffic had risen by 13 percent annually between 1950 and 1973, the growth rate had slowed to less than 6 percent, despite the CEOs' belief that deregulation would yield a significant increase in traffic.

High fixed costs gave each carrier the incentive to fill every last seat, even at a low fare. So although the direct attack of a no-frills competitor like People Express was no longer a threat, the majors created a cycle of price competition driven by a focus on capacity utilization. The operating margins for the major carriers fell from 6.1 percent in 1978 to −2.5 percent in 1990.

Increasing or maintaining the capacity of a weak business design only accelerates the Value Migration process (see Figure 6-4). It creates empty, profitless revenues. It happened in the steel industry. It is under way in several others. The incumbent airline players found themselves with obsolete business designs. Their options were limited by fixed, inflexible assets (both human and capital) and highly leveraged balance sheets. As the squeeze on profits intensified throughout the 1980s, they attempted to maneuver out of their corner.

FIGURE 6-4   VALUE FLOW OF BUSINESS DESIGNS

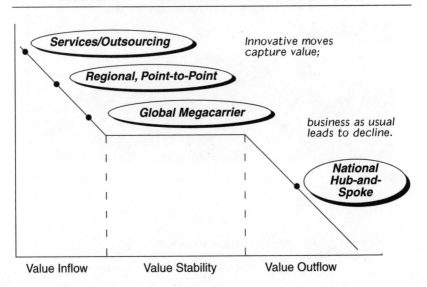

Acquisitions

A number of prominent deals were made as carriers sought economies of scale. Frank Lorenzo was among the most active, merging his Texas Air with struggling Continental in 1981. Raider Carl Icahn leveraged TWA in 1985 and then acquired Ozark Air two years later. Tiny Allegheny merged its way into the national league and adopted the name USAir. The merger madness did little to reduce operating costs, but it did severely leverage balance sheets.

Bankruptcy

Ironically, these highly leveraged carriers had a hidden source of competitive advantage—bankruptcy court. While some carriers, such as Braniff, failed completely, the courts often allowed bankrupt carriers to continue operating while they restructured. In 1983, Continental Airlines sought protection and temporarily shut down. A few days later, when it reopened, Lorenzo had voided union contracts, fired more than half the workforce, and dropped more than half his routes, lowering costs significantly. For example, labor costs, which had been 35 percent of operating costs, were soon down to 20 percent.

However, the continued operations of the bankrupt airlines ensured a high level of overcapacity in the industry. Load factors stayed in the 55–65 percent range. The incentives to compete on price were irresistible.

Differentiation: Frequent Flyer Programs

In a time of increasing cost scrutiny and downsizing, U.S. businesses restricted employee travel and encouraged workers to book less-expensive flights. The result was a further decline in the proportion of customers who were price-insensitive and paid full fare.

Instead of adapting their business designs, the majors initiated a variety of augmentation programs to preserve their franchises with business travelers who were still willing to pay higher prices. The most prominent was the frequent flyer program, which American Airlines instituted soon after deregulation in May 1981. It differentiated American from its rivals, but only for 11 days. United immediately countered with a frequent flyer program of its own. Once the other major carriers followed suit, frequent flyer programs simply became another costly requirement of doing business as a national carrier, a classic example of illusory differentiation.

Value Recapture: Creative Pricing

Increasingly, passengers viewed air travel as a commodity. In response to this fundamental change in customer priorities, the majors expanded their discount fares. In early 1991, for example, 93 percent of American's tickets were sold at a discount, and the average discount was 63 percent off full fare.

The discount fares cheapened air travel in customer's minds. The airlines had gone the way of the traditional department stores. They had a weak business design. They had a high-cost structure. There was no price integrity. Heavy discounting only confused the customer.

Recognizing the commoditization of air travel, Robert Crandall, CEO of American, decided to take dramatic action. In April 1992, he announced American's "value pricing" scheme. Like Sam Walton, Crandall saw that everyday low prices were more closely aligned with customer desires. Under the plan, there would be only four types of fares: first class, regular coach, 7-day advance purchase, and 21-day advance purchase. Although the restrictions on the advance fares were tightened, the regular coach fares had been cut by nearly 40 percent.

Unfortunately, although Crandall may have had a Wal-Mart vision, he had a Sears cost structure. His cost position was too high to pull off the low-price strategy. And he was depending on the cooperation of his competitors.

Predictably, most of the major carriers soon rationalized their fare structures. TWA undercut American's fares by as much as 20 percent, spurring a vicious price war. Northwest announced a two-for-one deal. In response, American dropped its advance purchase fares by 50 percent.

The fare war introduced hundreds of thousands of Americans to air travel, creating an even greater shift in the customer mix toward price-sensitive fliers. The war was devastating financially. By autumn, American abandoned its pricing scheme, but the damage had been done. In 1992, the airline industry collectively lost another $4 billion, making the combined loss $10 billion for 1990, 1991, and 1992. Value pricing merely intensified the downward spiral of the industry.

Chronic overcapacity continued to drive down fares and profits (see Figure 6-5). Crandall seemed resigned to the fact that he'd never make money in the air. The business design of the trunk carriers, like that of the traditional department store, was becoming economically obsolete. American's business system would have to be dismantled. American began to cede West Coast routes to Southwest. (The negative spiral of the majors was fueling a positive spiral for Southwest.) Hubs were closed. Except in the longest-haul or international services, the full-service airline business design could no longer meet customer priorities at a profit. "Unless the world changes, we will never buy another airplane," Crandall told the *New York Times Magazine* late in 1993. "When all the airplanes are worn out, the company simply won't be here anymore."[5]

Epilogue

The airline industry's performance had been discouraging. Long-term profitability seemed destined to trend toward zero. There were, however, pockets of profitability in this otherwise profitless industry.

FIGURE 6-5 **AIRLINE INDUSTRY PROFITABILITY**

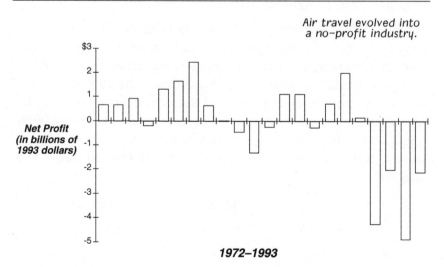

SOURCE: Air Transport Association.

A few innovative business designs created utility and recaptured value.

Airline Services: SABRE and Management Services

Crandall began to focus the investment resources of AMR Corp., American's parent company, on related businesses. The company's SABRE reservation system subsidiary and its management services group are both profitable. Understanding the advantage American would gain if it controlled ticket distribution channels, Crandall provided SABRE terminals to travel agents nationwide. American earned a fee for each booking. Crandall also sold SABRE to the new short-haul airlines. The newcomers could not afford the high costs of developing these systems internally so they outsourced them to American. The same airlines also contracted with American for management services like scheduling, yield management, and air-craft maintenance.

In 1993, SABRE had an operating margin of 19.6 percent, the management services group 10.6 percent. Although responsible for only $1.5 billion of AMR's $14 billion in revenue, SABRE and management services account for almost all of AMR's profits. One part of AMR's business was becoming the beneficiary of the same Value Migration that was destroying the value of the core business.

Southwest and Imitators

Southwest's business design consistently benefited from the airline industry's Value Migration process. Unlike Burr at People Express, Kelleher maintained a low-cost business design and expanded his airline at a carefully managed, sustainable pace. By 1994, Southwest transported more than 50 percent of the passengers in 80 of its 100 biggest markets. It targeted markets away from those coveted by the majors and built a strong leadership position in most of them. Its business design was powerful, as the year-end 1993 numbers indicated.

	Southwest	**American**
Load Factor	68.4%	60.4%
Cost (estimated cents per mile)	10.2	13.3

Profit (estimated cents per mile)	1.6	0
Passenger Revenue*	$2.2	$12.9
Shareholder Value*	$5.3	$5.0

* in billions

The majors found themselves even more disadvantaged. With Southwest's reputation for building dominant positions, incumbents often departed markets when Southwest arrived, allowing Southwest to expand significantly. At $2.2 billion in revenue, it was the seventh largest carrier in revenue passenger miles in 1994, and the only airline to have consistent growth in market value.

Southwest's old formula, meanwhile, again served as the model for a new breed of clones. Between 1991 and 1993, the Department of Transportation authorized 84 new airlines to operate, from Kiwi in Newark, to Mesa in Farmington, New Mexico, and to Reno Air in Reno.

By 1995, several major carriers had also decided to mimic the Southwest design. Continental and United announced subsidiaries that would offer low-cost flights. The Continental effort, dubbed CALite, has been launched in many East Coast markets. Two trips to bankruptcy court have given Continental a low-cost position that is closer to Southwest's than that of any other national carrier. But it is unclear whether United's effort, dubbed U2, will be able to bring down its cost enough, or if this experiment will go the way of Friendship Express a decade earlier.

More change is under way. For the first time in Southwest's 24-year history, Kelleher is attacking the majors directly. Unlike People Express, Southwest has much deeper pockets. The majors are also weaker than ever. But it is still a risky move—Kelleher will have to spend more time protecting his current position. Southwest has also outgrown its original design. Unless Kelleher creates the next-generation business design for Southwest Air, the clones will under-cut his fares and eat his profits. Southwest is at the inflection point between Phase I value growth and Phase II stability. The collapse of Southwest's stock price in 1994 indicates that Southwest might have already entered Phase II. Depending on the degree of competitive imitation, the stability phase could be short-lived. Southwest needs to be thinking about what its next business design should be.

Globalization: British Airways

The 16-year devolution of the U.S. airline industry is now taking place in compressed fashion in Europe. A phased, five-year deregulation of European air travel began to open the market in 1992. The industry has grown each year, yet virtually all of the subsidized national flag carriers are highly unprofitable. Upstart independents increased their market share from 40 to 50 percent in only two years (1991–1993) and account for almost all of the market growth. The commoditization of prices is happening rapidly. It appears that the demise of the U.S. airline industry is being replayed, with little or no strategic learning having been transferred to Europe. With one exception.

British Airways, the world's largest international carrier, has created a business design that has allowed it to escape the downward spiral under way on both sides of the Atlantic. BA chairman Sir Colin Marshall has several things going for him. His fleet is one-third the size of the big U.S. carriers. BA has developed a unique network of strategic alliances. It has the best load factor and yield in Europe, and both are higher than those of the U.S. majors. Although BA's costs are 12.5 cents per seat mile, higher than the U.S. average, they are among the lowest in Europe. In 1993, BA had an operating margin of 5.5 percent versus an average of .4 percent for the world's 18 leading fliers.

Part of BA's network of alliances includes a risky 25 percent investment in USAir. Marshall needed an airline that could feed passengers into his North Atlantic routes. USAir has traffic in 53 eastern U.S. cities. Furthermore, the two carriers won federal approval to share flight codes in those cities. This channels USAir passengers going overseas into BA's booking system.

The other component of BA's network is strategic alliances in other lucrative parts of the world. It has purchased a 25 percent stake in Qantas Airlines in Australia, 49 percent of a new German carrier called Deutsche BA, 49 percent of GB Airways in Spain and Morocco, and 49 percent of TAT European Airlines, the leading French independent.

A key part of the BA business design is careful focus on customer selection. By targeting the international flyer, British Airways has found a way to distinguish itself from both European and American carriers. It caters to the highest end of the market, the only one in which service is paid for. BA has a low-cost position, its service is excellent, its fares are aggressively priced, and it is making a profit. The business design has one potential flaw: USAir. The carrier is in such bad financial shape that even a modest rise in fuel prices could cripple it.

Even if that occurred, industry leaders would be wise to remember the lesson of People Express: A failed business does not indicate a failed business design. If British Airways isn't the dominant global megacarrier, someone else could be.

In 1995, Crandall, Kelleher, and Marshall face a common situation. The economic incentives of the remaining players make it unlikely that profitability will return. The European market is rapidly moving through the same profit-destroying process that has played out in the United States. Customers have repeatedly shown their preference for low-priced alternatives, proving that air travel is a commodity.

Two innovative business designs have been able to create and protect their value, but their uniqueness is being threatened.

Lessons Learned: Patterns

Customer priorities have moved in one direction in the domestic air transport industry: toward greater and greater price sensitivity. The hub-and-spoke business design of major U.S. airlines has delivered tremendous utility to the increasingly price-sensitive customer segments. What that business design has failed to do is recapture value for the airlines themselves. The regional, point-to-point business design, exemplified by Southwest Airlines, has been more successful at value recapture. However, recent margin erosion at Southwest raises the question of whether *any* business design can create sustainable profit and value growth in a hypercompetitive industry characterized by high fixed and negligible marginal costs. The only certain beneficiaries of Value Migration in the airline industry have been the customers.

Paradoxically, the regional airlines represent an opportunity for the beleaguered national carriers. To minimize the fixed-cost portion of their operating systems, regionals like Southwest have avoided building infrastructure, such as maintenance units and computer reservation systems. Troubled national airlines have identified these low-fixed-cost operators as a new customer set: AMR is now earning significant profits as an outsourcing provider of management and reservation services.

Another route to profitability may be a service-oriented international business design. British Airways has targeted international business travelers and built up a network of global alliances to offer them a seamless, high-service experience. Impending deregulation and sharpened competition in the European market will test the ability of the BA business design to continue to capture sufficient value.

Lessons from the evolution of the airline industry are that a major external event such as deregulation will create new customer segments and new opportunities for innovative business designs. Entrants will experiment and implement them. Since changing the course of a large corporation is difficult and time-consuming, incumbents should increase their flexibility to cope with nontraditional competitors by maintaining a portfolio of different business designs. When one design begins to attract value, it should also begin to attract commensurate investment to serve as a platform of future value growth.

Finally, when customers indicate a product or service is a commodity, even a successful business design will be profitable only as long as it presents a unique choice. People Express lost its edge when American matched its fares. If Southwest doesn't develop the next-generation business design, it will lose its distinction to the local carriers.

Replaying the Game

The airline chess game also illustrates the enduring power of institutional memory. In this case, conventional strategic behavior was exacerbated by a big case of industry-think versus customer-think. There was very little serious customer-think. All the majors responded to deregulation, to Southwest, to People's—to each other— in the same way. Instead of expanding, American or United or Delta could have strengthened its presence in a region of the country, just as Southwest did in Texas. The geography was plain: American's key hub was in Dallas, United's in Chicago, Delta's in Atlanta. In 1978, American was so much larger than Southwest it could have contained or even defeated the upstart with a highly focused strategy for achieving and maintaining regional leadership.

The failure of USAir would be cruel testimony to the risk of industry-think. Flying under the name Allegheny, the airline was one of the few regionals that enjoyed a low-cost position in 1978. It did not have a hub-and-spoke system. After deregulation it chose to develop one. It adopted the "bigger is cheaper" philosophy of the majors, merging its way to national scale. USAir, more than any other airline, could have taken off with the Southwest approach. It already had routes and terminal slots in the valuable Northeast. A business design focused on intense regional leadership could have created significant value growth. Instead, a business design focused on national growth led to value decline.

Two late-breaking chess moves will provide lessons further into the 1990s. Southwest's move to challenge the majors, and the threat it is under from imitators, closely parallels the situation that confronted Nucor, the steel minimill. Just as Nucor recognized that imitation and saturation threatened the power of its business design, Southwest needs to be aware of the eroding power of its previously successful business design. Nucor reinvented itself, using new technology and approaching new customer groups; it remains to be seen whether Southwest will be able to do the same.

Given the rapid pace of change in Europe, carriers there will either learn quickly from the Value Migration process in the United States, or replay the same value destruction game. Is there a People Express of Europe lurking in the wings? A Southwest? Will the burgeoning high-speed rail system undercut regional airlines? Will British Airways dominate international travel? What, if anything, will break the pattern toward zero profits?

Applications to Other Industries

Several other industries are in the midst of, or are about to enter, variations of the airline Value Migration pattern. Industries that invest in expensive, inflexible fixed assets are in danger of creating the zero-profit outcome. Chemicals, printing, and public utilities are all industries that have exhibited many of the early moves of the airlines pattern. The ability of the incumbents to escape the momentum of their previous moves will be critical.

The reaction of the incumbents to external shocks is visible in other industries. Whether driven by regulation or other discontinuities like new technology, the pervasiveness of industry-think often blinds the incumbents to newly viable business designs. Telecommunications, home entertainment, and, again, public utilities all have incumbents that have been slow to learn and to react. Ideally, executives in other industries will use the lessons of the airlines pattern to avoid a replay of the value destruction process that occurred in that industry.

Chapter **7**

Blockbuster Migration

Pharmaceuticals

- What new types of customers are making the decisions? What new priorities do they have? How well set am I to respond to these new customers?

- What effect will external shocks have on the economics of my business design? Is that design flexible enough to respond to these shocks?

- Is my organization capable of implementing a radically new business design?

THE PHARMACEUTICALS INDUSTRY has been one of the most enduring pillars of post–World War II prosperity in the United States and Europe. By applying extraordinary innovation, by creating breakthroughs that have improved health and longevity throughout the world (polio, smallpox, antibiotics), and by creating enormous wealth for investors, pharmaceutical companies have been long-term winners in the Value Migration game.

The formula for success, however, has been neither simple nor constant. Fundamental science has remained a core capability in creating utility. However, it is the treatment of disease that is paid for. Consequently, the business design required to maximize value recapture has changed dramatically over the past four decades.

As the customer base for pharmaceuticals has expanded, the priorities have also changed. Value has migrated from a design centered on *serendipitous science* (pre-1975), to a design focused on the creation of *blockbuster products* (1975–1990), to a design that responds to the changing structure of the customer base in the 1990s by focusing on low-cost distribution and market access—the *managed health care design* (see Figure 7-1).

Although numerous pharmaceutical companies have generated positive scientific, medical, and financial returns, none has played the Value Migration game as skillfully as Merck. At critical junctures, Merck has moved quickly and decisively to change its fundamental business design. As a result, it has significantly outperformed the rest of the industry in market value creation. Merck's ability to outperform its competitors has been a direct result of its agility and adaptability. Merck exemplifies the nimble incumbent that has minimized the negative effects of institutional memory and reinvented itself rather than be victimized as value stagnated or flowed out of an obsolete business design.

The lessons of the Value Migration pattern in the pharmaceutical industry are important for managers who find the decision makers in their customer base changing or find customers making demands that threaten the fundamental economics of the business. In addition, any research-intensive business will benefit from the lessons about R&D focus and portfolio management.

From Discovery to Safety

The modern pharmaceutical industry was the result of extraordinary parallel innovation in chemistry and medicine. As academic labora-

FIGURE 7-1   VALUE MIGRATION IN PHARMACEUTICALS

*In pharmaceuticals, the Value Migration pattern
was linear: the opportunity to maximize value growth
migrated to the blockbuster model in the 1980s and
the managed health care model in the 1990s.*

tories and chemical companies made more than 60 major break-throughs in the first half of the twentieth century, the medical profession was making great strides in understanding basic human physiology. These trends converged in the screening labs of pharma-ceutical companies, where scientists tried to find the right match between chemicals and disease mechanisms. This matching process was time-consuming, but when successful, it led to commercially viable products. More than 1,000 new products were introduced in the 1950s and the pharmaceutical industry emerged to legitimacy with worldwide sales of $2.75 billion by the end of the decade.

U.S. pharmaceutical companies and European chemical giants—Sandoz, Ciba-Geigy, and Roche in Switzerland; Bayer and Hoechst in Germany; Rhône Poulenc in France—quickly realized that the U.S. market was where innovative compounds became profitable products. The scale and relative wealth of the American economy in the 1950s made success in the U.S. market essential in maximiz-ing value recapture for R&D investment.

The business design that emerged in the 1950s was driven by science. A number of the pharmaceutical companies that we recog-nize as leaders today—Merck, Pfizer, Lilly—gained that stature by successfully investing in a business design reliant on large, efficient screening labs that could generate the most powerful chemical com-binations.

The Serendipitous Science Business Design

Fundamental Assumptions	Scientific breakthroughs are ran-dom events.
	All products will be profitable.

Business Design Element	**Choice**
R&D System	Mass screening of compounds, place many bets to increase odds
Customer Selection	Physician community
Differentiation	Breakthrough science
Value Recapture	Selling drugs paid for by insur-ance companies

Buoyed by the success of such early drugs as penicillin during World War II, physicians were eager to apply the results of pharmaceutical innovation. Concern about side effects was relatively low. Discovered in 1957 by Hoffman LaRoche, Valium was the first product to sell more than $500 million worldwide. Its success dramatically illustrated the economic power of unique, innovative products.

While the patient was the ultimate consumer, the physician was the customer who had the power to drive value. Patients were shielded from the manufacturers by custom, ethics, and regulation. The physician customer base was highly fragmented. From within independent practices, universities, hospitals, and clinics, physicians made decisions, usually with complete freedom, concerning the treatment of their patients for a wide variety of conditions. The pharmaceutical companies' marketing objective was to convince the doctor to prescribe their products.

Increasing the use of pharmaceuticals as a part of therapeutic programs was not difficult. The medical community was hungry for what the pharmaceutical companies were offering. Breakthroughs were the answer to their prayers. Suddenly they could actually treat diseases that had long been intractable.

Then came thalidomide. Thalidomide was a sleeping pill developed in Europe by William S. Merrill. After Merrill applied for approval to market the product in the United States in 1962, stories of birth deformities resulting from women taking the pill during pregnancy began to surface. A well-publicized resistance was organized by a single physician, Dr. Frances Kelsey. The Food and Drug Administration (FDA) did not approve the drug. Subsequently, several other approved products were found to have serious side effects. Physicians were alarmed. It was clear that the drug approval process needed changing. Safety was becoming the customer's highest priority.

In addition, new questions were raised about efficacy. Senator Estes Kefauver, the architect of regulations for several industries during the 1950s, turned his sights on the drug industry. He focused a critical spotlight on expensive products that had questionable efficacy. The thalidomide episode increased his commitment to limit the freedom that the pharmaceutical industry had enjoyed.

Throughout the 1960s, the FDA enacted a series of regulations governing the development and testing of new products that fundamentally changed the requirements of a successful business design. Suddenly a pharmaceutical company had to meet both the priorities of the physician (innovation and education) and the FDA (safety and rigorous statistical evidence).

The message to pharmaceutical companies was clear. Discovery research alone was no longer adequate. More rigorous testing and documentation supporting product safety and efficacy became critical elements of business design.

Most companies recalibrated their operations effectively. Legacy products continued to sell well, and powerful new classes of products were developed. The industry succeeded in responding to the priorities of physicians and the requirements of the FDA, generating steadily increasing revenues and profits through the 1960s.

Where the new requirements began to take their toll was on the cost side of the equation. During the 1960s and early 1970s, R&D spending in the industry grew from 4 percent of sales to more than 7 percent, with most of the increase coming from development (as opposed to discovery). The increase in the number and scope of clinical trials as well as the protracted development and approval processes were damaging the pharmaceutical companies' economics. Between 1962 and 1972, the average length of time from product discovery to market launch grew from two years to seven. In that same decade, the average cost of the development process grew from $1 million to $12 million.

While sales and profits continued to grow (return on sales was stable at 20 percent), the basic economic assumptions underlying the business design were changing.

U.S. patent law gives a pharmaceutical company a 17-year exclusive following initial registration of a chemical. In the 1950s, this meant that a company might get a product to market in 3–4 years and enjoy a patent protected position for 13–14 years. Since there were few competitive therapies, and the customer (the physician) really had no direct price sensitivity, the companies maintained significant pricing power. Profitability was virtually ensured. Popular products would pay back development costs over a long, profitable economic life.

With this design, companies average-resourced dozens of projects (investing in all equally) because finding the big winners was unpredictable. This science-driven process was sequential: from discovery to development to manufacturing to marketing. Marketing input came late in the process, if at all.

By the 1970s, this design was coming under increasing strain. FDA guidelines extended the length of the development process, shortening the patent-protected economic life of a product. These same guidelines also dramatically increased the cost of the development process (see Figure 7-2). The new demands of a key customer, the FDA, had both increased costs and reduced the revenue stream of pharmaceutical products, threatening the viability of a business design based on serendipitous science.

Many companies began to feel the new economic pressures acutely. In 1976, Roche lost its patent protection on Valium in the United Kingdom. Sales eroded as generic competitors entered the market. While its U.S. patent was valid until 1984, it was clear that Roche was vulnerable. The value inflow of the preceding 30 years was no longer a sure thing.

Merck was watching Valium and Roche with particular interest. Merck had grown in the 1960s to be the largest company in the U.S. pharmaceutical market. Merck's two largest products, Aldomet (for hypertension) and Indocin (for arthritis), were also facing patent

FIGURE 7-2   COST OF DRUG DEVELOPMENT

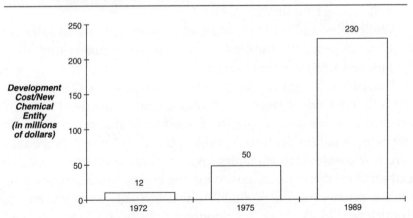

*With skyrocketing development costs, only a few
select projects could return the cost of R&D.*

SOURCE: Corporate Decisions, Inc. analysis.

expiration. At the same time, competitors were introducing products in categories led by Merck. Merck's leadership position was threatened; its basic business design was in jeopardy of slipping into value outflow.

It is 1978. As Roy Vagelos, head of Merck's R&D organization, you are in the predicament described above. This is the situation you see.

- The cost of developing a product has risen from $1 million in 1962, to $12 million in 1972, to $50 million in 1975.
- The success rate of products has diminished.
- Your flagship products, Aldomet and Indocin, face imminent patent expiration.
- Your pipeline has not delivered any new flagship products.
- Physicians have many more choices of treatment.
- You have adjusted your business design to accommodate the demands of the FDA by developing the capability to prove efficacy and safety.

What is your next move? What are the key moves that will prevent your business design from slipping into value outflow? How can you create a new business design that will continue to create and capture value?

Merck's Blockbuster Business Design

By 1978, it was clear that the economics of drug development had been altered dramatically. As the market leader, Merck had the most to lose. The patent expiration of Aldomet and Indocin would jeopardize fully 25 percent of its sales and 40 percent of its profits.

Merck's industry leadership could have created the kind of institutional memory that has destroyed many leading companies. The temptation to "stick to our knitting," to continue investing in research and development in the same ways, was formidable. Many in Merck's organization (as well as the rest of the industry) thought that the changing economics of drug development were minor and could be overcome with existing tools—that is, price.

Vagelos saw things differently. He knew that the old assumptions about customers and economics were no longer valid. As the FDA received more and more submissions, it moved even more slowly. Development costs continued to rise each year. Vagelos recognized that continued value growth would require fundamental rather than incremental changes in Merck's business design.

Drug development had evolved into a very high stakes game. Merck's research labs were pursuing dozens of promising compounds but the average expected return on any one project was decreasing rapidly.

In response to these new realities, Vagelos retooled Merck's business design. The first critical change was to focus greater development resources on fewer high-potential products and to ensure that those products reached the market ahead of the competition. Physicians hungry for innovation still flocked to the first product in a category. As a result, early entry translated into sustainable high market share (see Figure 7-3).

Vagelos created cross-functional teams around the most promising and important products. Responsible for the entire development cycle, these teams had freedom to create the most effective process they could. As an incentive, teams had to "compete" for resources (both people and dollars) throughout the organization, forcing pro-

FIGURE 7-3   MARKET SHARE BY ORDER OF ENTRY

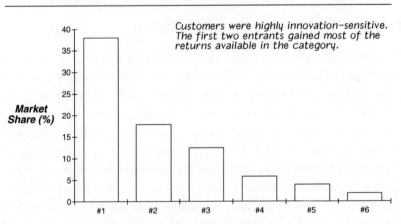

Customers were highly innovation-sensitive. The first two entrants gained most of the returns available in the category.

Competitors (by order of entry)

SOURCE: Corporate Decisions, Inc. analysis.

ject managers to "sell" and functional managers to "buy" into the hottest projects. From the start, marketing people were included to ensure that "hot" compounds would be translated into "big" products.

This free market allocated resources in a way that normal budgeting couldn't. Focus was automatic. People wanted to be part of a blockbuster team. Other projects could stay alive—the potential for breakthroughs could come from anywhere—but if they could not compete with other high-potential products, they withered.

To support this internal market, Merck developed a project management system to reduce cycle times in each step of the development process. The entire company focused on continuous improvement of the project management system, creating an experience and learning curve effect that competitors could not match. As a result, Merck began moving products through the development phase 30–40 percent faster than the industry average.

The second piece of the blockbuster business design was recasting the FDA as a valuable customer and treating its reviewers accordingly. Most of the industry thought of the FDA's reviewers as regulators, as external constraints on their business. The relationship was fundamentally antagonistic. Merck redefined this relationship. It invited the FDA into the development process early, and used FDA input to guide the company's efforts. Vagelos recognized that the FDA could make or break a product, not only by approval or rejection, but through the speed with which it acted on a product. Shrinking patent lives and crowded therapeutic classes meant that each month saved in the review process could be worth tens of millions of dollars.

Business Design
Serendipitous Science vs. Merck's Blockbuster Design

	Serendipitous Science Design	Merck's Blockbuster Design
Fundamental Assumptions	Discovery is unpredictable.	The ability to develop blockbusters is a given.
	FDA is a regulator.	FDA is a customer.
	Most successful drugs are profitable.	Only big drugs are profitable.

	Serendipitous Science Design	Merck's Blockbuster Design
Customer Selection	Physician	Physician and FDA
R&D System	Broad portfolio	Resources focused on fewer projects
		Intense project management

In 1986, Merck's new approach paid off. After only 11 months of review (the average was more than 30 months), it launched its ace-inhibitor Vasotec, in hot pursuit of the category leader, Bristol Myers' Capoten.

During the launch, Merck unveiled the third element of its blockbuster business design. High development costs had made commercial success more important than ever. To ensure an enthusiastic reception in the medical community, Merck concentrated its sales and marketing investment on the launch of Vasotec. It was no accident that Vasotec's sales exploded, catching up to and surpassing Capoten within five years of launch.

The blockbuster business design allowed Merck to satisfy the demands of the FDA and deliver a series of new products to the market in a way that no one in the industry had ever done. Physicians equated Merck with innovation. As Merck sales representatives became increasingly important sources of information, they gained preferential access to physicians while competitors' reps filled up the waiting room. By the end of the decade, Merck's blockbuster approach turned out *8 new products, each with more than $100 million in annual sales,* nearly double the number of blockbusters of its nearest competitor. (Given these products' disproportionately high impact on profitability, this feat contributed significantly to Merck's value growth in the next decade.)

Merck's success was not lost on competitors. Although many tried to emulate its blockbuster formula, few were able to put all of the pieces of the business design together. Several focused their R&D efforts but could not master the project management approach. Most tried to "adjust" their organizations to follow Merck's lead. But none could challenge Merck's effectiveness (see Figures 7-4 and 7-5).

FIGURE 7-4   MARKET VALUE CREATION

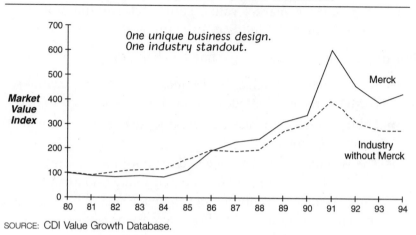

SOURCE: CDI Value Growth Database.

FIGURE 7-5   VALUE MIGRATION PHASES

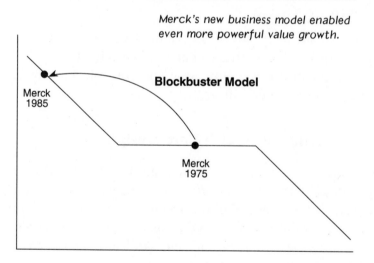

It's 1989. You are Roy Vagelos, CEO of one of the most admired corporations in America. You see a very positive picture.

- You have developed one of the most powerful product development organizations in history. Your success in launching new products is unparalleled.
- Your pipeline is full of promising new products. It is likely that you will launch innovative new products for at least the next decade.

- The financial markets have rewarded your business design with superior market value. Your stock has substantially outperformed the industry over the past decade.

But there are signs that things may be changing.

- New structures, such as health maintenance organizations (HMOs), have emerged, creating a new type of customer.
- Public attention increasingly has focused on pharmaceutical pricing practices.
- The Waxman-Hatch Act opened the door for generic competition by allowing approval based solely on bio-equivalence. While it has not yet developed as a credible threat, the largest economic hurdle—the cost of clinical testing for safety and efficacy—has been reduced.
- Looking to the future, a number of large, profitable products will lose patent protection. Generic competition will increase.

What's your next move? How should you adjust your business design in response to these changes? Which of these potential changes are real threats? How long will your blockbuster business design remain in value inflow?

Merck's Managed Health Care Design

The strategic crossroads that Merck faced in 1979 was created by the evolution of the FDA's priorities. Merck responded first and most effectively. But by the end of the 1980s, a new customer group was emerging—organized buyers. Once again, the new customer had different priorities from the old one. And once again, Merck was the first to anticipate and respond.

In 1991, Vagelos announced that Merck was going to reduce the size of its 2,700-member U.S. salesforce. He stunned the industry. The marketplace had not really changed significantly. Managed care organizations such as HMOs and preferred provider organizations (PPOs) were prevalent only in certain states (Minnesota, California, Florida, Massachusetts). Negative publicity about high drug prices had not translated into major restraints. All of the major players were adding reps each month.

Merck's business hadn't changed significantly either. Its development process continued to produce major products such as Pepcid for ulcers and Proscar for prostate conditions. Its development and approval cycle times were still 30 percent better than the industry average. The blockbuster development process was working. By 1992, Merck had 16 products, each with worldwide sales of more than $100 million. Vagelos couldn't be examining the same information that everyone else had.

In fact, Vagelos was looking at the exact same information. But what he saw was not current customer priorities but the trajectory of customer priorities into the future (see Figure 7-6). While the effects of managed care organizations, generic competition, and price pressure could not be felt today, they would be felt soon.

Furthermore, changes in accounting standards were forcing many large corporations to face up to a nagging obligation that they had successfully ignored for years. FASB 106 required companies to quantify their future health care liabilities for retired employees and this focused new attention on the costs of health care. The impetus to contain costs began to come from employers, symbolized by the $18 billion liability facing General Motors.

As organized buyers increased their use of generic substitution and therapeutic substitution (i.e., substituting one branded product for another branded product with similar efficacy but lower cost), the blockbuster business design would lose significant value-generating

FIGURE 7-6   CHANGING CUSTOMER PRIORITIES

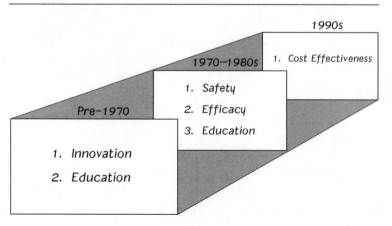

power. Profits would shrink and the capabilities that would create those profits would change. Key account management and low-cost distribution would displace sales and marketing as drivers of value growth.

The decline in profits was already foreseeable with a penetrating analysis of the components of overall industry profitability. Once adjusted for the effects of aggressive pricing and the contribution of legacy products, it was clear that sustainable profitability was 50 percent lower than reported profit levels (see Figure 7-7).

Vagelos anticipated the next cycle of value migration. He said that the future belonged primarily to bulk buyers of Merck medicines, and that these bulk buyers would, by 1995, account for 67 percent of his firm's U.S. sales. He added that marketing to bulk buyers would require a smaller and very different type of selling function than the one Merck was using.

The sales force announcement was only the opening move in Vagelos' plan to rebuild Merck's business design. Besides reducing the number of sales representatives, Vagelos fundamentally redefined the sales function, hiring MBAs and Ph.D.'s to develop a highly

FIGURE 7-7   ADJUSTED PHARMACEUTICAL INDUSTRY PERFORMANCE

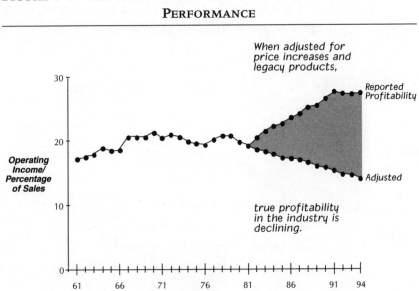

SOURCE: S&P (1981–1983), Value Line (1983–1994), and Corporate Decisions, Inc. analysis.

sophisticated account-management approach that catered to the more complex priorities of organized buyers. Finally, he recognized the need to tighten operations, looking for efficiency in anticipation of the price pressures that would squeeze margins. He also knew that responding effectively (and profitably) to the changing structure of the customer base would require two new capabilities— information on total health care costs and access to distribution.

While pharmaceutical sales were a relatively small portion of U.S. health care expenditures (7 percent in 1990), they attracted much critical attention. The industry's profitability and history of aggressive price increases drew the ire of public interest groups and politicians. Over the 1980s, the price of the average pharmaceutical product grew more than three times as fast as producer prices as a whole (150 percent versus 45 percent). Pharmaceutical prices had become an extremely sensitive issue.

Medicare, the single largest purchaser of many products, began to ask for limits on the price increases. Employers that paid for large portions of their employees' health care began to look for ways to limit their overall costs. In response to these priorities, pharmacy benefit managers (PBMs) emerged, offering employers and insurers a way to limit the pharmaceutical portion of their total health care expense. A basic tenet of the old business design for pharmaceutical companies—pricing flexibility—was being challenged.

Most health professionals agree that drugs are among the most cost effective ways to treat patients. Common sense suggests that spending $500 per year to prevent a heart attack is enormously preferable to the cost (both financial and human) of treating the heart attack victim. Generating the data required to prove this cost effectiveness traditionally had not been a part of the drug development process. Even more important, comparative cost-effectiveness data among alternative drug therapies had never been developed. Merck's blockbuster design, with its in-depth focus on a handful of major development projects, was the perfect launching pad for developing the first cost-effectiveness data, allowing it to differentiate its products for highly price-sensitive organized buyers.

The growing power of the managed care industry in the early 1990s changed the way that pharmaceutical prescribing decisions were made. In an effort to control costs, HMOs and PBMs created mechanisms that limited the physician's freedom of choice. Through formularies (i.e., lists of approved products), these organizations influenced physicians' prescribing behavior toward lower-cost therapies. From the pharmaceutical company's point of view, these formularies became critical vehicles of market access. The leverage of restrictive formularies and growing membership lists enabled the managed care organizations to extract significant discounts from pharmaceutical manufacturers. As large buyers continued to grow in both membership and influence (both of which were predictable), the ability to sell to and negotiate with them was critical to manufacturers.

The most influential of the PBMs was Medco Containment Systems. Medco was responsible for the pharmaceutical benefits of more than 33 million patients. Selling products to Medco had a significant impact on overall market share. Merck, with its portfolio of blockbuster products, was especially dependent on Medco.

In November 1993, Merck bought Medco for $6 billion. The purchase price astounded both industry insiders and Wall Street. Merck was valuing the company far beyond anyone's previous estimate. Why did Merck see so much value in a company with no patents, no scientists, no laboratories, no manufacturing facilities, and no hard assets?

The most immediate and obvious value of Medco was its ability to affect market share by influencing prescribing behavior. Merck products could be substituted for other equivalent products with a phone call. In an increasingly cost-conscious environment, the ability to position Merck's products as *the* cost-effective alternative was a critical advantage. But not worth $6 billion.

There were four aspects of Medco that Merck felt justified its valuation.

1. *Sales force substitution.* Increasingly large numbers of physicians were having their choices limited by formularies that listed insurance reimbursable products. Consequently, the need for the traditional go-to-market mechanism—a direct, face-to-face selling force—diminished. In the new environment, the productivity advantage provided by Medco's tele-sellers was compelling.

2. *Information.* The sales of pharmaceuticals traditionally involved a one-way flow of information. Sales reps called on physicians. They wrote no sales orders; they received no direct feedback on the effectiveness of their efforts. In fact, until very recently, it was impossible

to know what drugs a given physician was, in fact, prescribing. By aggregating patient records, PBMs created a new flow of information. Treatment history could be captured on a patient-by-patient basis. The value of this information would be immeasurable. For the first time, Merck could get data on how its products were actually being used, allowing it to more effectively and efficiently improve the way that it differentiated its products and focused its sales and marketing efforts.

3. *Compliance.* Another aspect of information value was in the area of compliance. Studies indicated that 50 percent of patients failed to take their prescribed drugs at the recommended dosages and intervals (25 percent underdosed, 15 percent left prescriptions unfilled, and 10 percent overdosed). Noncompliance led to ineffective treatment, potential medical complications, and higher total medical costs as well as substantial lost revenues for pharmaceutical manufacturers. Medco gave Merck access to patient behavior data. Proper use of Merck products would increase confidence in their efficacy and improve value recapture.

4. *Disease management.* The potentially most valuable aspect of Medco was that it allowed Merck to transform itself from a company that sold pills to one that applied its knowledge and expertise to manage diseases and reduce their cost to both patient and payor. Merck had invested billions of dollars in understanding the mechanisms and treatment of diseases. Traditionally it had applied this information only to the development of submissions for FDA approval. Since the priorities of health care providers now included managing the costs of patient care, Merck would be able to transform its information and expertise into a performing asset, changing both the scope of its activities and the value recapture on the investment of drug development. Earning a per-patient fee, Merck could manage patient treatments more cost effectively. Medco would give Merck a direct connection to these health care providers as well as the patient information to develop the most effective treatment protocols.

By acquiring Medco, Merck had acquired capabilities that allowed it to continue to meet its new and existing customers' most important priorities. Merck's blockbuster design of the 1980s remained an important core of its new design. Getting big products to the market quickly would still be critical. But the changing customer base dictated that Merck invest to expand that business design to match customer priorities in the new world of managed care.

Epilogue

Merck's announcement of the Medco purchase was the final and clearest signal that Merck had radically overhauled its business design. Many competitors did not, and still do not, understand the rationale and economics of that decision. The capabilities that Merck invested in might not earn returns for many years—evolution of the customer base is slow and gradual. From the traditional competitor's perspective, Merck made a colossal mistake.

Viewed in the context of the 40-year pattern of Value Migration in the pharmaceutical industry, the logic of Merck's move becomes clear. In the 1950s, success depended on serendipitous science. As the demands of one customer, the FDA, became more complex, companies created new development capabilities. The economics began to change, prompting Merck to create its blockbuster design, which ensured that Merck would continue to earn superior returns on its investment in the development of innovative products. As the customer base began to shift from individual physicians to large buyers in the late 1980s, new pressures again threatened Merck's ability to earn those returns. Merck responded by developing the capabilities and skills necessary to recapture the value that its science created. By acquiring Medco, Merck will be able not only to earn a return on its drugs, but also to earn a return on the information and expertise that previously sat on the shelf at the FDA in the form of drug applications.

Lessons Learned: Patterns

In many industries, pure technological innovation is no longer enough. Only with a flexible and innovative business design is it possible to capture value on an ongoing basis. This is true for many reasons. First, customers learn. As they become more literate and comfortable with technologies and products, they don't need or want to pay for being educated. For example, physicians had long ago stopped needing Merck (or any other pharmaceutical company) to teach them about cholesterol. Second, true technical innovation has become more difficult. In many industries, advances are more incremental than breakthrough. Despite a slightly better side-effect profile, it was hard for Merck to command premium pricing for the development of the third H_2 antagonist (an ulcer drug).

The moves that Merck made, both in the late 1970s and in the early 1990s, required foresight and courage. The company moved against the currents of conventional wisdom. In both cases, however, Merck was able to define the rules of the game for all who followed. Merck took the initiative and created unique business designs that have proven difficult to imitate. Merck preempted the market.

Replaying the Game

Merck's continuous transformation in response to changing customer priorities serves as a vivid reminder that even entrenched giants can read customers and move adroitly. Unlike U.S. Steel, IBM, or United Airlines, Merck refused to let institutional memory compromise its future value growth.

Several pharmaceutical companies would like to have moved as quickly and successfully as Merck. The blockbuster design was accessible to all, but executing it successfully demanded a willingness to focus. Few competitors could meet the challenge. As a result, many pharmaceutical companies now have relatively empty pipelines. Average resourcing has diminished their ability to deliver economically viable products. Merck's second dramatic move, the purchase of Medco, touched off a round of imitation, as Lilly, Smith-Kline Beecham, and Pfizer all either purchased or entered into alliances with PBMs.

Applications to Other Industries

Why should bankers or publishers, or consumer packaged-goods companies, or chemical companies invest time to understand Merck's key moves and business design changes? More generally, what types of companies would profit from understanding the Merck success?

Merck's two major transformations are relevant to different audiences for different reasons. The development of the blockbuster design should interest companies under increasing pressure to focus their resources on fewer, more valuable investments. "Investments" can refer to R&D projects, new books, or customer accounts. Value growth for publishers, for example, may be driven by a few block-busters rather than by countless smaller, marginally profitable entries.

In consumer packaged goods, the same dynamic is at work, in a different guise. At issue here are both projects and accounts. Procter & Gamble will not fund a product unless it can be launched globally. It is moving in the right direction. But as important for P&G, and for other consumer products firms, the opportunity for value growth resides increasingly in a small number of key accounts (Wal-Mart, Target, CVS), which need an attention level dramatically higher than five years ago. These firms need a blockbuster account management process. Many are still without one.

Companies experiencing a sharp shift in the relative value-generating power of key functional areas can learn from both of Merck's major transitions. Historically, sales, marketing, and pricing drove the value growth in pharmaceuticals. As customers and economics shifted, the ability of these three functions to drive value growth diminished. The relative importance of development, FDA management, and account management rose rapidly. Merck understood this shift and managed it, despite the organizational trauma in cutting back on the role of the sales force and traditional marketing activities.

Numerous other companies and industries confront the shift of the relative importance of different functional areas. In business forms, the historical generators of value growth were manufacturing and sales; today they are account management, software technology, marketing, and purchasing. In computing, for many companies the shift is one from technology to marketing. In banking, the historical generators of value growth were lending and the consumer banking network. Today they are marketing and new product development.

In all these industries, there has been a significant lag between signals from customers and response from product and service providers. When that lag is too great, companies miss opportunities to create and capture value, and make themselves vulnerable to new entrants and nontraditional business designs.

Finally, any company with a combination of inefficient systems and declining product magic can profit from considering Merck's transition to the managed health care design. Merck understood that the aura around its product was vanishing (just as it has in PCs and is about to in many industrial products, including chemicals, equipment, and instrumentation), and that power was shifting from manufacturer to distributor. It also understood that the dominant method of moving product from manufacturer to customer was characterized by high costs to the seller and high costs and hassle to the buyer.

Merck's move into distribution was both about power (customer contact, customer control) and efficiency (lower selling and buying costs). The challenge of this pattern of shifting power in the value chain is one confronting many manufacturers today. Some do not even recognize it as an issue. Those that do are puzzled by what to do about it. The Merck–Medco precedent, when truly understood, provides a cluster of guidelines and cautions that can be used to help make the right decisions for managing this pattern of value flow.

Chapter **8**

Multicategory Migration

Coffee

- How do my customers think about the functionality of my product? How has that changed in the past five years?

- How might new business-design alternatives affect the way that customers will consider all incumbent designs?

- What opportunities are there to differentiate products that are becoming commodities?

WHAT BUSINESS AM I IN? A simple question that often cannot be answered simply. In many industries, the definition of the product, the customer, and the benefits that are being sold all depend on point of view. In most industries, tradition answers the question. Competitors are defined, industry classifications are established. Too often, however, an overly categorical answer to the question "What business am I in?" becomes an impediment. It limits the field of vision. Worse, it can become a filter through which you see the customer—incorrectly.

In the coffee industry, a mis-answering of the question has led to Value Migration (see Figure 8-1). As recently as 1987, three major brands held 90 percent of the $8-billion retail market. Only six years later, new gourmet roasters have created more than $1 billion in shareholder value—all of it at the expense of the traditional coffee

FIGURE 8-1   VALUE MIGRATION IN COFFEE

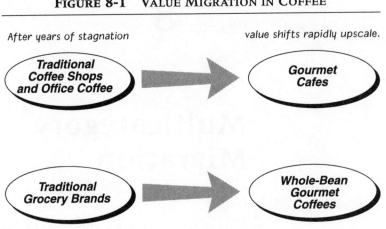

leaders. Procter & Gamble alone was perfectly positioned to create $2–3 billion in new value, had it defined the business it was in by asking customers what they wanted, not by what P&G had historically given them.

The lessons of the coffee industry apply to any company that has seen its product become a commodity. Commoditization is a function of the product or service that is offered as well as the business designs in which it is embedded. When competitors all employ identical business designs, the customer is often left to differentiate products only on price. These commodity categories can only be reinvigorated by new business designs that create new types of utility for customers.

The Coffee Industry

In the early 1980s, Howard Schultz had the opportunity to go on a week-long coffee-buying trip to Milan, Italy. He was a buyer for Starbucks Coffee Co., which sold fresh, whole coffee beans in five specialty stores in Seattle. In Italy he saw crowds of city dwellers begin each day with a stop in a coffee bar. The cafes were bustling, boisterous, filled with rich aromas and unique drinks with exotic names like *latte macchiato, espresso con panna.* The same crowds returned to the cafes in the evenings to sit and talk with friends. This could happen in America, Schultz realized.

MULTICATEGORY MIGRATION **159**

Back in Seattle, he insistently petitioned his two bosses to let him start a cafe. They refused, because they wanted to be in the coffee bean business, not the restaurant business.

Schultz quit to try the idea on his own. He pursued 200 investors for more than a year. Finally, he raised $1.7 million—some of it from his former bosses. In April 1986, Schultz opened his first cafe in downtown Seattle. The coffee he served was Starbucks'.

In less than a year, Schultz had opened two more cafes. He bought out his former bosses for $4 million. By August 1987, Schultz had the Starbucks name over his three cafes.

Meanwhile, in the "real" coffee industry, a national battle had been under way for many years between Maxwell House, owned by General Foods, and Folgers, owned by Procter & Gamble. The two brands commanded more than 60 percent of the coffee market. To the palate, the coffees were blandly similar. To the eye, they were barely distinguishable. Both were ground coffees made from inexpensive Robusta beans sold in tin cans. Competition among Maxwell House, Folgers, and the third big player—Nescafé, owned by Nestlé—was based on price. Coffee was treated as a commodity. The major players' business designs were built on this assumption.

Traditional Coffee Business Design

Fundamental Assumptions	Coffee is a commodity for which consumers will never pay a premium.

Business Design Element	**Choice**
Customer Selection	Entire grocery-buying public
Differentiation	National brands
	Price
Manufacturing System	Ground coffee, mass produced and vacuum-packed for long shelf life
Value Recapture	High-volume loss leader (ineffective value capture)
Go-to-Market Mechanism	Grocery stores, national advertising

During this competitive battle, the market had been declining slowly but steadily. Americans were drinking less coffee. Sales of the three major brands were down. Still, the brand owners spent millions on advertising to maintain share in the shrinking market. Coffee was promoted every week as a supermarket loss leader.

The majors had made partial attempts to reinvigorate the market. Maxwell House introduced its Private Collection label in 1985. It was a whole-bean coffee. The beans were displayed in a big plastic case in supermarket coffee aisles. The grocers furnished machines so customers could grind the beans in the store and brew their coffee at home. General Foods spent millions to advertise the product. Sales were poor.

Folgers introduced Gourmet Supreme and French Roast, both premium grinds. Both failed miserably. Folgers had thought there might be a niche for a higher-quality product. Now company executives guessed not. Coffee drinkers just did not want to pay more. They were happy with what they had—or so Folgers concluded. The only aberration was in the South, where customers preferred the rich, strong-tasting blends sold there by regional roasters. The regionals had very strong market share in their territories. But the southern markets were small, and the regional roasters made up only 3 or 4 percent of the national market. They were an annoyance, not a serious competitive threat. "Just a fad, this whole-bean coffee thing," executives concluded.

Schultz's little crop of stores were not a competitive threat either. Nor were the gourmet shops that had also opened in a few cities like Seattle, which sold fresh, whole coffee beans by the pound. The entire "gourmet coffee" segment, as it was classified, accounted for less than 5 percent of the total market.

It is January 1988. You're the general manager of Folgers. This is the situation you see.

- Your core coffee business is becoming less attractive. Price competition for market share is expensive and is destroying profitability.

- Your attempts at high-end coffees have not succeeded. Your customers appear to be motivated only by price.

- These high-end roasters that have sprung up seem successful, but they have very small niche markets. They do not sell to your customers.

What's your next move? What adjustments to your business design will allow you to create and capture value growth? How can you get out of the dead-end price wars that are devaluing your once attractive business?

Invention

By the end of 1988, Folgers was winning the grocery store battle. Maxwell House had slipped to 26.4 percent market share, a tick behind Folgers. To shore up profit margins, General Foods also started using an even higher proportion of cheap, bitter, Robusta beans in its blends.

Both companies were losing the war, however. Coffee was becoming a profitless industry. In 1988, General Foods lost $40 million on its domestic coffee business; P&G saw its margins disappearing. Middle-aged and increasingly health-conscious Baby Boomers seemed to be moving away from caffeine. U.S. coffee consumption, which had peaked at 3.1 cups a day per person in 1962, was at 1.67 cups a day, an all-time low.

Industry executives did not know how to respond. In the good old days, coffee accounted for nearly one-third of General Foods' operating profit. Managers worried about GF's reliance on its coffee business. Yet they had not introduced a single significant new product in a decade. Institutional memory prevailed. The new players in the industry—the regional whole-bean sellers, Starbucks, a few mom-and-pop cafes—were growing at double digit rates, but they were minuscule in terms of total dollars. Starbucks' 1988 sales were $10 million. It was hard to measure or even imagine the momentum in such tiny numbers, relative to a $5-billion industry.

One thing was clear. The customer was not driving decision making at P&G, General Foods, or Nestlé. There was little or no improvement in product quality or packaging—little or no improvement in customer utility. And despite the claims in commercials, there was also little difference among the taste of major brands.

The majors' failures in premium brands only reinforced their belief that gourmet coffee was a passing fad. A look at a few other industries might have given them a clue that it was not only a real segment, but a threat to their core business. Several companies in other categories were testing the upper end of the consumer quality spectrum: Haagen-Dazs in ice cream, TCBY in frozen yogurt, Perrier in bottled water, Mrs. Fields in cookies. Sales were soaring. Gourmet foods at gourmet prices would indeed sell among a growing population of discriminating customers. The question was how to convert the customer.

An important part of the answer had not escaped the whole-bean coffee providers. The fundamental change was product quality. They, like Schultz, used Arabica beans exclusively (which were much more aromatic, flavorful, and expensive). The coffee tasted better. And its delivery to the customer, whether in groceries or at cafes, was novel and highly differentiated. Millstone Coffee in Everett, Washington, which was pushing whole bean in Seattle groceries while Starbucks built cafes there, had grown 30–80 percent each year since 1981. Sales in 1990 topped $30 million. Boyer Brothers Coffee Co. created a powerful leadership position in Denver. Since incorporating in 1985, sales to grocers increased 100 percent a year, reaching $18 million in 1990. The company was already marketing to retailers in 22 states. The majors had tried to offer a high-end product with their same old business design. It could not be done. The new players had developed completely different designs.

Coffee drinkers were enjoying the first major expansion in customer options in decades. Although gourmet coffee was priced 80–100 percent higher than traditional coffee, people bought it. Even at $6 a pound, the pleasure worked out to only 10¢ a cup. Furthermore, despite the recession, the go-go 1980s had created a status-conscious consumer. When office workers bought a frothy latte, they were buying coffee as good as any CEO, movie star, or yachter could buy. They could not afford a $40,000-car, not even a new CD player, but they could reward themselves with a $6-bag of great coffee. Or a cup of exclusivity, custom-made by an expert cafe brewer for $1.95. Coffee was an affordable luxury—a fundamentally different concept than coffee in a can (see Figure 8-2).

None of the majors was examining customer desires—or the business designs that served them, which supported the small but

FIGURE 8-2   CUSTOMER PRIORITY EVOLUTION

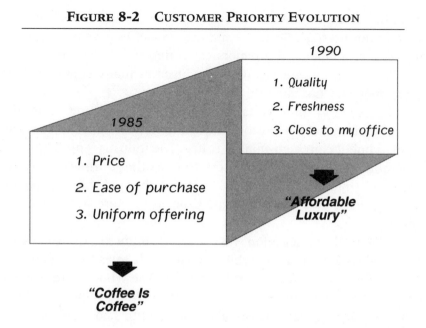

As always, changing customer priorities create opportunities for new business designs and vulnerability for traditional models.

rapidly growing number of players on the fringe of the competitive radar screen. One design, the cafe, was so different that neither Maxwell House nor Folgers thought it a threat. The other design, whole-bean displays in groceries, was, however, annoying. The upstarts presented a broad array of flavors. Their delivery people did not merely deliver the product; they set up displays, cleaned the bean-dispensing bins, even held live tastings for shoppers.

These new business designs were "too complex" a chore for the nationals to copy. They were not mere adjustments to what the nationals were already doing. These designs were based on new assumptions. The scope, differentiation, go-to-market mechanisms, and value recapture were all different. Instead, the majors continued to invest intensely in their existing business, resigned to shrinking profits at the supermarket. They now saw coffee as a loss leader. Phillip Morris, owner of Kraft, which had absorbed General Foods, quadrupled the Maxwell House ad budget to $100 million. Maxwell House and Folgers escalated the war with perpetual rounds of discounting, and millions of cents-off coupons. These moves did not raise brand prestige. To make matters worse, in a vain attempt to improve profitability, the majors converted their cans from 16 oz. to 13 oz., claiming the contents produced as many cups of coffee. Consumers did not view this as value-added.

Imperceptibly, but certainly, value was migrating from the canned, ground-coffee business design to new designs built around fresh, whole-bean, high-quality coffee. The industry's profit growth was shifting to the gourmet roasters. In 1990, the gourmet companies had $717 million in sales, a 13.5 percent share of the $5.3-billion market. Profit margins on whole-bean sales were as high as 25 percent.

By 1991, the penetration was even more dramatic. Gourmet sales had reached $800 million, while industrywide sales had dropped to $4.5 billion, led by declines at the majors. The whole-bean players' market share had climbed to 17.7 percent. More important, their share of value, by any reasonable calculation, had climbed to 30 percent.

At the same time, the cafe, the second new business design, was reaching critical mass in a few select cities. Seattle, already dubbed "Latteland" by a local newspaper columnist, led the way. By 1992, there were 150 cafes in the city. Chicago had 40; Vancouver was close behind. The customers' desire for quality coffee was the same, but the business design that met their priorities was Schultz's Milan cafe design. The cafes were taking share, not so much from national brands on store shelves, but from mediocre coffee shops, and the even-worse-than-mediocre office coffee services. However, the volume of whole-bean coffee sold by cafes began rising rapidly too.

Dominating select cities brought name recognition for the whole beaners. Starbucks was a phenomenon in Seattle. The cafes created a culture and a loyal customer base.

Back in the war rooms at Folgers and Maxwell House, product managers were still arguing over coupons.

These innovative business designs were not only about the "product." Starbucks was also building a highly innovative and effective human resource system. Back in 1988, when he had only 26 cafes, Schultz started hiring experienced executives from corporations like Pepsi to manage finances and human resources. Their expertise showed. They named their counter servers *baristas*, Italian for bartender. Each new *barista* was given 25 hours of classes on coffee history and lore, quality, drink preparation, and brewing that perfect cup at home. With friendly conversation, the knowledgeable *baristas* educated consumers in the romance and sophistication of Starbucks' products.

All employees, even part-timers, were eligible for health and dental benefits. In 1991, Schultz introduced Bean Stock, a stock option plan for full-timers *and* part-timers. Turnover of counter help was less than 60 percent, very low for the food service industry.

In addition, the scope of Starbucks' business design was built on the concept of strict sequential focus. It took enormous discipline on Schultz's part to conquer cities in depth, rather than to spread his investment thinly across a broad national geography. The success of Starbucks in every market it had entered confirmed both the demand for the product as well as the power of the business design. City share mattered. It made delivery efficient and preserved product freshness. It was an enormously cost-effective way to build brand loyalty without advertising. Finally, it created a powerful profit engine Starbucks could use to drive enormous future value growth.

Starbucks' city-by-city approach had one major vulnerability: it left space for other players. Would anyone exploit it?

It's June 1992. You are the CEO of P&G. This is the situation that you see.

- The gourmet roasters of coffee are no longer just a distraction. They have taken significant share from your business. Your share of a shrinking market is falling.
- The rise of coffee cafes is a positive sign. Maybe fashion will bring the younger generation back to coffee. Maybe the coffee business is not dying.

What's your next move? What can you do to reverse the tide in the grocery store? How can you take advantage of the new interest created by these cafes?

You are Howard Schultz of Starbucks. Here is the situation that you see.

- Your business design has great economic power. You have been able to establish leading positions in every city that you have entered.

- The market opportunities seem unlimited. The challenge is maintaining product quality—the core of the business design—while moving quickly enough to take advantage.

What's your next move? How can you maximize the power of your design? Are you vulnerable by failing to move rapidly enough? How long can you count on inaction by the majors or by other whole-bean providers?

Acceleration

The impact of the whole-bean coffee business designs on the market was undeniable. In the fall of 1992, Starbucks' sales were running at $28 million a quarter. Remarkably, neither cafes like Starbucks nor grocery suppliers like Millstone and Boyer Brothers had any well-known national competitor. The majors were still not responding.

In late 1992 and early 1993, an industry that had been characterized by very little national news for more than a decade experienced several major events that made the headlines.

The first big move was in cafes. Starbucks' 1992 sales forecast was $90 million. Operating income would be $6 million. But the cafes were not generating enough cash to allow expansion as fast as the customer opportunity would allow. Schultz took his company public in July 1992. He offered 2.1 million shares at $17 apiece, hoping to raise $35.7 million. He did, valuing his company at $115 million. Two quarters later, the company's market value was $500 million. Employees suddenly found themselves with a liquid, and valuable, asset.

Starbucks brilliantly leveraged its own IPO to generate name awareness without advertising. It tempted dozens of newspapers and magazines with articles about itself. Stories appeared everywhere. People across the country were mentally prepared for the arrival of a Starbucks cafe in their city.

Other chains were catching on: Barnie's in Florida, Coffee Beanery in Michigan. New channels for gourmet coffee were also surfacing. A few select restaurants started to offer custom blends.

La Creme Coffee, a Dallas roaster, supplied top eateries in several cities. Value continued to migrate to these new channels of "the affordable luxury."

The second big move was in grocery whole bean. Boyer Brothers, which had been renamed Brothers Gourmet Coffees, had its own route system in the Rocky Mountain states, and had contracted with leading direct-store-delivery (DSD) distributors elsewhere. By the end of 1991, its sales were $30 million. Brothers had put whole-bean coffee dispensers in 2,500 food stores. It augmented the stations with gourmet ground coffees in cans. Its drivers stopped as often as three times a week to clean and fill bulk bins in high-volume stores to ensure quality (roasted beans stay fresh no more than two weeks).

In December 1992, Brothers engineered a big merger with Specialty Coffee of Bow, New Hampshire, which itself had been built through acquisition, having previously purchased Nicholas Coffee Co. and Elkin Coffee. The new company, Gourmet Coffees of America (GCA), would be headquartered in Boca Raton, Florida. It was a lone merger, not a sign of widespread consolidation in the industry. Yet it *was* a sign that you might need to be bigger to compete in the supermarkets. GCA had three manufacturing and distribution facilities, multiple brands, 130 varieties, and $100 million in sales. It began a just-in-time manufacturing and inventory system to ensure fresh product. It also built a packaging line, using a new type of plastic bag that would keep prepackaged gourmet whole-bean and ground coffees fresh on supermarket shelves.

GCA fueled its own expansion with acquisitions. It acquired Gloria Jean's, the number one, mall-based whole-bean supplier with 180 stores, and Hillside, a California based company, which was Chock Full O' Nuts' entry into the whole-bean business. Then GCA went public in December 1993 and formally changed its name to Brothers Gourmet Coffees. Its market value at the time of the IPO was $200 million. One quarter later it fell to $130 million and stayed there. Despite impressive sales and growing market share, Brothers gourmet whole-bean business design lacked the power of the Starbucks design. This should not have been a surprise. In fact, Ted Lingle, executive director of the Specialty Coffee Association of America, had told *USA Today* several months earlier: "People who own coffee-bean stores are shifting into coffee cafes. The most profitable part of the business is in retail sales of coffee as a beverage."[1] Brothers moved quickly in response to the message from the stock market, opening cafes under the Brothers name.

Meanwhile, Starbucks' first quarter sales for 1993 were $41 million, up 97 percent from the prior year. Profits had grown by 60 percent. By year's end, the approximate market value of the majors would be $4 billion.[2] The market value of the new business designs was more than $1 billion. Activity in the coffee industry was intensifying. The developments that had been hidden below the surface were driven upward into clear view. No one could deny that whole-bean sales in groceries, and coffee sales in cafes, were unstoppable trends (see Figure 8-3).

It's December 1993. You're the CEO of Brothers, or Starbucks, or P&G. This is the situation you see.

FIGURE 8-3   RADAR SCREEN: FOLGERS (P&G)

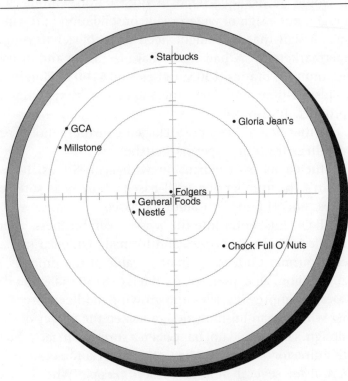

When value begins to shift,
fringe players become the most dangerous rivals.

- Competitors are appearing in every market across the country, trying to fill the opportunity space. Competition will intensify.

- Starbucks has created a superior business design that appealed to the investment community. Brothers' whole-bean grocery design appears weaker.

- The major coffee incumbents, General Foods and P&G, have not yet responded to the challenge of gourmet coffee.

What's your next move? What can you do immediately to take advantage of the market opportunity? What moves will create a dominant position as the category becomes more crowded and competitive? What might the deep-pocketed majors do? How should you position yourself to defend the value that you have already created?

Convergence

Answering these questions was complicated because what was important to the customer was changing again. When whole beans first hit the market, what mattered was availability. Now, with burgeoning choices, consumers developed brand loyalties. They wanted assured quality. They wanted convenience.

The abundance of market opportunities had created hyperactivity, just like that in the personal computer market of the 1980s. Newcomers arrived in force. There was intense competition for scarce grocery-shelf space.

The traditional players were still conspicuously inactive. Despite a demonstrated ability to develop and launch new products, they did not focus that skill on launching a new gourmet coffee brand. Part of this inactivity can be attributed to a lack of information. They still tracked grocery sales with check-out scanner data. Whole-bean coffee was not scanned. So although they knew the market was growing, they did not have an easy way to analyze how fast and they did not develop new methods to find out.

The Value Migration pattern was entering a new phase. The two business designs that had created gourmet coffee—cafes and whole bean in grocery—were converging. And competition and imitation challenged each design's ability to continue value growth (see Figure 8-4).

Although Starbucks had a major lead in cafes—it now had 280, mostly urban, compared with 180 for Gloria Jean's mall-based stores and fewer for other chains—a significant portion of the gourmet market was in grocery. Starbucks had no presence there. Yet. On the other hand, Brothers was strong in the grocery market and was opening more cafes.

Brothers had captured 30 percent of the coffee shelf space in Denver. It built strong loyalty through direct promotion to an extensive database of local customers. Millstone had a secure position in Seattle. But elsewhere competition was wrecking the whole-bean business. Early warnings of commoditization were visible. There was an increasing number of signs reading $3.99/lb. for fresh whole beans. Grocery stores like Stop & Shop installed dispensers with their own whole-bean brands.

How could the whole-bean companies combat commoditization? Only by building a strong brand. This would allow them to convince grocers that they would make more profit on the high-margin branded regional coffees. The question was, what business design would create and capture the value of that brand?

A student of Value Migration patterns could identify the relevant model: the Coca-Cola business design. Once preeminent, Coke was

FIGURE 8-4   VALUE MIGRATION IN COFFEE: THE NEXT PHASE

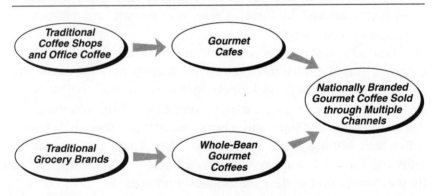

The next phase of Value Migration may lead to convergence of and competition among previously noncompeting business models.

seriously challenged by Pepsi. Coke advertises to maintain brand in the retail channels. While it fights to a draw with Pepsi in supermarket sales, it wins 2:1 in restaurants, 3:1 in vending machines, and 4:1 in international sales. It accepts lower margins in the highly competitive retail channel in order to build a brand that earns spectacular returns in the other channels. Retail is the strategic space of the market that allows significant value recapture in the other spaces. The emerging coffee market had clear distribution channel spaces. Which would be strategic? Which would allow them to earn a sustainable return?

The success of the Starbucks business design demonstrated that the most cost-effective way to build loyalty and brand recognition was to dominate local markets with cafes. Cafes were the strategic space in the gourmet coffee game. Although the number of cafes in the United States had mushroomed from 200 in 1989 to more than 5,000 in 1994, there were still many East Coast cities to conquer. Competition had become much tougher, however. In New York City, for example, the number of coffee bars had doubled from 55 to 110 from the spring to fall of 1994. There was such a foot race for the best storefronts that Starbucks, Brothers, Timothy's, and local chains such as New World and Coopers were offering to pay rents that were 10–15 percent higher than what the landlords were asking—as much as $230 a square foot in midtown Manhattan.

Starbucks had 425 cafes in place by October 1994. Schultz announced plans to open 200 more, moving into Philadelphia and Las Vegas. He also began to look for other places where Starbucks could maximize value recapture on the brand equity created in its cafes. It began positioning its "darker roast" against the "brownish," less flavorful coffee to be found in the grocery. It also developed a brand (Meridian) for the discount channel. It struck a deal with Pepsi to prepare a grocery offering. It pursued other new channels as well (Starbucks is offered on Delta Airlines as well as in restaurants).

Whether Starbucks' cafe business was leveling off was not yet clear. But Schultz was not going to wait and see. His eye was clearly on supermarket trade (see Figure 8-5). The company's 1993 annual report stated, "Management believes that the supermarkets pose the greatest competitive challenge, in part because supermarkets offer customers the convenience of not having to make a separate trip to [our] stores." It also noted that "In virtually every major metropolitan

FIGURE 8-5   STARBUCKS MARKET VALUE

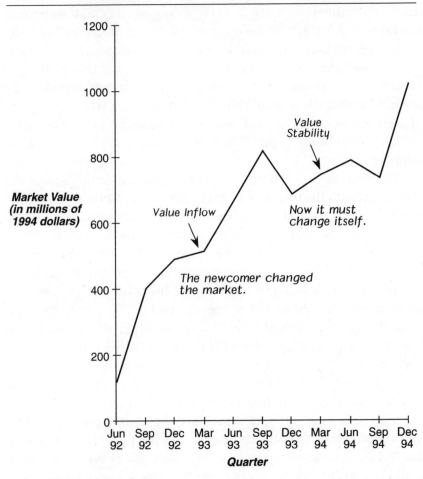

SOURCE: CDI Value Growth Database.

area where Starbucks operates and expects to operate there are local or regional competitors with substantial market presence." The battle in the gourmet coffee business was now crossing categories and channels.

Indeed, in 1994, Brothers announced plans to open 80 Brothers cafes. Another company, Seattle's Best Coffee, planned to franchise nearly 500 stores nationwide within the next five years. Espresso stands were popping up on every corner. Big players like McDonald's and Dunkin' Donuts were even offering coffee made from high-quality Arabica beans.

However, Schultz's attempt to make inroads into supermarkets while opening so many cafes required more than just broadening distribution. Many elements of the business design had to be recrafted. "Starbucks . . . requires a whole different level of organizational growth,"[3] noted analyst Jean-Michel Valette of Hambrecht & Quist in *Business Week* in October 1994. Starbucks needed to substantially expand its infrastructure as it moved from a series of cafes to a multi-channel retailer. Schultz began focusing on internal operations to improve efficiency, investing heavily in a computer network to link his expanding empire, and designing a PC-based point-of-sale system that allowed managers to track sales carefully.

Was Starbucks' business design moving from the value inflow phase to the value stability phase? It had several of the classic characteristics. Retail prices were softening. So was Starbucks' stock price; by December, it had drifted down to $27.50 from a high of $32.50 in June. Schultz was plowing immense resources into opening 200 more stores when the market was getting tougher for each successive cafe. Although 1994 estimated sales were $285 million, a huge leap from $158 million the year before, sales were slowing in stores that had been operating for a year or more.

Epilogue

In 1995, the value growth game in coffee is far from over. Folgers, Maxwell House, Nestlé, Chock Full O' Nuts, Starbucks, and Brothers all have an array of moves to consider. While the geography is getting crowded, there are still distribution points that have remained largely unexplored. The coffee cart trade has large untapped potential. There are also huge institutional contracts to be won at universities, airlines, stadiums, and so on. There are restaurant contracts too. Even bookstores and department stores represent potential new channels. Mail order sales continue to rise.

As noted, some whole beaners like Brothers are starting to sell prepackaged ground coffees because the new packaging guarantees freshness. This approach taps a large number of people who do not want to grind their own coffee. Customer surveys show that freshness is the number one concern, not whether the bean is whole or ground.

Finally, there is national advertising. None of the whole-bean companies do it. And big as Starbucks is, its name is not recognized from shore to shore.

Lessons Learned: Patterns

During the 10-year course of Value Migration in the coffee industry, the major roasters had a break-even business as the result of price wars. The gourmet coffee companies generated pretax returns of 18 percent. From 1988 to 1993, the market value of the traditional roasters actually declined, while the gourmet providers (grocery and cafe) created nearly $1 billion of shareholder value (see Figure 8-6).

Why were the majors unable to stop the flow of value to these new business designs? There are several reasons. They used low-grade beans, producing mediocre coffee. They failed to switch to packaging that was attractive and preserved freshness. And, through rock-bottom pricing and heavy couponing, they trained the consumer to regard their product as a commodity.

Figure 8-6 U.S. Gourmet Coffee Value Growth

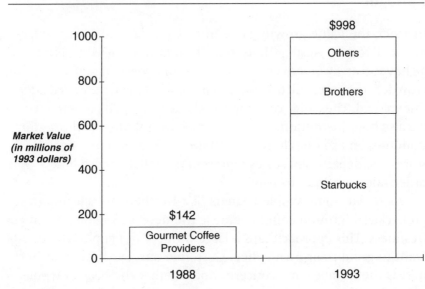

Source: CDI Value Growth Database.

Had the majors stayed focused on changing customer tastes, bought better beans, changed their packaging and delivery systems, and restructured prices, they would have made it much harder for the gourmet companies to break into the market. Instead, the majors were blinded by their institutional memory and inertia.

The majors will continue to be burdened by underpowered economic engines that generate empty revenues (see Figure 8-7). Meanwhile, Starbucks, GCA, and the others have the potential to achieve significant growth in sales, profits, and shareholder value. They also have the capacity to build strong new consumer brands with enduring value.

Replaying the Game

Value Migration in coffee is a case of three important missed opportunities, one by the traditional leaders, one by the gourmet whole-bean roasters, and one by the cafe superstar.

What might P&G have done? Suppose that it redefined its position. Instead of saying, "We sell canned coffee of moderate quality in groceries," the company could have said, "We sell coffee," and

FIGURE 8-7   VALUE MIGRATION PHASES

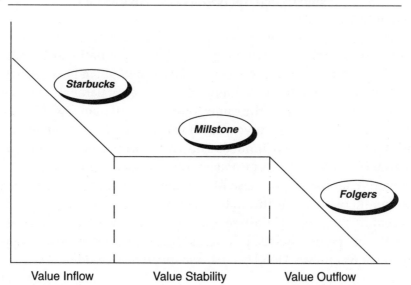

| Value Inflow | Value Stability | Value Outflow |

recognized that customers' preferences were changing. What matters is creating and protecting a strong national brand to meet these customer needs.

The next step in the logic of value growth for P&G would have been as follows. The brand we've built to sell our mid-tier coffee in the groceries will not carry over to the gourmet coffee position because it's made of Robusta beans, and because it would not work with the consumer. So we need to introduce a new brand in the category (something P&G has done countless times, and more skillfully than anybody else) that preempts the quality position (call it Mountain Blend). To make this work, we need a new business design, namely DSD delivery. This is a stretch, but not a radical one (the development of our Wal-Mart account management system was far more radical).

Preempting the quality coffee position would require going beyond establishing a whole-bean brand in the grocery. The cafe design has become a powerful new brand-building tool. It shapes preferences—and sells large quantities of whole-bean coffee. For P&G, this would be a radical new business design, but it also would be a highly efficient one, building strong brand loyalty without tens of millions of advertising dollars.

The grocery store coffee, however, did require massive advertising. That is why whole-bean penetration into grocery took so long. None of the regionals had the resources to engineer a national product launch.

P&G did. That was its business. P&G could afford to invest $50–100 million over two years to build a new national brand. It had the potential to create a branded gourmet-coffee business with $500 million–$1 billion in potential revenue. A parallel launch of the cafe business, under the same gourmet brand name, would have reinforced the brand with very favorable economics. Brand building through cafes was self-funded. Plus, cafes would be a major new channel for whole bean, and a major opportunity to provide consumers with coupons to purchase Mountain Blend at the grocery store, further increasing pull-through and making P&G even more difficult to beat in the grocery. Cafe revenue potential was $1–1.5 billion.

At this point, the really interesting opportunities would open up. Most restaurants, food chains, and institutions today sell branded cola (Coke or Pepsi) and *unbranded* coffee. Once Mountain Blend is established as the "Coke" of coffee (high quality, the "standard"), P&G's clout would enable it to market the nationally accepted quality coffee brand to restaurants and institutions. A third space also worth more than $1 billion.

All these moves would have required creating new business designs. But value growth is about new business designs. In this case, the opportunity existed to create $2–3 billion in new value. Even for a giant like P&G, that is meaningful growth.

There are second-order implications from playing the game this way. In a time of incredible retailer power, the supplier's only recourse is increased innovation and the ownership of powerful new brands. Owning the lead brand of quality coffee would have further strengthened P&G's hand in its negotiations with the Wal-Marts and Targets of the world.

The other missed opportunity? A whole-bean provider could have built a brand by opening a cafe division. Though not as large as P&G's, this lost opportunity was significant nonetheless. Not one of the regional whole-bean roasters opened a cafe business—until 1994. Fully seven years after Starbucks' success was sending un-heeded signals to Millstone's in Seattle. Fully three years after the Starbucks design and its superior customer and economic perfor-mance were (or could have been) evident to all. In a way, the regional roaster oversight was more poignant than P&G's. The regionals did not have the cash flow to advertise their way to creating a brand. Here was a business design (the gourmet cafe) that not only gener-ated profit, but as important, brand recognition and brand loyalty.

One of the cruelest aspects of the logic of value growth is timing. A regional roaster launching a cafe design in 1991, staying one step behind Starbucks, could have built a national brand by 1994, with incredibly favorable economics. By 1994, it was too late. The influx of Starbucks' imitators numbered in the dozens. Thousands of locations were opened from 1991 to 1994, rapidly filling what had largely been an empty space in 1991. Thirty-six months of delay, a billion dollars in value lost.

The third major missed opportunity was Starbucks'. It had built a marvelous, unique business design based on quality, city focus, an outstanding human resource system, and an extraordinarily efficient operating system. It was much like the design established by McDonald's in the late 1950s. Unlike McDonald's, Starbucks chose not to franchise. Perhaps it should have.

The decision not to franchise was motivated by Schultz's desire to maintain quality. Fair enough. But although it is difficult, franchising can be managed to maintain high quality; that is the essence of the McDonald's design. Had Starbucks made a well-managed franchising move, the window of opportunity for its dozens of imitators would have been shut almost completely. Starbucks would have won the retail game, and today could focus all its energy on the vast territory of the grocery and institutional businesses.

Applications to Other Industries

The lessons of Value Migration in coffee apply to many categories of branded consumer products. Because traditional retail go-to-market mechanisms for these categories are often shared (brands compete for shelf space in stores), competitive business designs attempt to differentiate their offerings based on brand and price. Too often, these common business design elements speed the commoditization of products. The battle for market share points is expensive and too often focuses competitors on each other rather than on innovative ways of delivering utility to customers.

The value growth created by the new entrants in the coffee industry suggests that many commodity products are merely the result of stagnant or undifferentiated business designs, not the product itself. In both industrial and consumer markets, the opportunity to reenergize a commodity category should be examined. The battle to become low-cost producers to gain market share points can be value destroying. Instead, business design reinvention can create value growth by delivering higher-utility offerings to customers for which they will gladly reward you with profits.

Chapter **9**

From Integration to Specialization

Computing

- What are the points of strategic control in my industry?

- Is a standard emerging in my industry? If so, what are its implications for my business design?

- Can my customers disaggregate my product or service and choose what they are willing to pay for and what they are not?

THE COMPUTING INDUSTRY is one of the most dramatic value-growth stories of the twentieth century. The primitive ENIAC crunched out its first calculation in the closing phases of World War II. Fifty years later, the total value of computing companies was greater than the *combined* value of the entire U.S. steel, textile, and aerospace industries.

At the root of this growth has been a remarkable spread of computers and an evolution of computing functionality from large-batch number crunching to a vast range of text, data, and image manipulation. For decades, computers existed only in glass rooms with special environmental controls. Even within major companies, research universities, and government agencies, computing was the exclusive preserve of a handful of specialists. While many of its original functions continue, they have been supplemented by myriad additional applications. Computing is now an integral part of daily life in the home, in the classroom, and in every aspect in business for companies large and small.

Since the immediate postwar decades, the computing industry has thrived. But the traditional incumbents, mainframe companies such as IBM, and the minicomputer companies such as Digital Equipment Corporation (DEC), Prime, and Wang, have not: Prime is out of business; the others are in the midst of painful and humbling restructuring. A new cadre of companies now controls the direction and evolution of the industry, firms like Microsoft, Intel, Novell, EDS, and Hewlett-Packard.

In the past 10 years alone, more than $100 billion of value changed hands. Why were the leaders in the old world unable to extend their dominance to the new? For most of the postwar era, corporate, institutional, and government users constituted the entire computing market. In the 1980s, the influx of millions of individual users, both in households and in businesses, radically changed the customer base of computing companies. The evolution of its needs drove the shift in successful business design from integration to specialization (see Figure 9-1).

FIGURE 9-1   VALUE MIGRATION IN COMPUTING

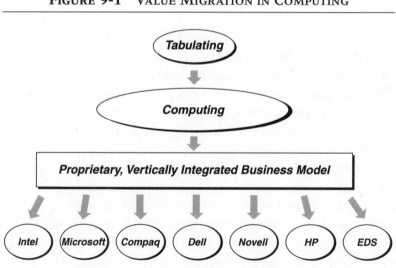

Over four decades, value migrated from tabulating to computing, to the integrated model, to an array of specialist models.

Who can learn from the computing story? Any industry incumbent with a strong leadership position. Any industry in which value is shifting from integration to specialization. And any industry in which successive waves of enormous customer frustration give rise to the invention and growth of new business designs.

The Rise of the Integrated Computer Company

The genetic code of the first phase of the computing industry was set in the decades immediately following World War II. Although each pioneer—IBM, DEC, and Data General—had different cultures and primary market niches, their fundamental approach to customers and markets was largely the same. Together, they defined the integrated computing business design that created extraordinary value growth.

Back then, relatively few entities could afford processing power that was, by today's standards, absurdly expensive. The organizations that could afford it were eager to take advantage of computing capability to order, automate, and accelerate their internal processes. Since practically any electronic means of large-batch data processing was preferable to tabulation or human calculation, the key customer demands focused primarily on basic computing functionality.

The pioneers responded with a highly integrated business design that rested on several pillars. The first was a proprietary architecture and a proprietary operating system, which meant that competitors' systems could not communicate with one another. Although the lack of compatibility discouraged the purchase of different systems within one organization, it did not impair basic functionality because the vendors offered comprehensive support and service for their products. Cementing this long-term bond between the organizational customer and the computer vendor was a knowledgeable, highly effective direct sales force. Sales reps sold hardware based on the ratio of price to processing power, then provided a raft of very profitable, proprietary follow-on items—basic software, customized applications, and peripheral equipment.

For the customer, the integrated business design meant commitment. Since switching hardware essentially meant writing off all previous computing investment, customers tended to remain with

one hardware vendor. For the computer companies, the proprietary
approach and the mutual commitment it created were powerful
mechanisms for creating utility and capturing value. Once an account
had chosen a supplier, there was little competition for the myriad
peripherals, software upgrades, and support functions. Over the lifetime of the basic hardware, these follow-on products and services
provided a steady stream of highly profitable revenue.

The First Wave: IBM and the Mainframe Computer

The first computing company to successfully implement the integrated business design was IBM. The firm's early and decisive imprint
on the shape of the industry was remarkable, and all the more so
because at the close of World War II, IBM was not a computing
company. As the leading player in tabulating machines, it was the
one company with the most to lose from the development of electronic calculating and data processing.

It was not an easy decision for the tabulating leader to think about
entering this strange new business called computing. A computer
company executive summed up the perspective:

> Denial can blind people. We found it very, very hard to face up
> to the . . . decision. Financially, it should have been easy. In
> retrospect, it should have been easy strategically too. Yet we,
> . . . management, were at each other's throats over this.
>
> Our people have navigated successfully through one transi-
> tion, so perhaps it won't be as hard to sign them up for another
> one. But success can trap you. The more successful we are as
> a . . . company, the more difficult it will be to become some-
> thing else. To take advantage of some of the opportunities I see
> ahead, we are going to have to transform ourselves again. The
> time to do it is while our core business is still so strong.[1]

This quote appeared in *Fortune* in 1993. Ironically, it was an
excerpt from discussions at Intel in 1984 concerning the issue of
whether to stay with memory chips or to move to microprocessors.
It also precisely describes the environment at IBM in 1952 and 1953.
Thomas Watson, Sr., who had built a company to a dominant position
in tabulating, and who had built what was perhaps the industry's
best direct sales force, was dead set against the move to computing.
Thomas Watson, Jr. saw it as the only move the company could

make. Debate between the factions was intense and bitter, but the younger Watson carried the day. IBM's tradition of taking great gambles for great gains had begun.

What Watson, Jr. appreciated was that IBM's real engine of value creation was not its tabulating technology but its relationship with its customers. Like their computer progeny, tabulating machines required a steady stream of service, support, and peripheral products. As IBM developed its computing capability, its reps worked diligently to transition their accounts from tabulating machines to computers.

In 1952, IBM was a computer newcomer. By 1959, it was the dominant player, with 70 percent plus market share in the sales of mainframe computers. The first major wave of Value Migration in computing had begun.

The IBM Mainframe Business Design

Fundamental Assumptions	Customers require assistance in the purchasing, servicing, upgrading, and maintenance of their computing systems.
	Importance of proprietary architecture
	Computing companies must offer the full range of products and services to meet all of their customers' computing requirements.
Business Design Element	**IBMs' Choice**
Customer Selection	Large organizational users (corporations, governments, and academic institutions)
Scope	Full line of hardware, software, and support
Differentiation	Proprietary architecture
Value Recapture	Per-unit hardware sales
	Ongoing software and service contracts

Manufacturing/Operating System	High cost overhead
Capital Intensity	High
Go-to-Market Mechanism	Direct sales force

By the beginning of the 1960s, organizational customers were beginning to use computers not only for special projects but essential ongoing functions, such as accounting and inventory. Consequently, they began to demand increased functionality and reliability from their vendors. To meet this need, IBM embarked on the development of the 360 mainframe. The company invested the equivalent of $5 billion in the project, more than its total sales in 1966. While its existing product platforms were selling well, IBM realized that its existing business design would not protect its leadership position. For customers, the 360 delivered both increased functionality and reliability, and rapidly became the standard by which mainframe hardware and computing utility were defined. For IBM, the 360 created robust product sales, a growing number of captive customer organizations, and a rich stream of demand for follow-on support and services.

Like the transition from tabulating to computing, the development of the 360 was a "bet the company" move, another great gamble to achieve great gain. It worked. It built the foundation for the firm's value growth for the next two decades. In 1960, IBM's revenue was $1.4 billion, its market value was $11.3 billion, and its market value/revenue ratio was 8:1 (higher than Microsoft's today). By 1970, IBM's market value had grown to $37 billion, an extraordinary value growth of 13 percent per year.

IBM's third major move was entering the Japanese market. The IBM of the 1960s was a company with a very finely tuned competitive radar screen. Although it had created a dominant position in computing by 1959 and had reinforced that position with significant new technology in 1964, it also had excellent peripheral competitive vision, at least as far as mainframes were concerned.

IBM realized that much of its potential customer base was in Japan. Unless IBM could lead in Japan as it did in the United States and Europe, its value growth would be threatened. It took years of work, and extraordinary efforts (such as engaging the help of the

State Department), but in the end, IBM prevailed. The company was allowed to enter the Japanese market, and it took the lead.

By achieving a position in Japan, IBM had developed a global business design whose basic tenet was leadership in every market. The IBM customer was the large, computing-intensive, security-seeking information technology department. There were hundreds of these entities—in the United States, Japan, and Europe. There was more demand than the company could comfortably meet. (It was growing so rapidly that field representatives were promoted and moved every two years. The sales staff used to say that IBM stood for "I've Been Moved.") It ran flat out to meet its customers' priorities and to respond to new ones. It displayed all the characteristics of the value inflow stage: growth in profits, growth in organization, and a powerful ability to attract the most talented technologists, marketers, and business managers in the industry.

The Second Wave: DEC and the Minicomputer

IBM's success made it easy to overlook the second major value migration in computing, the migration to the minicomputer-based business design. As IBM was consolidating its position in mainframes, an MIT-trained engineer named Ken Olsen founded the Digital Equipment Corporation (DEC) in an old textile mill building in Maynard, Massachusetts.

The principal difference between IBM and DEC was customer selection. Olsen opened up computing power to a broader set of users—computer literate scientific and engineering departments of companies and universities. Where the keepers of the mainframe and the nexus of the IBM relationship had always resided at the corporate or organizationwide level, DEC's product/service offering matched the requirements of computing-intensive *departments.* These customers were more sophisticated. They could program the machines themselves or enlist the help of value-added resellers (VARs). More important, they wanted direct access to computing power, without having to beg and kowtow to the IT monopoly within the company.

Although DEC had identified new customers with some different priorities from those of IBM, its underlying business design was still based on integration. Whereas average IBM contracts would be measured in millions of dollars, DEC's would be measured in hundreds of thousands. Where IBM would write 100 percent of its customers' software applications, DEC would provide 30 percent outright and collaborate on an additional 30 percent. Proprietary architecture, comprehensive product service bundles, and long-term customer relationships nurtured by an effective direct sales force formed the foundation of DEC's ability to create utility and recapture value.

DEC's product offering and its modification of the integrated business design matched precisely what this new customer set wanted. The customers voted for DEC en masse. DEC's value exploded. A crop of minicomputer companies sprang up such as Data General, Wang, and Prime. By the mid-1970s, minicomputer companies had created $7.5 billion in market value. The second major value migration in computing was in full force.

The Rise of the Individual User

By the late 1970s, the rapid and even predictable advances in microprocessor chips had begun to create a whole new category of customer: the individual. This group's new priorities had profound implications for computing companies' business designs.

A few early personal computers such as the Commodore Pet and the Altair had been on the market in the early to mid-1970s. But the spiritual birth of the personal computer was the release of the Apple II in 1977.

When Stephen Jobs and Steve Wozniak founded Apple in a California garage in 1976, they were inspired by a radically new vision of what computing would mean. Until then, the essence of computing had been helping large organizations automate and accelerate their internal processes. To Jobs and Wozniak, this definition was woefully incomplete. Computers and software would not fulfill their marvelous potential until they became tools to empower the individual, in the office, in the classroom, and in the home.

Jobs and Wozniak offered a product that created enormous demand among people who had never really considered themselves "unserved customers." Just as the minicomputer had given access to and control of computing to research scientists and department heads, the personal computer was giving access to individual users.

It is 1980. You are the CEO of IBM or DEC. Here is the situation you see.

- Apple's early success has tapped a powerful new opportunity: computing for the individual.

- The rise of the minicomputer companies has proved that value growth can be created by expanding downward into the customer set.

- Most of your managers have little experience with personal computers and little regard for individual users.

What is your next move? Are these new computers toys, a fad, or the future? How can a giant organization cope with a challenge from a nimble, entrepreneurial rival? Does continued healthy demand for mainframes and minis reduce the urgency to address the issue of personal computing?

The Third Wave: Development of the PC

When IBM surveyed the changing customer landscape, it kept in mind the meteoric rise of DEC during the 1970s. Being number two in minis had always rankled IBM. As the computing customer set expanded downward once again, IBM was determined not to cede the opportunity to Apple or any other player.

It was 1953 again. Just as Thomas Watson, Jr. had dragged the tabulating giant into the computing age, so a crack team of managers and technologists was charged with leading Big Blue into the age of the personal computer. It was a daunting task. The PC was unfamiliar territory, ripe with opportunities to commit strategic errors.

To make the transition to the world of personal computing, IBM drew on its great-gambles-for-great-gains strategy. The shift was one of the most difficult—and most astute—moves in corporate history. It had to be made quickly. The PC simply could not go through the normal product development cycle that had led to the successful products of the past.

To produce the PC quickly, IBM took several bold measures. It installed the managerial and technical project teams in Boca Raton, as far as possible from the wing-tipped warriors in Armonk. It outsourced the processor chip to Intel and the operating system to a tiny company called Microsoft. (Bill Gates, the owner of Microsoft, did not have the operating system that IBM sought, but he agreed to produce it. To deliver on this commitment, he and Paul Allen acquired a product called 86-DOS from Seattle Computer for $50,000.)

IBM was as bold in developing a new business design as it was in developing a new product. The PC would benefit from IBM's first mass-market advertising targeted at the individual user. It would be sold through dealers and computer stores in addition to the traditional sales force. Finally, IBM determined that the hardware sales would have to be profitable as a stand-alone value-recapture mechanism. Unlike organizational customers, individuals would not place high value on follow-on services, upgrades, and "systems-lifetime" contracts.

Business Design
IBM Mainframe vs. IBM PC

	Mainframe Business Design	PC Business Design
Fundamental Assumptions	Computers improve organizational productivity.	Computers improve personal productivity.
Customer Selection	IT departments	Individual users
Scope	Multimillion dollar systems	$3,000 machines
	Full vertical integration	Outsourced microprocessor and operating systems
Differentiation	Proprietary architecture	Open standard
Value Recapture	Per-unit hardware sales	Per-unit hardware sales
	Ongoing software and support contracts	

	Mainframe Business Design	PC Business Design
Go-to-Market Mechanism	Direct sales force	Direct sales force
		Dealers
		Computer retailers

The development of IBM's personal computer was truly an example of an elephant learning to sprint. Design and testing were completed in 11 months. The first PC rolled off the assembly line in August 1981. Within three years, PC sales went from under one million units to more than seven million. By 1984, annual PC sales for the industry were $12 billion. IBM owned a 37 percent share. The third major migration of value had been triggered.

By mid-decade, IBM's brilliant gamble on the PC seemed to be paying off. In evaluating its portfolio of business designs, it had reallocated resources to a high-growth area and was beginning to reap the benefits. While other corporate giants such as GM were stumbling badly, IBM seemed to be the only Western company able to compete with the surging Japanese. By 1985, IBM's value reached $130 billion (see Figure 9-2). In the eyes of competitors, executives in other industries, young business school graduates, and investment analysts, it was the best managed corporation in the world.

The Unraveling of the IBM Business Design

In developing the PC, IBM had met an unfamiliar challenge from a nimble upstart, improved the offering, persevered, and triumphed. But in the successful fast-tracking effort that had stunted the momentum of Apple, IBM had sown the seeds of its own downfall.

The supplier contracts that IBM negotiated with Microsoft and Intel fundamentally recast the structure of the computing industry. IBM and DEC had relied on their proprietary architecture and operating system to keep hardware margins high, customers loyal, and revenues from ongoing service extremely profitable. But IBM did not insist on exclusivity in its contractual agreements with Intel and Microsoft. They were free to provide the essence of the IBM PC to other hardware assemblers. IBM no longer controlled the parts of the computing equation that delivered what the customer of the

Figure 9-2   Value Growth in Computing

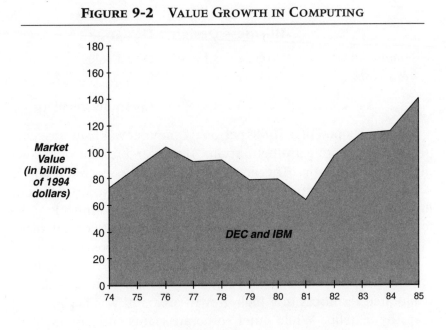

Market
Value
(in billions
of 1994
dollars)

DEC and IBM

*Until 1985, the integrated
model drove value growth.*

late 1980s would pay a premium for—applications software and the processing power to run it. IBM had put a quality product on the market quickly, but at a terrible price: loss of strategic control.

Microsoft and Intel now had strategic control in the burgeoning personal computer industry. They held patent rights, and valuable product development lead times, to the components of the PC that delivered utility to the customer. Of course, IBM's design, standard-setting architecture, and disk drives also delivered utility to the customer. But unlike the chip and the operating system, the assembly could be supplied by practically anyone. That point was lost neither on Intel nor on Microsoft, which began selling their products to other assemblers. Since the lion's share of the cost for chips and MS-DOS was in the up-front R&D, the incremental sales had a dramatic effect on profitability. But more important, the wide distribution of the microprocessor and the operating system created a virtuous circle of compatibility and market share. As more and more PCs adopted the Microsoft–Intel standard architecture, the safer it became for consumers and software writers alike to choose it too. A standard was being set. In an industry that had previously been dominated by proprietary systems, a common architecture was emerging for the first time.

Standardization set a basic assumption of the integrated computing design on its head. Integrated producers such as IBM and DEC had created enormous value growth by developing hardware and then selling whatever solutions and support they wanted to a captive customer base. In the open architecture world of personal computers, the integrated computing giants could no longer control their customers.

The Splintering of Customer Priorities

Clearly, the world of personal computing was taking on a very different shape from the world of corporate computing. But just as computer vendors were struggling to adapt to the individual, changes were also taking place among their primary and core customers—the organizational users.

In 1980, a typical manufacturer with $2 billion in revenue performed all of its corporate financial functions on a mainframe. Its R&D department had ignored corporate's relationship with IBM and purchased a VAX. So had manufacturing. The marketing department had Wang word processors as did the legal department. The other administrative areas all used IBM MTST word processors. Documents and data flowing between departments had to be retyped, reformatted, reentered. The organization had 175 working applications. Most were incompatible. Over the past ten years, the cumulative cost of this dysfunctional system had mounted to $170 million and a Tower of Babel effect that caused customers to complain, "Our technologies can't talk to each other and incompatibility is costing us a fortune in time, attention, and hard dollars."

When customers had hardware problems, the integrated computer companies provided support. However, a long period of exclusive customer relationships had deprived vendors of experience in knitting together different proprietary systems. Having captive customers had also dulled the integrated vendors' problem-solving edge. They developed passable solutions, but not extraordinary ones. They lacked the business perspective and customer service orientation necessary to translate IT spending into improved organizational performance. For decades, these shortcomings mattered little. If a 1980 IBM customer could get 80 percent of the solution needed, it would smile and open the checkbook. After all, 80 percent of a solution was preferable to writing off decades of IT investment. By 1990, this was no longer true.

For both the organizational and the individual customer, the integrated business design was becoming increasingly irrelevant. For individual users, open standards meant freedom from the crushing embrace of hardware vendors. PC owners enjoyed a vastly expanded range of options not only for basic hardware purchase, but also for software, support, and peripherals. For the organizational customer, the need for comprehensive, high-performance solutions and advice had never been greater. Disappointed by the integrated vendors, organizational customers were beginning to turn to a new crop of problem-solving specialists and consultants.

As they defected from the integrated vendors, organizational customers began to realize what had always been true for individual users: There was no need to accept mediocre levels of performance in all categories from an integrated provider. This change in customer priorities struck at the very foundations of the dominant computing companies (see Figure 9-3). Value growth in the future would depend not on providing a wide but middling-quality range of services for captive customers, but on doing one thing better than

FIGURE 9-3   EVOLUTION OF CUSTOMER NEEDS

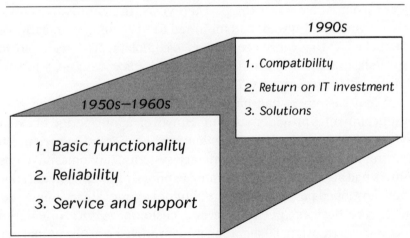

1990s

1. *Compatibility*

2. *Return on IT investment*

3. *Solutions*

1950s–1960s

1. *Basic functionality*

2. *Reliability*

3. *Service and support*

anyone else. It would depend not on integration but on specialization.

It is 1990. You are the CEO of IBM or DEC. What is your next move? What will be the key value-generating activities for a computing company to survive? Hardware? Software? Services? Is there a way to recapture some of the profit stream that Microsoft has diverted from the hardware manufacturers over the past five years?

The Specialist Providers Take Center Stage

By 1990, there were two distinct sets of customers: the organizational IT department and the individual user. The large-scale IT department continued to use mainframes and minis, but had supplemented its hardware arsenal with high-end workstations and, increasingly, networked PCs. Individuals used PCs exclusively. In some organizations, information technology managers represented both customer groups: they were in charge of the large mainframe and also served as a help desk, LAN manager, and purchasing agent for all of the organization's PC users.

What the two different customer sets were willing to pay for was becoming increasingly clear (see Figure 9-4). The individual

FIGURE 9-4   CUSTOMER PRIORITIES

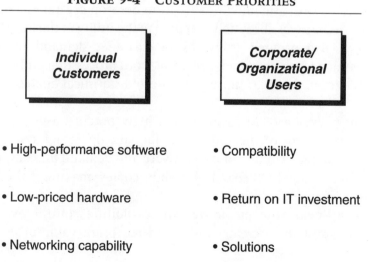

wanted state-of-the-art software, the processing power to run it, low-price, reliable assembly, and the ability to communicate with other PCs. The IT department wanted productivity returns that justified their computing investment, protection from obsolescence, and, increasingly, top-quality advice about how to adapt their IT systems to the constantly changing scope and functions of their organization. What both customers realized was that they were no longer constrained to satisfy their priorities at a single source. So they began to assemble a portfolio of suppliers for their diverse priorities.

The cast of effective specialist providers was growing rapidly. Lurking in the background in the mid-1980s, they were now claiming market share, generating cash, and raising capital to make the next major step forward. They also knew customers' priorities extremely well, and knew how to tailor their business designs to meet them. These aggressive, highly focused firms were poised to create tens of billions of dollars in market value.

Microsoft

The most conspicuous master of specialization has been Microsoft, whose extraordinary profit growth since the late 1980s made CEO Gates the richest person in America. By relentlessly developing higher-functionality operating systems and applications, Microsoft, more than any other company, demonstrated that the future of the computing industry lies not in hardware but in software.

The customer priority that drove Microsoft's initial growth was the need to get basic functionality from desktop computers. Microsoft's MS-DOS was absolutely essential to the utility of the PC. Microsoft has also profited from strong customer demand for basic applications (such as spreadsheets and word processors) and specialized programs (such as more sophisticated statistical analysis packages).

The keystone of Microsoft's amazingly potent business design has been control of the industry's standard operating system. As IBM encouraged cloning of its hardware and demand for computing skyrocketed, MS-DOS sold 100 million copies, making it the best-selling software of all time.

Gates' next strategic move was exploiting control over the operating system to create utility and recapture value in desktop applications such as spreadsheets, word processors, and database programs. While developing the Windows-based operating system, Microsoft began writing high-performance applications to run on it.

Most of the incumbent applications leaders that had the overwhelming share of DOS-based applications were investing their scarce development resources in designing applications for a DOS follow-on operating system being developed by Microsoft under contract to IBM called OS/2. Microsoft let the industry believe that OS/2 would be the successor to DOS and that Windows would have a minimal level of importance. When Gates finally launched Windows 3.0 and OS/2 development lagged, developers were unable to offer Windows versions of their products. Buoyed by the momentum of Windows, Gates quickly released Excel for Windows, which usurped Lotus 1-2-3 as the dominant spreadsheet, and Word for Windows, which seriously eroded the share of the WordPerfect word processing program. He then acquired Foxpro and launched an internally developed database called Access, decimating Ashton-Tate's DBase, whose Windows version was only released three years later. Today, applications supply more than half of Microsoft's revenue.

The Microsoft Business Design

Fundamental Assumptions	Software, not hardware, will become scarce and therefore the value-creating area in computing.
	Control of the operating system creates opportunity for profit in other areas.

Business Design Element	**Microsoft's Choice**
Scope	Operating systems and applications
Differentiation	Control of industry's dominant operating system
	Independent developer marketing

Business Design Element	Microsoft's Choice
Value Recapture	Upgrades
	Control of industry's dominant operating system
Go-to-Market Mechanism	Bundling of operating system on new machines
	Independent developer marketing

Finally, Microsoft has consolidated its powerful industry position by aggressively marketing the Windows platform to independent software developers. A vast array of Windows-based applications reinforces the dominance of the Windows platform, which, in turn, provides an economic incentive for software developers to write to the Windows standard. To fuel this virtuous circle, Microsoft holds teach-ins, symposia, conventions, and workshops for hundreds of independent software writers, to educate them about the subtleties of Windows and to encourage them to develop programs for it. The combination of Microsoft's own basic applications and the hundreds of specialized applications provided by independent developers constitutes a formidable entry barrier for any other operating system.

The final element in Microsoft's business design is a highly focused acquisition policy, as evidenced by its purchase of the original DOS, Foxpro, CD-ROM companies, and the attempted acquisition of Intuit. Since its IPO in 1986, Microsoft has been the most powerful value creator in the computing industry, reaching $35 billion in market value by 1994.

Intel

The media attention lavished on Microsoft and its visionary CEO has dwarfed that received by Intel. But the microprocessor company from California has, by some measures, become every bit as dominant in its own corner of the computing industry.

The customer priorities that Intel has identified and met have been twofold. When individuals were just beginning to develop an appetite for personal computers, Intel positioned itself as the microprocessor supplier for the DOS operating system. As one hundred million customers made DOS the best-selling software of all time, the Intel architecture became a de facto industry standard, which competitors had little choice but to copy. The second driver of Intel's growth has been the premium that customers place on processing speed. Users will pay handsomely for a faster chip that enables cutting-edge software applications. The most sophisticated software code creates no utility without the chip to make it run.

The key to Intel's business design has been industry-leading product development speed. Guided by the decisive hand of CEO Andy Grove, the company has steadily invested more than 10 percent of sales in R&D. Relentless efforts to maintain its design and manufacturing speed and skill have given Intel a lead of several quarters that chief competitor AMD has been unable to erode. Unmatched advances in chip speed encourage software developers to write for the Windows-Intel standard, which builds consumer confidence about the enduring utility of their computing systems.

This upward spiral has enabled Intel to recapture enormous value. Since 1984, the market value of Intel has grown more than six-fold to $27 billion.

Compaq

Microsoft and Intel effectively disaggregated the PC, claiming vast slices of value for themselves at the expense of unhappy assemblers such as IBM. Yet Compaq has flourished in this hardware niche that might seem at first glance to be bereft of value.

Compaq's early success was built on founder Rod Canion's realization that the customer areas of highest utility (software and the chips that made it run) had been captured by other players (Microsoft and Intel). Consequently, earning a profit as an assembler would depend on providing a low-priced product. Beyond basic requirements such as reliability, reasonable weight, and decent screen quality, there was simply nothing else consumers were willing to pay for.

Powered by an innovative low-cost business design, Compaq rose rapidly, breaking the ranks of the *Fortune* 500 in its fourth year of existence. Its early success was driven by three factors: privileged relations with independent dealers, a highly experienced management team, and speedy product development. In the early 1980s,

Compaq halved the industry's average development time from 12–18 to 6–9 months.

In the mid-1980s, the company's success presented it with a dramatic strategic choice, to remain a low-cost clone manufacturer or develop a differentiated product. Compaq chose to innovate and in five years drove its market value to $5.5 billion.

But the company's differentiation proved ultimately unsustainable. As Compaq was at the height of its success, it found itself being ruthlessly undercut by other clone makers. Under new leadership, Compaq has successfully executed a hybrid strategy since 1992: providing an acceptably low-cost product with just enough brand equity and quality to command a slight price premium. To wring a profit from this strategy, Compaq has furiously cut prices, while cutting costs even faster. Between 1991 and 1993, Compaq shed 15 percent of its work force and reduced manufacturing costs by 52 percent while revenues increased from $3.3 billion to $7.2 billion.

In 1994, Compaq eclipsed IBM in world PC production (Compaq rose from 8 percent in 1993 to 10.3 percent in 1994; Big Blue declined from 10.8 percent to 8.5 percent) and reached $10.3 billion in market value. By fundamentally rethinking the role of an assembler, it has created value where traditional players such as IBM have suffered.

Novell

In the 1980s, speedy chips, low-cost assembly, and high-performance software created tens of billions of dollars of market value by raising the productivity of individuals both in the office and at home. What Novell of Provo, Utah, astutely grasped was that once PCs had spread across the desktops of America, the newly empowered users would want to communicate with each other.

Among the largest demanders of complex networks are the *Fortune* 500 companies that spent the early 1990s reengineering their operations. With fewer people responsible for more information on a global basis, these organizations now depend on improved communications to remain competitive. In short, companies have discovered that sharing data between PCs is one way to realize the elusive return on organizational IT investment. The key vehicle for linking PCs together is a custom-designed network, and the dominant provider of networking software is Novell.

Like the other specialist providers, Novell has created a highly innovative business design focused on meeting the customer priorities in its chosen field profitably and better than any competitor. One important factor in Novell's business design has been astute customer selection. As corporate customers downsized, Novell focused its marketing resources on weaning computer-literate young managers away from the central IT departments still wedded to IBM and DEC. It was in the more remote outposts of computing, such as sales and marketing departments and regional offices, that PCs first gained a foothold, and the demand for networking first emerged. As larger, more sophisticated networks have supplanted some of the functions of minis and even mainframes, Novell has redirected its marketing attention back to central IT managers.

Another key facet of Novell's business design is mobilizing powerful sources of external leverage to reinforce the market dominance of its software. First, to build more durable strategic control over the networking market, Novell has assiduously cultivated a vast number of small, independent network installers, who perform the thorny task of grafting Novell software onto a company's existing computer system. By offering workshops, product education seminars, and a basic course through which installers earn a Certified Network Engineer certificate, Novell has created a following of effective and loyal constituents. This approach is one significant reason that competitors' products have failed to make inroads against Novell's Netware, which still commands 70 percent of the networking software market.

Novell's second source of external leverage has been what former CEO Ray Noorda calls "coopetition," or cooperating with competitors. Rival Microsoft has earned fear and loathing from its software competitors by pursuing complete and total domination of its markets. In contrast, Novell has opted for an inclusive approach, fostering a loose confederation of hardware and software companies to promote jointly the virtues of networking. For example, Novell has actively assisted rival software developers such as Banyan, IBM, and DEC to design products that work more effectively with Novell's offerings.

Novell's ability to identify an emerging customer need and to build an innovative business design has made it extremely successful. Since 1984, Novell has created $6.2 billion in market value.

Systems Integrators

The same fundamental priorities that have powered the rise of Novell have also created opportunity for another group of specialists, the systems integrators. Functioning much like consultants, they diagnose a large organization's daily computing requirements and overall, long-term strategy, then assemble the appropriate combination of hardware and software to serve them.

IT departments require the services of a systems integrator because many aspects of large-scale computing have grown dauntingly complex and costly. Managers trained in the age of mainframes need advice in converting an organization to an unfamiliar computing paradigm such as the PC networks made possible by Novell. Companies consummating mergers or globalizing their operations often face communications challenges beyond the experience of any one existing department. Finally, companies are coming to appreciate the fact that getting the right information to the right people at the right time can make the difference between being an industry leader and an also-ran. These organizations are hiring outside expertise to ensure the best performing match between their IT system and business strategy.

Leading systems integrators have deployed business designs that reflect the diversity of their cultures and origins. For EDS, which has built a strong franchise in particular vertical markets, customer selection has been a key aspect of business design (see Chapter 11). Arthur Andersen has leveraged its accounting and finance background to link clients' IT architecture to its broader business strategy, and IBM's ISSC recaptures value by cross-selling IBM hardware and software. Other essential elements of a systems-integration business design include relationships with a wide range of hardware and software providers, problem-solving skills, and a strong customer-service orientation.

Although difficult to measure, the value growth of systems integrators has been substantial. Since 1984, market leader EDS has created $16 billion in market value growth. It accounts for less than 10 percent of parent GM's revenues, but it represents more than 25 percent of its market capitalization. In a belated move to adjust its business design portfolio, IBM is aggressively seeking to create a high-return business with ISSC.

Epilogue

The specialist providers have created more than $100 billion of value since 1980. As they have delivered utility to millions of users and enriched their shareholders and employees, these companies have gained tremendous power and influence (see Figure 9-5).

But as the experience of the integrated giants has demonstrated, leadership in the computing industry can change extremely rapidly. If the specialist providers fail to track changing customer priorities and competing business designs, they will experience a quick and painful transition through the stability zone to value outflow.

What developments could threaten today's leaders? Microsoft's all-important control of the operating system faces twin challenges, from IBM's O/S Warp, and from Apple's newly licensed Macintosh system, which has a proven track record with millions of individual users. Meanwhile, Novell must ensure that its policy of coopetition

FIGURE 9-5   VALUE MIGRATION

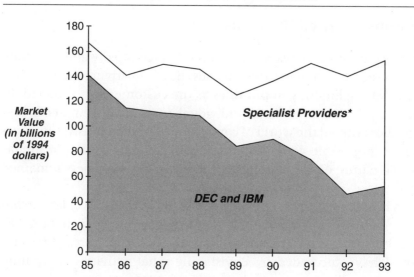

After 1985, nearly $100 billion in value changed hands, flowing from the traditional computing model to the new specialized business design.

SOURCE: CDI Value Growth Database.
*Lotus, Microsoft, Intel, Novell, EDS, HP, Compaq, and Dell.

does not cede strategic control over a key element of its software. But before worrying about threats from within its own confederation, the Utah firm must contain Microsoft's assault on its networking niche. Intel's value growth hinges on maintaining its slim lead in chip development. Even more significant a threat is the IBM–Apple–Motorola alliance, which is trying to create an alternative architecture to outperform Intel's current offering. In systems integration, robust demand has encouraged competitive entry; consequently, the leading players face the specter of margin erosion and commoditization.

But the specialists in the most precarious position of all are the low-cost hardware assemblers such as Compaq. It is far from clear whether these companies will find a formula for sustainable differentiation. As Rappaport and Halevi argue in a brilliant *Harvard Business Review* article, the future of the computing industry may very well belong to software, leaving dominance in hardware manufacturing a hollow victory.[2] IBM's acquisition of Lotus in the spring of 1995 indicates that it may have learned that lesson.

Lessons Learned: Patterns

In the computing industry, value has migrated rapidly and forcefully from integrated to specialized business designs. Driving this shift was a dramatic splintering of priorities as the customer set expanded. In the early 1980s, millions of individual users with new needs and priorities entered the world of computing. Simultaneously, the priorities of large-scale computing customers shifted, while the fundamental nature of the offerings of the integrated providers remained static.

A host of specialists seized the opportunity, taking over leadership of the industry. Microsoft, Intel, and Compaq disaggregated the PC, each capturing enormous value in a highly focused area. EDS and Novell have succeeded by envisioning what activities computing customers will place a premium on in the future.

What can managers learn from the pattern of Value Migration in computing? First, that the customer base can change in at least two ways. A vast influx of new customers can unearth a whole new set of priorities (the rise of the individual user). In addition, the evolving priorities of long-standing customers can undercut a previously successful business design (the defection of the institutional customer). Second, that companies in transition must never lose sight of the true source of strategic control. IBM's rapid development of the PC was a masterful campaign but one that ultimately failed to recapture long-term value because of the surrender of the chip to Intel and the operating system to Microsoft. Finally, the dramatic value redistribution among computing companies is a warning to strong incumbents everywhere: In times of turbulence, examine your portfolio of business designs carefully and move swiftly to reallocate resources from the successes of the past to the opportunities of the future.

Replaying the Game

By 1985, the integrated computing giants had amassed vast arsenals of expertise, industry relationships, employee talent, and financial resources. Yet in the ensuing 10 years they suffered staggering value loss and lost industry leadership. What might they have done to preserve their enormous gains of the previous decades?

Although constrained by institutional memory, DEC was the natural candidate to develop and popularize the personal computer. Its culture was built on empowering new customers and distributing computing power closer to individuals and farther from the central mainframe.

Instead it was IBM that saw the potential of the PC and executed a brilliant strategy of rapid market entry. Once the PC was established, however, IBM could have, and should have, taken back the chip and the operating system, which it is belatedly trying to do through its alliance with Apple and Motorola.

Once the growing power of Intel and Microsoft sealed off that option, IBM could have exploited its manufacturing expertise to become a low-cost assembler and distributor of PC hardware. Perhaps the more potent engine of value creation would have been to leverage years of support and service experience to become the first, truly top-quality systems integration and IT outsourcing provider. It was IBM, not EDS, that won the watershed Kodak outsourcing contract in 1989. Seizing leadership in systems integration and networking was perhaps an even more realistic possibility for DEC. No one had more experience in working with networked systems and countless, small affiliated organizations than DEC did with its enormous army of value-added VAX resellers.

The tragedy of the integrated giants was that they possessed powerful assets in their tremendous wealth and deep pools of talent and experience built up over decades of providing bundled services. If they had been as sensitive as the new entrants to the changing priorities of the customer base, both IBM and DEC could have picked one or two areas of focus, sharply upgraded their capability, and become specialist providers. Such a move would have enabled them to maintain their value—an awesome achievement in a decade of massive value redistribution. More important, they would have been well positioned to capture the next phase of value growth in the industry.

Perhaps the most interesting chance to replay the game in the computing industry belonged to Apple. In the early 1980s, its revolutionary Macintosh operating system delivered unparalleled utility to the user—a full six years ahead of Microsoft's Windows. At that time, an intense debate raged in Cupertino over whether or not to license the operating system and focus on being a software company. But John Sculley and his team chose to define Apple as a hardware manufacturer, consigning it to a marginal future at the edge of the computing industry.

A different decision in the mid-1980s might have made Apple what Microsoft is today, a dominant supplier of both operating systems and applications software, an industry leader, and a fantastically powerful engine of value growth. In a belated attempt to realize some portion of this vision, Apple began licensing its Macintosh operating system in 1994.

Applications to Other Industries

Who can learn from the dramatic migration of value in the computing industry? Any company whose customer set may expand rapidly, either because of changing technology (as in computing), changing regulations (as in airlines,) changing demographics (as in mall-based suburban retailing), or changing infrastructure (as in automobile-accessible fast-food restaurants). Other students of the computing story might include dominant incumbents with a wealth of resources, skills, and experience, but no sense of urgency about channeling those toward areas of future value growth. Under the leadership of Robert Allen, AT&T is effectively upgrading specialized capabilities in high-end business solutions, and linking telephones to televisions and computers. Are venerable giants in such areas as electric power generation, integrated chemicals production, and integrated financial services moving as aggressively?

In one sense, Value Migration in computing is about tabulating, mainframes, minis, PCs, and operating systems. In a deeper sense, it is about the long-term evolution of customer priorities and frustrations: the need to automate computation; the frustration with centralized computing; the frustration with departmental computing; the frustration with proprietary systems, incompatibility, character-based (versus graphical-based) user interfaces, lack of connectivity, lack of integrated solutions, and lack of global support.

Understanding this deeper sense demands a new way of thinking. It demands seeing an industry's evolution through the minds and pocketbooks of customers. It is difficult to learn to think this way. But anyone who does has a tremendous competitive advantage in an age of intensifying Value Migration.

Chapter 10

From Conventional Selling to Low-Cost Distribution

- Are my customers becoming more price-sensitive?

- Is the sophistication of my customers increasing faster than that of my products or services?

- Does my organization use a direct sales force? Why? How have customers changed since our direct sales force was created?

FOR MOST OF THIS CENTURY, manufacturers dominated the business landscape. The mass-production techniques of Henry Ford created tremendous leaps in productivity. In the process, the cost of manufactured goods has declined, opening up vast new markets of consumers. Manufacturers' innovations, and their ability to make products accessible to all, drove value growth for decades. Downstream functions, such as distribution, were necessary but secondary. Manufacturing was the center of gravity in the value chain.

The classic go-to-market mechanism in the age of manufacturing was the direct sales force. Although the sales force was costly, manufacturers could afford the expense because product margins were so high. Key functions of the sales force included providing basic product information, a point of contact with the vendor, and a human face to associate with the product. Customers were willing to pay for these benefits. By providing them, the sales force generated demand, and in a world of high gross margins, incremental demand had a dramatic effect on profit levels and profit growth.

The traditional direct sales force was not the most cost-effective mechanism by which to bring product and customer together. Nor did it possess the expertise or support system to deliver complex, customized solutions. The direct sales force occupied the middle ground, serving customers who required moderate levels of service and product information. In the age of the product, that's where all the value was (see Figure 10-1).

In the late 1970s, customer priorities began to change. Both individual and corporate customers became so familiar with and knowledgeable about certain classes of products that they no longer

FIGURE 10-1   THE COLLAPSE OF THE MIDDLE

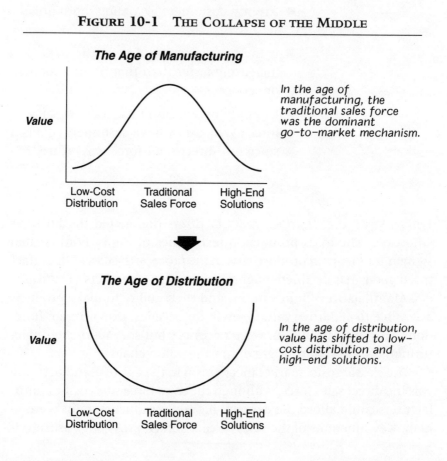

required the information and service that direct sales representatives provided. Customers wanted the product, period. And they wanted it at low cost. While many traditional product manufacturers ignored this fundamental shift in customer priorities, distribution experts were eagerly experimenting with new, low-cost business designs.

Nowhere was this shift in customer priorities and adroit response by a distribution-focused company more vividly played out than in the world of personal computing. In 1983, most American consumers needed the counsel of a manufacturer's representative to purchase a personal computer. By the end of the 1980s, many buyers found purchasing a computer scarcely more daunting than purchasing a stereo. This growing group of consumers was willing to trade the storefront, sales representative, and package of basic product information for $500 off the purchase price. They bypassed computer retailers and the local IBM product office to buy PCs over the phone.

The companies that capitalized on this dramatic shift were Dell and, later, Gateway 2000. While rivals such as IBM were still employing high-cost manufacturing and traditional sales methods, these upstarts were creating billions of dollars of market value by giving the customers what they wanted: quality merchandise at a low price.

This increased customer sophistication, decreased need for information and support, and growing sensitivity to price is now a fundamental pattern in both retail and business-to-business purchasing. In pharmaceuticals, chemicals, groceries, and financial services, traditional product offerings have been demystified. Low-cost distribution business designs, such as those of Wal-Mart, The Home Depot, Medco, Costco, and Charles Schwab, have responded, creating dramatic value growth and shifting the value chain's center of gravity from manufacturing toward distribution.

However, the sophisticated, price-sensitive customers and innovative, low-cost distributors compose only half the threat to the traditional sales approach. While some customers knew the products and no longer required basic information or support, others sought not to diminish, but to augment their service bundle. For this new breed of customer, value no longer resided in the product itself. The real source of utility was an entire problem-solving system, a system in which the product was only one element. These buyers no longer wanted products, but solutions.

A growing cast of companies is developing business designs to meet the need for solutions. In retail, Nordstrom is combining unparalleled product selection, easy-to-navigate store layout, over-the-top service, and a no-questions return policy to take the frustration out of shopping. In business computing, EDS has created billions of dollars of shareholder value by becoming a strategic computing partner, and, in some cases, by taking over all of a company's information technology activities. These providers of high-end solutions have embedded traditional products and services in a broader offering that includes comprehensive information, advice, and ongoing support.

The traditional sales approach is being undercut by low-cost distributors and overpowered by high-end solutions providers. Together, these trends have led to the collapse of the middle.[1] In industry after industry, value is flowing out of middle-of-the-road sales mechanisms and into either low-cost channels or high-end solutions. Directly challenging the dominant selling paradigm of the age of manufacturing, these two business designs represent powerful new vehicles of value growth.

Low-Cost Distribution

This chapter focuses on low-cost distribution (the next one addresses high-end solutions). Five case studies show how low-cost distributors have displaced traditional sales channels. In retail, grocery, financial services, personal computing, and basic supplies purchasing, innovators have watched consumer sophistication outpace product complexity, creating an opportunity for a low-cost offering. In each industry, business design innovators have combined customer knowledge, sophisticated expense management, and leading-edge logistics to take value away from traditional selling.

Wal-Mart

Although Wal-Mart's success is typically explained by its economic advantage over traditional retailers, its opportunity for success resulted from a significant shift in the priorities of a large segment of American consumers. Over two decades, this group became increasingly price-sensitive. With tax, interest, medical, and social security payments growing from 25 percent of personal income in 1970 to 34 percent in 1990, the average middle-income family faced a real decline in its purchasing power. A fundamental change in lifestyle also favored the Wal-Mart business design. With a lengthening work year and a doubling in the number of women in the workforce, the average head of the household had less time to shop.

Wal-Mart responded to these trends by offering inexpensive access to a vast range of nationally branded basic goods. It built giant 100,000-square-foot stores, whose tremendous volume enabled the company to undercut small variety store incumbents. The discount a Wal-Mart store offered had a significant effect on consumers' finances (for many, it freed up 30–50 percent of their discretionary income). By consolidating many merchandise categories under one roof, Wal-Mart made shopping easier, trimming an average of two hours a week off shopping time. By placing its stores in C and D counties, Wal-Mart was able to open more than a thousand stores across the country without going head-to-head with another major retailer.

Another critical aspect of Wal-Mart's success has been its obsession with expense reduction. By 1970, it had already established a hub-and-spoke distribution system to its stores. In 1978, it began automating these distribution centers. Five years later, it had launched a satellite system to coordinate shipping and ordering. By 1984, it had implemented electronic data interchange systems. Each of these changes used cutting-edge technology and systems, and each contributed to lowering the company's operating expense ratio, even as Wal-Mart was offering lower prices than every traditional department store.

The Wal-Mart Business Design

Fundamental Assumptions	Price and time saving are the dominant purchase criteria.
	Target and secure unserved customer segment.
Business Design Element	**Wal-Mart's Choice**
Customer Selection	Middle- to low-income residents of C and D counties

Business Design Element	Wal-Mart's Choice
Scope	Extremely broad line of discounted merchandise
Differentiation	Low prices
	Breadth of merchandise
Purchasing	Aggressive, large-scale purchasing, using volume to gain concessions from manufacturers
Manufacturing/Operating System	Superior logistics, distribution, and merchandise replenishment
Organizational Configuration	Employee stock ownership plan

Wal-Mart has also succeeded in part because it deliberately and relentlessly redesigned its business. In 1983, it created a new business design: Sam's Clubs. Wal-Mart found that within the price-sensitive segment it served, there existed an even more price-sensitive group. Sam's Club serves these customers by offering almost the same products but in bulk. Stores have little display or floor help. The prices are lower, the margins thinner, but the customers are loyal—and the club is impervious to attack from competitors.

Wal-Mart's logistics, purchasing clout, and constant willingness to reformulate its business design to match evolving customer priorities have permanently altered the world of retail sales. While the traditional formats of Sears, JC Penney, and May's have experienced stagnation, Wal-Mart alone has generated more than a third of all the wealth created in the retail sector over the past decade (see Figure 10-2).

Aldi

A similar phenomenon has evolved rapidly in Europe's grocery business in the past decade. In the 1970s and 1980s, traditional food shops were being rendered economically obsolete by hypermarkets—large superstores that sold every kind of grocery under one roof and had fresh selection, favorable prices, and a significant range of household items. The hypermarket business design created value by fulfilling

FIGURE 10-2   SEARS VS. WAL-MART BUSINESS MODEL

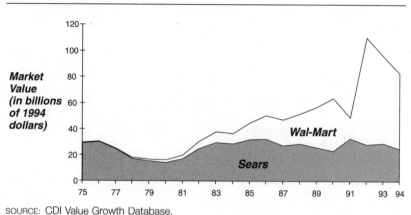

SOURCE: CDI Value Growth Database.

the emerging customer priorities of low prices and one-stop shopping.

In the 1990s, however, radically different "hard-discount" stores are responding to customers' even sharper focus on price. Before 1980, the hard-discount business design existed only in Germany, the birthplace of Aldi. The first Aldi store opened in 1948 and thrived in the depressed, war-torn regions of the country. Financially strapped Germans, already famous for their thriftiness, turned to small, urban Aldi stores for their food staples. The selection was limited, quality was passable, but prices were rock bottom. Today, quality remains just acceptable, but more store locations have created convenience, and prices are still the lowest around. Even wealthy consumers shop Aldi because in Germany, as the Germans say, "Poor people must save, and rich people like to save."

Several elements distinguish Aldi's business design and drive its success. Unlike hypermarkets or conventional grocers, Aldi stores are small and sparsely furnished, located primarily in cities. Store size averages 8,000 square feet. Product range is limited to about 600 items, mostly nonperishable, high-turn staples such as canned produce, paper goods, snacks, and frozen foods. The strategic goal is to limit spoilage and sell product even before payment is due suppliers (see Figure 10-3).

Hard discounters are stingy about overhead. Employees are non-union and are expected to mop floors and stock shelves when not

FIGURE 10-3   ALIGNING BUSINESS DESIGN WITH CUSTOMER
PRIORITIES

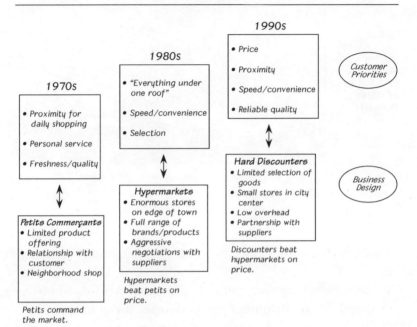

attending the check-out. Customer service is minimal, keeping labor costs to a low 3.5 percent of sales, compared to 6 percent for traditional supermarkets. Goods are sold out of the shipping box. There are few fancy displays. There are no stock boys and checks are not accepted. Advertising is almost nonexistent. Chains like Aldi rely on word-of-mouth and market presence. This attention to overhead creates a significant cost advantage. Aldi's typical city store has $2,500 sales per employee hour versus $1,900 for a supermarket. The result is the lowest prices in town—the greatest priority of modern customers.

Aldi started expanding into other European markets in 1979. In the late 1980s, it moved into Britain and France, where it challenged the hypermarkets by building stores in poor regions devastated by economic recession. Beset by double-digit unemployment, falling incomes, and an increased concern about the future, French consumers rapidly gravitated to the Aldi alternative. When expanding internationally, Aldi also attempted to modify its design to meet country-specific customer preferences. In France, for example, Aldi stocked more fresh produce.

Between 1988, the year Aldi opened its first store in France, and 1994, the number of stores grew 74 percent annually. The penetration of other hard discounters like Lidi & Schwarz and Kwik Save into other European markets has been just as dramatic. Hyper-markets have been slow to react. An article about the hard discount-ers in *The Economist* noted, "Their small size, cheap fittings, and lack of brand names meant they were not taken seriously at first in France."[2] Blinded by their own success, the hypermarkets failed to realize that customer priorities were shifting. In 1990, Carrefour, the French hypermarket, finally made a countermove by founding Europe Discount, its version of the hard-discount design. In the following two years, Continent, another hypermarket, began to open its hard-discount Dia stores.

Charles Schwab

One of the most striking examples of growing customer sophistica-tion and timely development of a low-cost distribution business design is in financial services. While trading stocks and bonds for individuals used to be the exclusive turf of full-service brokerages, San Francisco-based discount broker Charles Schwab has given Main Street access to Wall Street—at very low cost to the individual. Since 1990, Schwab's shareholder value has nearly quintupled to more than $1.5 billion, significantly outperforming the Dow Jones Securi-ties Dealers Index (Figure 10-4).

FIGURE 10-4   CHARLES SCHWAB VS. BROKERAGE FIRMS INDEX

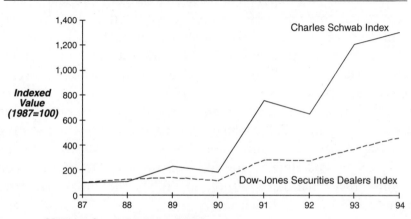

SOURCE: CDI Value Growth Database, Dow-Jones.

As in other industries, it was the changing consumer that created the market opening for Schwab. Throughout the 1980s, the general public's interest in financial markets increased dramatically. The extraordinary proliferation of business and financial media was both an indication and a driver of American investors' sophistication. More than 1 million people bought Peter Lynch's *One Up on Wall Street*, a folksy how-to book, which claims that the man on the street possesses all the tools to pick the next boom stock. Business magazines such as *Forbes, Fortune, Business Week,* and *The Economist* have seen their circulation to individuals take off, while on-line services like America Online and CompuServe are giving individuals a much wider range of information about companies and markets.

The greater sophistication of individual investors coincided with two other developments: First, heightened anxiety among Baby Boomers about their financial future, and second, a roaring bull market that caused returns on stocks and mutual funds to dwarf those on more conservative investment vehicles. Together, greater sophistication, a sense of urgency about savings and investment, and propitious market conditions drew many who had never ventured beyond a savings account into the public markets.

But heightened awareness of the principles of investing also had a powerful effect on savers who were already in the market, trading through pricey full-service brokerages. Increasingly confident in their investing capabilities, a growing number of these clients began to realize that they were paying for services they no longer required. Rose Wunder, a 32-year-old sales rep at Pitney Bowes, exemplified the disgruntled customer. "I don't need a broker," she said. "I don't want to talk to a real person. I don't have the time. I know what I want done—I just need a way to implement it."[3]

Charles Schwab responded to the priorities of both customer groups. The heart of Schwab's value proposition was empowering customers to make their own trades and investments. Schwab offered no investment counsel, only market access. With no costly network of advisers to support, Schwab operated at a much lower cost structure than full-service houses, and it passed a piece of those savings along to the customer in the form of lower commissions. Small-volume trades that cost $75 through a full-service broker often cost as little as $39 through Schwab.

This attractive pricing structure lured a rapidly growing crowd of customers. In 1980, discount brokers handled a tiny fraction of all retail stock trades. By the mid-1990s, the share of discount brokers had risen to a significant 14 percent. By the end of the decade, it is projected to be 20 percent. Value is migrating from the traditional brokerage design to the new discount business design. With a 44 percent share of the discount broker business, Schwab is the greatest beneficiary of this Value Migration process.[4]

A key to Schwab's fast growth has been relentless business design innovation. Realizing that customers are less interested in advice and more interested in executing their own financial strategies, Schwab has regularly rolled out new offerings focused on providing increased trading functionality to individual investors. In 1989, it introduced automated telephone touchpad trading; in 1993, it introduced StreetSmart for Windows, a software package that allows customers to trade via modem; in 1994, it released Custom Broker, a phone, fax, and paging service for active traders.

Perhaps Schwab's greatest innovation has been OneSource, a smorgasbord of hundreds of no-load funds run by dozens of money managers. Dubbed "a financial Wal-Mart" by the *New York Times*, OneSource has transformed the company from a discount brokerage into one of the country's top three mutual fund distributors.[5] By using its marketing and distribution clout, Schwab has boosted volume and turned itself into an industry powerhouse. In its second year of operation, OneSource claimed 6.4 percent of all fund sales handled by brokers.

The Charles Schwab Business Design

Fundamental Assumptions	Individual investors quickly gain confidence and comfort with basic financial instruments.
	Financial advice and market access can be unbundled.
Business Design Element	**Charles Schwab's Choice**
Customer Selection	More experienced individual investors

Business Design Element	Charles Schwab's Choice
Scope	Multiple financial instruments (stocks, mutual funds, money market funds)
	Multiple-channel access and information (storefront, telephone, fax, pager, PC)
Differentiation	Price
	Selection (OneSource)
Value Recapture	Commissions (from individual investors)
	Fees (from mutual fund companies)
Purchasing	Aggressive bargaining with money managers to impose fees and retain investor names

Both discount brokerage and mutual fund distribution continue as powerful engines of profit and shareholder value creation. Schwab has a margin of 90 percent on trades above a breakeven level of 22,400 per day. In February 1994, it averaged more than 38,000.[6] Although the margins on fund distribution are thinner, fund-based revenue is more stable. In 1994, when most brokerage profits fell by 30 percent, Schwab continued its profit growth. While stocks of investment houses tumbled 20 percent, Schwab increased its shareholder value.

W.W. Grainger

Wal-Mart's opportunity was created by the consumer's concurrent desire for low prices and a faster way to buy simple household items. There is an analog among large industrial companies, whose purchasing agents buy so-called MRO (maintenance, repair, and operation) supplies. These include everything from spare parts to bottled industrial bleach. The corporation that buys both heavy industrial equipment and janitorial cleaning supplies is no different in need or economics from the consumer who buys a refrigerator and Lysol. MRO products require far more time to buy than they are worth. The purchase price is a small fraction of the company's total cost to acquire them.

As cost cutting and reengineering drove much of corporate America's budgets in the 1980s, purchasing became a strategic function. Companies moved toward vendor partnerships and alliances, and electronic data interchange. Purchasing managers tended to focus on the large-ticket items and vendors, but they didn't lose sight of the costs associated with the many small, mundane products. They did have trouble finding an effective solution, however.

The elusiveness of the solution was due to the characteristics of MRO supplies. There are thousands of individual products from thousands of individual suppliers. Complicating matters even more, purchasing decisions tended to be made at local plants. Under such conditions, it was nearly impossible either to establish purchasing leverage or to consolidate and increase the efficiency of the buying infrastructure. Further difficulty arose because the purchasing needs varied widely. A spare part needed in an emergency was best acquired from a local supplier. The need for cleaning supplies was more predictable, and their delivery could be planned for and optimized.

W. W. Grainger in Skokie, Illinois, offered a solution. It grouped 1,100 suppliers and 73,000 products in a single catalog and became the first one-stop shop for MRO supplies. Between 1983 and 1993, it created $2 billion in new shareholder value.

This one-stop shopping enabled customers to consolidate their vendors, dramatically reducing the time and paperwork involved in purchasing supplies. In addition, it consolidated billing, eliminating hundreds of individual transactions. By bundling this work into one mail-order package, Grainger was able to lower the industrial customer's cost and time to buy.

To optimize delivery, Grainger separated its system into distinct segments and tiers. It created three regional distribution hubs, which efficiently supply 300 local branches—storefronts that keep common and emergency items on hand and can order the rest. The local branches are located within a 20-minute drive of more than 60 percent of the market. A general distribution system meets the priorities of larger customers and takes care of periodic replenishment transactions. A consulting service provides purchasing support. Grainger invested significantly in state-of-the-art management information systems; the key is effective use of a computer-satellite communications system, which links its branches, distribution points, and many suppliers. This system, together with the pooling of multiple suppliers through the hubs, turns inventories more quickly, reduces the amount of unproductive capital, and improves service. These factors enable Grainger to lower its costs enough so that it can still profit while lowering the customer's cost to buy.

Although Grainger gains volume with low prices, its economic advantage and profit are based more on its ability to lower the cost to serve customers, in comparison to manufacturers. Manufacturers' economics are driven by the concentration and disparity of customer sizes, which can range from a $100,000 annual account to a $50 one. A manufacturer's distribution system is not optimized to serve either type of customer, and would never be able to achieve the scale required at the lower end to reduce the inefficiencies there.

This disparity is prevalent in many industries, and can be quite striking. One company found that the cost to serve its large accounts was 12 percent of sales; for small customers it averaged 46 percent of sales. The replication of the Grainger business design to other arenas of industrial purchasing will create significant new value growth opportunities in the next two decades.

Dell Computer

By 1990, the PC was ubiquitous. Customers understood how to use the technology. Apple's Macintosh and Microsoft's Windows made operation even easier, and customer need for service also declined. Competition based on an undifferentiated product drove prices down. Gross margin per PC declined from $1,600 to $500 in just the three years between 1989 and 1992. Customers didn't need the old sales and service business design. The specialty computer retailers collapsed under their own weight. Computerland went out of business. Radio Shack entered an extended period of stagnation and profit decline.

Distributors were being replaced with another business design made famous by a precocious college-student-turned-entrepreneur, Michael Dell. From its dorm room beginnings in the mid-1980s, Dell Computer, now based in Austin, Texas, has created almost $2 billion in market value.

If customers only wanted a quality machine for a low price, Dell realized, the mode of delivery was almost irrelevant. A large segment of customers would be willing to get their machines through the mail. Given the availability of cheap component parts, Dell efficiently assembled the machines for less than the big manufacturers, and his cost for selling them was far less than the cost to maintain a storefront and a sales force.

Mail-order PCs were not new: The original IBM PC could be purchased through mail distributors as early as 1983. But IBM and Apple relied on small independent mail-order companies, many of which were fly-by-night, did not deliver when promised, made numerous shipping mistakes, and hassled customers. In contrast, Dell delivered basic service and stood behind its merchandise, with a money-back guarantee. Its system won extraordinarily high-quality scores with independent rating agencies and consumers.

Dell further cemented the trust of the customer by transforming his business, through highly focused marketing efforts, into a brand in the customer's mind, re-creating a first-mover's advantage by redefining the necessary offerings of the business. He also realized that customers still valued emergency support services, but only when they needed it. So he established a telephone hotline that could answer 90 percent of customer questions immediately and accurately.

Once Dell had established a reputation for quality and superior service in the home PC market, he was able to tap into the rich business market, further driving his company's scale economies versus other mail order distributors and computer manufacturers. Dell's selling and administrative expenses are 14 percent of sales, compared to 24 percent at Apple, and 20 percent at Compaq (even *after* restructuring). This economic disparity is driven by the simple difference in cost and productivity of each company's sales force. IBM's direct sales force costs $150,000 per person annually, with each person bringing in slightly less than $2 million in sales. Dell's tele-marketers cost only $40,000 per person, but each produces more than $4 million in sales. That isn't a productivity advantage—it's a productivity knockout.

Epilogue: From Manufacturing to Distribution

As low-cost distributors have been gaining market share and market value from traditional selling designs, they have been raising new questions about the balance of power in the value chain. Although it is difficult to measure the flow of market value from manufacturers to distributors, it is clear that the success of distribution experts is forcing manufacturers to reevaluate the robustness of their brands, question the economic power of their business designs, and rethink their approaches to future value growth. For example, consider the effect that Wal-Mart's success has had on packaged goods companies. By the early 1980s, Wal-Mart had become a purchasing power with the ability to achieve extraordinary price concessions. Now the new low-cost distribution design directly affected the business design of manufacturers. It forced them to cut their own costs or lose the high-volume sales channel.

Wal-Mart's latest effort is to compel its suppliers to streamline their distribution techniques to conform to its requirements. Wal-Mart's cooperative effort with P&G, for example, led to a dramatic increase in inventory turns, lower handling costs, and significantly lower systems costs—in this case for both companies.

In its discount broker business, Schwab has grown primarily at the expense of traditional, full-service channels. But with the introduction of OneSource, Schwab has begun to take value from the product "manufacturers," the fund managers themselves. Schwab has used its distribution clout to force the fund families to pick up the 25 basis point (25 cents per $100 invested) fee formerly borne by consumers. This has boosted Schwab's volume, allowed the individual to pay lower fees, and delivered a harsh jolt of reality to the high-flying money management industry. In the future, Schwab will probably use its power to squeeze fund families further: The latest families to sign up for OneSource are already being charged more than the original 25 basis point fee.

Even more disquieting to money managers is the shift in the customer contact point. To take advantage of Schwab's marketing and distribution prowess, they must forfeit control of the customer relationship. When Schwab sells a fund for a money manager, it passes along the assets, but not the customer's name. This destroys the ability of the fund family to cross-sell and establish a deeper relationship with the investor. OneSource not only makes it impossible for fund families to woo shareholders with direct mail and phone calls, but actually facilitates defection because switching among OneSource funds is so easy. (And conveniently, Charles Schwab itself maintains a line of low-risk money market funds, often a favorite destination for panicky investors in market downturns.) To gain access to Schwab's distribution network, fund families must accept all of its conditions, which makes some fund operators extremely nervous. As one noted, going through Schwab is like "dancing with the devil."[7]

Unlike the low-cost retail players, Grainger did not gain value primarily from other distributors. From the outset, it has grown by having a lower cost to serve than the manufacturers it buys from. With an average customer worth less than $1,900 and an average transaction size less than $130, Grainger is significantly more cost-effective in serving the low end of a manufacturer's customer base.

Dell's effect on conventional computer retailers was swift and dramatic, but it also made a profound impact on computer manufacturers. For virtually all the major hardware players, value shifted sharply to the low end. The lesson: Where there is no more product magic, don't pretend there is. IBM, DEC, and HP were buffered by other product lines. Compaq was on its own, and nearly went under. Apple saw its share of the PC market dwindle from 15 to close to 10 percent. Only HP responded early. Christening its low-end products "information appliances," it gave the customer what it wanted by driving down manufacturing costs and outsourcing its distribution function to low-cost distribution channels. IBM and DEC followed— four years later! They shifted only after losing billions of dollars of value through the continued excess cost of their direct sales forces, and through lost revenues.

Lessons Learned: Patterns and Business Design Success Factors

Low-cost distribution becomes a powerful engine of value creation when customers grow more sophisticated and products and services lose their differentiation in the marketplace. Then price becomes the dominant purchase criterion. Value migrates quickly to those companies that can streamline their business designs accordingly. Although the low-cost distribution revolution began with consumer goods, it has successfully entered, and will continue to spread through, the service and business-to-business sectors.

An important dynamic that follows the growth of low-cost distribution in an industry is the transfer of power from manufacturers to distributors. In numerous industries, low-cost distribution specialists have become the dominant player, forcing manufacturers to cut prices or significantly modify their operations (see Figure 10-5).

Although drawn from a diverse range of industries, the low-cost distribution specialists examined in this chapter share key capabilities. These organizational skills are the critical building blocks of the low-cost distribution business design.

Figure 10-5 Increasing Channel Concentration

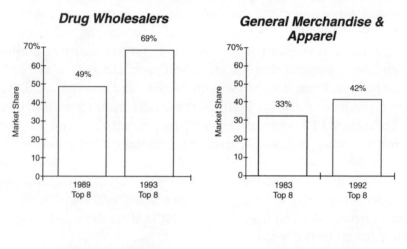

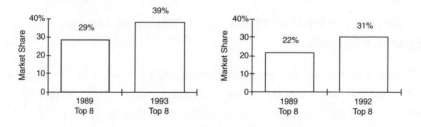

The age of distribution is marked by
rapidly concentrating distributor power.

SOURCE: Corporate Decisions, Inc. analysis.

Customer selection. In most industries, only a subset of the customer base is interested in the low-cost distribution option. Of these customers, only some can be served profitably. Wal-Mart's move into C and D counties, Aldi's selection of recession-hit urban areas, and Grainger's focus on the small accounts and small transactions of the major supplies distributors all exemplify astute customer selection.

Differentiation. The most conspicuous part of low-cost distributors' value proposition is rock-bottom prices. However, other important elements in the successful distribution specialists' offering are reliability and basic minimum quality. Delivering on these criteria, as well as price, has differentiated Wal-Mart and Dell from their competitors and allowed them to revolutionize their industries.

Manufacturing/operating system. Low-cost distributors are challenged to squeeze high operating margins out of low gross margins. Schwab and Wal-Mart achieve these operational efficiencies though innovative use of technology such as highly computerized back-office operations and electronic links to suppliers and customers.

Purchasing. Once low-cost distributors have gained critical mass, an important driver of profitability and value growth becomes their ability to bargain effectively with suppliers. The parameters on which a low-cost distributor can influence manufacturers include pricing, delivery systems, and relationships with the end-consumer.

Applications to Other Industries

In a broad range of industries, the collapse of the middle is just beginning to undermine the foundation of conventional sales designs. Where products have become commodities and opportunities for augmentation are low, astute manufacturers are moving quickly to adopt low-cost distribution. This process has started to unfold in sectors as diverse as plastic resins, semiconductor chips, and on-line computer services. The migration of value in these cases is being driven by the same pattern of customer priorities and changing economics.

Consider Speedplast, a service established by A. Schulman, a European plastics distributor based in France. Traditionally, resins were sold by a manufacturer's direct sales force to big customers, and by distributors to smaller customers. The specialized nature of the product demanded a high level of technical service and support, which required a trained salesperson. Today, plastics compounders view most resins as pure commodities.

Speedplast is essentially a Dell Computer for the plastics industry. Through a mail-order catalog, it offers 500 of Schulman's most commonly distributed products with an everyday low price, phone ordering, a guarantee to meet specifications, and 24-hour delivery anywhere in France. Customers even receive a 5 percent discount if they pay by credit card. Although European analysts said the Dell business design would never work in an industrial setting, Speedplast is proving them wrong. Why? Because like soap and socks (and PCs!), plastics are now commoditized—the customer needs little information or technical support, and the delivery system can be low cost.

While some product manufacturers such as Dell and Speedplast have developed their own low-cost distribution systems, others have captured some of the value migrating downstream by purchasing a low-cost distributor in their industries. One high-profile example of this pattern was Merck's purchase of Medco in 1993. Merck saw the changing health-care climate in the United States shifting value to cost-effective drug distribution. It chose to capitalize on Value Migration rather than fight it.

AgrEvo, a $2.3-billion crop-protection products manufacturer saw structural changes in the European agricultural sector driving value toward low-cost distribution. In response, it acquired a majority holding in Stefes, a low-cost agricultural supplies distributor. "Only by resolutely orienting our activities to customers' priorities can the highest possible degree of customer satisfaction and thus customer loyalty be achieved at an optimum level of marketing costs," said AgrEvo Chairman Gerhard Prante. "In acquiring a majority interest in Stefes, we are taking account of a market segment in which farmers are willing to dispense with extensive customer services, but in turn demand cheaper crop protection products."[8]

Some of the newest low-cost distribution designs have evolved in the form of brokers. One example is NECX, a $200-million entrepreneurial company in Massachusetts. Semiconductor manufacturers with unpredicted surplus chips can unload them through NECX. A manufacturer that is short of a specific chip can pick it up in a hurry from NECX. Neither the seller nor buyer needs technical help because each has its own cohort of engineers. NECX is enormously popular because of its ability to source or sell these complex parts anywhere in the world. A manufacturing chief at one of NECX's large customers commented that NECX, like Dell, has brought a positive reputation to a distribution channel that was once considered no more than a source of poor-quality products. To support its business design, NECX has developed the world's largest database for tracking computer components and their specifications, availability, and prices in recent trades. Again, the pattern is the same: The product is commoditized, the customer needs little sales or technical support, and the delivery system is inexpensive.

The low-cost distribution design extends to services as well. Information has become a commodity to be traded, distributed, and controlled. Today, many companies are attempting to establish themselves as the leader in electronic commerce, to create *the* low-cost electronic channel to the information superhighway. One such firm is CommerceNet. Founded in April 1994, CommerceNet aims to shape the development of standards that dictate usage of the Internet, and to facilitate electronic commerce for computer and financial-services companies. The key elements of its design are an on-line product catalog, order and transaction processing, security encryption for financial transaction safety, and transportation scheduling. While the victor of the electronic communications battle has yet to be declared, once again the same pattern is emerging: The product is commoditized, the customer needs little sales or technical support, and the delivery system is low cost.

The questions prompted by the low-cost distribution pattern for any executive are clear: Is my product becoming commoditized, either because of a competitive offering or because my customer no longer needs the service and information I've historically provided? Are there economic or other forces changing the priorities of my customers, making them more aware of their cost to buy my product relative to others? How large is the disparity between my cost to serve large customers versus small customers? Could these costs be dramatically lowered if a distribution channel bundled my products with others and offered the customer low-price, one-stop shopping? In a growing number of industries, the answers to these questions are positive, and a migration of value is imminent. Despite enormous value growth in the last two decades, the impact of low-cost distribution is just beginning.

Chapter 11

From Conventional Selling to High-End Solutions

- Are technology, regulation, and industry paradigms changing faster than my customers can keep up with them?
- Are my customers facing unprecedented demands from their customers and shareholders?
- Is globalization changing the way my customers think about supplier relationships?

THE PREVIOUS CHAPTER examined one facet of the obsolescence of the direct sales force business design. The direct sales force occupied the middle ground, serving customers who required moderate levels of service and product information. This worked reasonably well in the age of the product. However, it was not the most cost-effective way to bring product and customer together. In certain industries, customer sophistication has outstripped product complexity, and new players are undermining traditional sales channels by offering low-cost distribution of product and services.

There is a second facet of the collapse of the middle. Traditional sales forces lack the expertise to deliver complex, customized solutions. But in the age of business design, that is what more customers need. They are increasingly dissatisfied with the level of service, advice, and support that is delivered with new products. Furthermore, in many cases they do not even need a product so much as a new way to carry out a significant portion of their company's functionality. These customers are demanding high-end solutions (see Figure 11-1).

This customer desire represents a tremendous value growth opportunity, but crafting a business design that delivers solutions, and delivers them profitably, is daunting. Nevertheless, a handful of companies have successfully developed business designs that provide high-end solutions. Over the past five years, solutions pioneers such as Hewlett-Packard and EDS have created billions of dollars of market value. They created this substantial value growth when many of their competitors were suffering.

A growing number of sophisticated companies are entering the high-end solutions arena. Often, their new business designs offer an extremely valuable alternative—at times a company-saving move—to the traditional sale of manufactured goods.

FIGURE 11-1   EVOLUTION OF CUSTOMER PRIORITIES

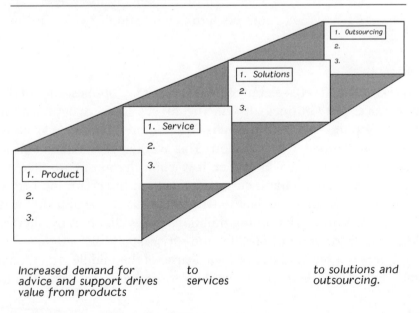

Increased demand for   to   to solutions and
advice and support drives   services   outsourcing.
value from products

Hewlett-Packard and Solutions-Based Global Account Management

Hewlett-Packard has been one of the most dramatic value growth stories of the 1990s. It has a strong, multibillion dollar business base with such leading corporate customers as General Electric, Ford, and Citicorp, and a reputation as a leader in providing computing business solutions. It was the most admired computer company in a *Business Week* poll of senior executives. In addition, HP significantly outperformed its larger competitors in terms of value growth, increasing its market capitalization by 70 percent (to $26 billion) in a period when IBM and DEC collectively lost almost $50 billion in market value (see Figure 11-2).

FIGURE 11-2   MARKET VALUE CREATION

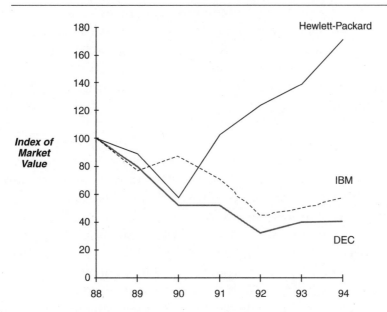

Hewlett–Packard moved away from the traditional computing business model to meet customer needs for low–cost distribution and high–end solutions. Within five years, its value growth performance significantly outdistanced IBM's and DEC's.

SOURCE: CDI Value Growth Database.

While HP's successful family of printers has certainly played a role in this success story, much of the company's performance is the result of its high-end solutions innovation, Global Account Management (GAM). A powerful tool for creating strategic partnerships with top corporate customers, GAM has been recognized as an industry-leading business design that HP's competitors are still struggling to match.

As recently as 10 years ago, HP was a solid if unexceptional performer in the crowded world of computing. Along with Sun, DEC, and Apollo, HP enjoyed a reputation for making technically excellent products. But its narrow product focus, dominant engineering culture, and traditional, geographically organized sales force left it undistinguished in the eyes of the corporate customer.

What enabled HP to capitalize on the migration of value toward high-end solutions was careful observation of changing customer priorities. Although the cost of computing power continued to fall through the mid-1980s, processor time, particularly for proprietary mainframe systems, was still extremely expensive. As a result, MIS departments tended to ration computer time and focus on hardware price/performance as the critical determinant in purchase decisions. In addition, mainframes and minis were complex and temperamental machines, often requiring elaborate specialized facilities and full-time technical experts to keep them running smoothly. This generated demand for reliable service and support.

Most computer companies responded to this demand with a direct sales force to sell hardware and a service force to provide support. To forestall switching based on hardware performance, vendors relentlessly focused on continually improving their products' price per unit of processing power.

Then customers began to change. As hardware prices fell further, MIS managers focused more of their attention and discretionary dollars on other aspects of computing. More sophisticated, they began to see that it was not only hardware but also software, applications, and services that made systems valuable to employees. Traditionally, computers had been used to speed the performance of routine back-office processes. As computers spread throughout the organization, applications became more strategically oriented. Computing systems were now important business management tools, critical enablers of revenue and profit growth.

The result was a changing set of customer priorities and decision making. The MIS emphasis shifted to minimizing total systems costs, particularly by cutting the wasteful investment in proprietary applications. Furthermore, the increasingly strategic and global nature of computing meant that decisions were no longer left to local MIS managers, the nexus of the old direct-sales relationship. Instead, senior management was playing an increasingly important role. Therefore, the ability of a vendor to offer business solutions and seamless global support became an important factor in purchasing decisions.

These changing customer priorities created a new business opportunity. Hewlett-Packard's executives firmly believed that the largest and most sophisticated international customers would not only demand seamless, global support from computer vendors, but also new levels of partnering and commitment to jointly tackle complex business-computing issues.

Having understood the trajectory of customer priorities, HP in 1990 set about creating a business design that met them. First, it limited the scope of the new effort to its most important customers, painstakingly selected on the basis of current and potential HP sales, their need for global support, and their industry leadership position. By designing solutions for the leaders, HP could grow profitably by replicating solutions within vertical industry segments.

After developing only a few pilot accounts, HP de-emphasized its traditional direct sales approach and focused on making two key transitions. The first was to move from selling products to providing knowledge-based services—that is, to define solutions, not products, as its value-added. For example, it was willing to recommend third-party hardware for part of a system it had designed in collaboration with the customer. The second change was to switch the customer relationship from the purchasing-agent level to the CIO- and senior-management level. Elevation of the relationship allowed HP to redefine itself as a strategic partner contributing to the customer's overall competitiveness and economic performance.

To cultivate and sustain these deeper relationships, HP deployed a Global Account Manager in the headquarters city of each GAM customer. This manager was a senior-level HP sales executive whose primary contact was with the chief information officer and whose primary mission was to manage not the revenue, but the profitability of the account on a global basis. The Global Account Manager focused HP's efforts on meeting customer priorities and, with HP support staff and local field people, on delivering solutions. As the GAM program grew from the original few to a significant number of accounts, HP made each of its top 100 managers serve as a liaison with a number of GAM customers. For instance, Lew Platt, HP's CEO, is personally responsible for having quarterly discussions, setting objectives, and building a top-level relationship with several large HP customers.

To support the new business design, HP radically reconfigured its sales and marketing organizations. HP's global account program was developed as a separate entity within HP's sales and marketing function, which had been organized along product and geographic lines. For HP's global accounts, the GAM program and its managers have authority that supersedes that of the traditional sales organization. The head of Global Accounts reports directly to the VP of sales and marketing. In addition, the individual global account managers can reach into local HP operations anywhere in the world and deploy resources to service their accounts' needs.

The Hewlett-Packard Global Account Management Business Design

Fundamental Assumptions	Rapid changes in the world of corporate computing exhaust the time, attention, and resources of large customers.
	The globalization of many companies has created the need for equally global computing systems and vendor relationships.
Business Design Element	**Hewlett-Packard's Choice**
Customer Selection	Program limited to most valuable customers
	Vertical market rollout
Scope	Computing partner, offering advice, support, service, and solutions
	Equipment sales

Organizational Configuration	Global Account Manager on site in client headquarters city
	Global Account Manager can mobilize HP resources worldwide to create solutions
Go-to-Market Mechanism	Senior-level selling

What has HP gained? First, it has managed to capture an important share of its global customers' senior management attention. In an environment where customers can only afford a few select partnerships, such a position creates significant strategic advantage. In addition, success with these customers positions HP to achieve its goal of earning 70 percent of its revenues from outside the United States by the year 2000. HP has also seen its set of global accounts grow in importance. Today they account for a substantial share of the Computer Systems Organization's revenue and have growth rates and operating margins significantly higher than those of HP's smaller accounts.

The strength of HP's new business design has not been lost on the investment community. While the market value of traditional computer vendors has been heavily discounted by investors, HP has seen its market value grow steadily. HP now enjoys a market value/sales ratio of 1.0, versus 0.7 and 0.4 for IBM and DEC, respectively, and 0.6 for HP's old archrival Sun.

HP's success has also not been lost on its competitors. In early 1994, IBM announced a sweeping reorganization to become more customer focused, realigning its traditional regional and product group businesses into industry groups. IBM also developed its own global accounts program in the summer of 1994, four years behind HP.

EDS: The Outsourcing Leader

Global account management is one type of high-end solutions business design. A second design—the outsourcing provider—further develops the partnership between buyer and supplier.

For the purposes of this chapter, outsourcing can be defined as the comprehensive subcontracting of an entire function or a cross-functional set of activities to a specialized provider. Numerous academics and executives have examined the outsourcing phenomenon from the point of view of a company relinquishing activities. In the *Sloan Management Review*, Quinn and Hilmer argue that "by strategically outsourcing and emphasizing a company's core competencies, managers can leverage their firm's skills and resources for increased competitiveness."[1] They cite the example of Nike, which is the largest supplier of athletic shoes in the world and which has created more than $2.5 billion in market value over the past decade, yet subcontracts all shoe production and manufacture to suppliers in Southeast Asia. In fact, Nike is essentially a product design and marketing firm. Academics like Quinn and Hilmer point to "the leveraged corporation" as a powerful new business design.

The other point of view, however, is that the provision of outsourcing solutions is an important opportunity for value growth. For every Nike, there must be high-quality manufacturers able to interface seamlessly with the shoe company's upstream design and downstream marketing functions. As corporations revisit their traditional assumptions about vertical integration and formal ownership of all functional areas, the demand for focused, expert outsourcing providers has soared.

To understand the tremendous value growth opportunity for outsourcing providers, it is necessary to examine the changing priorities, mind-set, and capabilities of large corporate customers. Since the 1980s, corporations have come under unprecedented pressure to optimize financial performance. Reengineering and core competency strategies have encouraged companies to retain crucial activities in-house and subcontract activities that cannot be optimized or fail to provide competitive advantage.

Technology has provided more powerful tools to implement these ideas. Distributed computing power, electronic data interchange, and tracking systems such as bar coding have enabled large corporations to assess more clearly the costs and benefits of each internal process. Together, increased pressure for performance, new managerial techniques, and heightened organizational capabilities have created a new customer priority: extracting the maximum value from each step in the value chain.

One of the early companies to capitalize on the shift in priorities was IBM. Its giant 1989 deal to take over all of Eastman Kodak's IT functions was the lightning that ignited the outsourcing firestorm. As David Togut noted in *The Data Processing Outsourcing Market*, "This watershed event put internal MIS departments under intense scrutiny. Unlike many internal MIS departments, a sophisticated outsourcer uses its technology expertise, consulting experience, and financial resources to provide a complete business solution, not just a technology solution."[2]

In the next five years, outsourcing providers in a range of industries and functional areas emerged. Although primarily an overnight express mail company, Federal Express has also become a provider of mission-critical distribution services for medical supplies and consumer goods companies such as Williams-Sonoma. A host of firms have entered the field of clinical research services, enabling pharmaceutical and biotech companies to outsource the whole clinical trial function. At the other end of the pharmaceutical value chain, pharmacy benefit managers such as Medco and PCS have carved out the entire pharmaceutical portion of the managed health-care industry. Customized Transportation Inc. offers comprehensive logistics-outsourcing solutions to midwestern manufacturers, while Servicemaster has become the leader in facilities management. Together, this group of companies has created more than $12 billion in market value since 1989—a strong reflection of the migration of value toward high-end solutions.

One of the most successful outsourcing providers is also one of the most venerable. In 1962, an ambitious IBM salesman named H. Ross Perot left Big Blue to start his own computing company, Electronic Data Systems (EDS). While IBM sold hardware, software, and service, EDS began selling computing time. Although many of the largest corporate and government users could fully utilize an expensive mainframe system, Perot recognized a growing number of customers that could not justify the mainframe's massive fixed cost. EDS enabled these customers to convert IT from a fixed to a variable cost, shed their computing assets, and simply rent time, memory, and processing power from EDS's regional "data centers."

The first customers Perot targeted were in the health care and insurance industries. From 1964 to 1969, EDS' revenues increased from $100,000 to $5.3 million, thanks largely to time-share contracts with Medicare, Medicaid, and state Blue Cross/Blue Shield organizations. Over time, EDS became the preferred provider for the industry, winning contracts because insurance customers were confident that "EDS knows our business."

Following this successful formula, EDS has built a business design around vertical market conquest. From its position of strength in insurance, EDS has methodically entered other vertical markets like banking, manufacturing, transportation, and energy. Its strategy in entering new territory has been to acquire the highest-value customers, develop industry-specific solutions, then replicate them profitably throughout a broader set of customers. For example, after gaining experience in automotive applications with General Motors, EDS captured accounts with Saab, Caterpillar, Chausson, and Cummins Engine. After sealing a landmark IT-outsourcing contract with First Fidelity Bancorp in the late 1970s, EDS has gone on to build a powerful franchise in banking.

As EDS has cultivated these markets, it has expanded its breadth of offerings. IT outsourcing in the 1990s means not only time-sharing but also network management, specialized processing, and applications software such as round-the-clock order placement and instant stock quotations for brokerage houses. Because few large companies can break even on these functions and even fewer can use them to generate competitive advantage, they are a prime opportunity for outsourcing. Increasingly, EDS and its competitors are moving into general business-strategy consulting because it enables them to begin a dialogue with senior-level management that may eventually result in long-term outsourcing contracts that are focused on the right business issues for the client.

The EDS Outsourcing/Systems-Integration Business Design

Fundamental Assumptions	Computing is essential to the success of, but outside the core competence of, many corporations.

Business Design Element	**EDS' Choice**
Customer Selection	Systematic vertical market conquest

Value Recapture	Sophisticated contracts that maximize account profitability through basic rates, volume increases, and add-on services
Differentiation	Vertical market expertise
Manufacturing	Rigorous project methodology
	Replication of solutions across accounts
Capital Intensity	High
Organizational Configuration	Vertical market operating units
	Matrixed organization (vertical market/function)
Go-to-Market Mechanism	Senior-level selling

The benefits that EDS delivers as a full-range IT outsourcing provider are threefold. First, EDS offers customers an attractive financial proposition: cutting IT costs by as much as 30 percent and bolstering the balance sheet through the sale of nonproductive assets. Second, it enables customers to focus time and attention on their core businesses. Third, it facilitates large-scale organizational changes within the customer organization—such as consolidating IT departments after a large merger.[3]

Because of its extraordinary expertise, EDS was acquired by General Motors in 1984. EDS consolidated GM's 70 worldwide data centers, rationalized 17 CAD/CAM platforms into three, and created on-line links between GM and its thousands of upstream suppliers and downstream dealers. EDS also played an integral behind-the-scenes role in the development of the Saturn, the first car to be engineered entirely on computer screens. Togut identifies cost containment as EDS's most visible achievement at GM. "Before GM acquired EDS in 1984, GM expected its IT costs to grow in excess of 10 percent annually. Since then, EDS has kept costs flat while providing additional functionality."[4] GM's huge volume of business quadrupled EDS' revenues from $947 million in 1984 to $3.4 billion in 1985, making EDS the clear leader in the IT outsourcing industry.

Since being acquired by GM, EDS has posted an impressive record of revenue, profit, and value growth. As revenues tripled from a little more than $3 billion in 1985 to more than $10 billion in 1994, the proportion of business from GM dropped from 71 percent to 34 percent. EDS' market value has increased from $3.5 billion at the time of the acquisition to more than $19 billion (see Figure 11-3). In 1994, EDS continued to pace the outsourcing industry, reaching an agreement to provide all of Xerox's IT requirements worldwide over 10 years for $3.2 billion. The deal transfers 1,700 IT personnel and some $150 million worth of hardware from Xerox to EDS and is predicted to reduce Xerox's IT spending by 25 percent over the life of the contract.

One key to EDS' business design and impressive record of value growth has been its focus on account profitability. In contrast to a sales representative who targets quarterly revenues or a plant manager who aims for high-capacity utilization, an EDS account execu-

FIGURE 11-3   VALUE CREATION

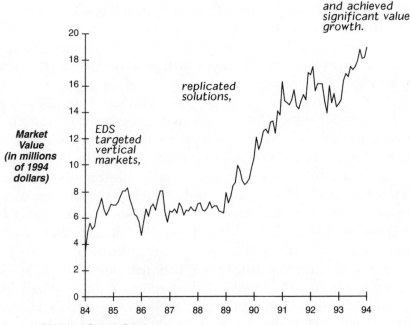

SOURCE: CDI Value Growth Database.

tive manages a multiyear outsourcing contract for profitability over the lifetime of the account. By maintaining a performance database of past project costs, EDS is able to estimate very accurately its own costs, and how they will change over a long-term outsourcing relationship. With costs established, EDS can price its services to ensure target profitability.

Another pillar of EDS' business design has been its organization and human resource policies. Although each client situation is to some extent unique, EDS' approaches are all based on a well-developed, companywide project methodology. This uniformity and shared knowledge base allow EDS consultants and technicians to enter a project at any stage and add value with minimal ramp-up time. For account managers, a consistent platform of skills and approaches to client problems creates flexibility and leverage in staffing. They can comb the EDS organization for functional expertise and deploy it quickly and efficiently on behalf of a client.

EDS' success in IT outsourcing has attracted many entrants, including CSC, Arthur Andersen, and IBM. While this entry is a tribute to EDS' impressive record of profit and value creation, it also signals that the company will have to reinvent its business design if it hopes to avoid the eventual commoditization of its offering.

Lessons Learned: Patterns and Business Design Success Factors

The opportunity for high-end solution business designs emerges when customers face daunting new challenges or increased claims on their scarce resources. In the consumer world, rapidly disappearing leisure time has created opportunities for solutions in the food and apparel categories. In the business-to-business realm, the push to globalize and pressure from aggressive competitors and restive shareholders have created the need for high-end solutions in many functional areas.

When corporations or individuals face these kinds of challenges, successful solutions providers create value for clients and themselves by taking over activities that are critical to the success of the customer but outside the customer's core competences. The initial basis of a solutions partnership is often the customer's desire to reduce costs. But the most successful solutions providers avoid the commoditization of their offerings by adding to the customer's top-line growth and by making the customer organization not only more efficient but also more effective.

Global Account Management and outsourcing are two distinct business designs that both deliver high-end solutions. But despite their differences, GAM and outsourcing require similar organizational competencies. Both designs involve a much higher degree of daily integration with the customer than the traditional supplier of goods or services. Both strive to create a long-term relationship with the customer. Revisiting the experiences of Hewlett-Packard and EDS reveals the critical factors for mastering any high-end solutions business design.

Customer selection. To ensure maximum long-term profitability, both HP and EDS have deployed a strategy of vertical market penetration. First, they focus on a few large or leading-edge customers. With a proven track record, they can more easily add other accounts in the industry, which become highly profitable because much of the systems design is transferable. HP has multiplied the size of its GAM program but limited its own learning investment to only eight vertical industries.

Differentiation. The key to long-term profitability is making products unique and services difficult to replicate. For Hewlett-Packard's GAM program, a key defensive barrier is its first-mover advantage. Other players such as IBM have followed HP's lead and established GAM programs, but how long will it be before IBM is capable of measuring worldwide profitability by account? EDS has exploited its lead time in certain markets, such as insurance, to build up a formidable base of industry-specific knowledge, which competitors cannot match.

Value recapture. One of the greatest challenges to developing a high-end solutions business design is pricing. Products can be priced by the unit. Services can be priced by the hour. But high-end solutions, which bundle product, service, and knowledge over a long period of time, often defy traditional approaches to value recapture.

EDS has raised the sophistication of typical buyer-supplier contracts to include an elaborate schedule of volume surcharges and add-on services. As relationships between outsourcing partners become deeper and longer in duration, however, the contracting corporation may increasingly ask outsourcing providers to assume a share of the business risk. The pioneers in this regard are the pharmaceutical companies and PBMs that have launched a flurry of new risk-sharing ventures in an attempt to come to grips with the changing health care environment. Innovative contractual agreements have appeared in other industries as well—for example, Ford and Asea Brown Boveri's pricing of the design and construction services for Ford's paint-finishing plant in Oakville, Canada. Discarding the traditional request-for-proposal/fixed-price bid approach, Ford and ABB structured a process in which they collaborated on design, giving each party an economic incentive to lower total costs and improve quality.

A final component to value recapture within a high-end solutions business design is focus on account profitability. HP has invested considerable financial resources in an information system capable of capturing worldwide profitability for each account. The key measure HP uses is return on sales and marketing investment, against which all HP Global Account Managers are judged.

Manufacturing/operating. Solutions providers must be able to convert innovations into off-the-shelf products that can be rolled out at a fraction of the original development cost. The tools that enable EDS to effectively replicate its solutions are vertical market focus and proprietary project methodology. In its sales and marketing groups, HP is actively seeking to replicate solutions within and across GAM accounts.

Organizational configuration. National markets, currency controls, and cumbersome communications processes made national or regional selling organizations an appropriate structure 15 years ago. The globalization of capital flows, communications networks, and the operations of corporate customers have rendered that model obsolete. Increasingly, companies are being forced to configure themselves to meet the priorities of distinct customers or customer segments, regardless of geography. The HP Global Account Manager, the EDS vertical market teams, and the planned reorganization of IBM by vertical market all exemplify this trend. Customer-centric structure must be accompanied by a strong problem-solving and customer service orientation. Companies that traditionally have been technology or product driven must cultivate these skills within their organizations or acquire them externally.

Go-to-market mechanism. The success of the high-end solutions pioneers has been attributable, in large part, to aggressive senior-level marketing and ongoing customer contact. EDS maintains dialogues with each customer's CIO, CFO, or even CEO. By consciously elevating the level of its dialogue with customers, EDS becomes a valued business partner, not merely a supplier of commodity processing time. Companies in all industries can learn from this successful practice. The most conspicuous example is Jack Welch, who regularly calls on CEOs at large clients such as Ford to discuss how GE's plastics division can provide automotive engineering solutions that will improve the customer's systems economics.

Applications to Other Industries

The success of both HP's and EDS' high-end solution business designs has attracted attention, envy, and waves of imitation. As the collapse of the middle plays out in a broad range of industries, the demand for high-end solutions will increase dramatically.

The opportunity to create value as an outsourcer will emerge wherever companies, under intensifying pressure for better financial performance, rely on processes outside of their core competence. The opportunity will be even greater when the process or activity in question is complex, and potentially crippling to the organization when poorly executed.

Global account management represents another rapidly growing area of opportunity. Large corporations are integrating their worldwide operations, rationalizing their suppliers, and coming under increasing pressure for rapid product development and higher-quality standards. These trends generate demand for reliable, innovative business partners capable of providing global product, support, and service.

Consider the well-publicized effort by Ford to globalize its operations and its design process. One of the early results has been the Mondeo/Contour, a car manufactured according to a single set of specifications, which will be sold globally with only minor customization for regional markets. To ensure consistent availability of supply and worldwide support and service, Ford has had to rethink its supplier relationships, creating an opportunity for vendors with

Global Account Management. The nascent globalizing initiatives of manufacturers like Xerox, Whirlpool, Hyundai, and Unilever may also create opportunity for comprehensive, high-end solutions.

The collapse of the middle has turned the dominant selling paradigm of the manufacturing age on its head. As discussed in Chapter 10, in industries where customers have become more sophisticated and products demystified, manufacturers must act rapidly to strip away service and provide low-cost distribution. Conversely, in a growing number of industries customers are demanding long-term partnerships and a more comprehensive service bundle. For companies able to recognize these changes in their customer base and transform their business designs accordingly, high-end solutions will be a powerful source of value growth for the next decade.

PART III

Prescription

Introduction:
Applying Value Migration to Your
Organization

Parts I and II of this book presented a tool set for examining Value Migration and a series of Value Migration patterns. Part III is about prescription. It provides you with a tangible, systematic method for applying Value Migration to your own situation.

Chapter 12 outlines a process for anticipating Value Migration. This methodology will help you determine whether Value Migration is already under way in your industry, whether migration is likely to occur in the near future, and how that migration will look once it has begun. Anticipating Value Migration activates your early warning system.

Once a call to action has been signaled, the challenge becomes moving your organization to response. Chapter 13 provides methods for overcoming the institutional memory that can block detection of—and response to—Value Migration. These methods help you see the pattern of Value Migration more clearly within your own business and enable you to make the moves that your early warning system suggests are necessary.

Chapter 14 then describes the basic elements of response—the moves you must make to profit from Value Migration. It answers the fundamental question: What do I do about Value Migration? It shows how you can apply your knowledge of Value Migration to respond to threats, take advantage of opportunities, and capture the next cycle of value growth in your industry.

The final chapter challenges you to master the new game of

business chess. Value Migration demands that executives make the right moves. Learning to make those moves with the confidence required to implement them successfully is the fundamental challenge for management in the new game.

Chapter **12**

How to Anticipate Value Migration

- What are the early warning signs of Value Migration in my industry?
- How can I detect them early enough to respond to their threats and opportunities faster than my competitors?
- How can I predict the timing, trajectory, and rate of Value Migration?

VALUE MIGRATION HAS NOT BEEN KIND TO MANY INDUSTRY GIANTS, as illustrated by the case studies in Part II. Many erstwhile leaders have seen their profitability, their market value, and their leadership position erode. Value Migration is not, however, new. It has been a part of business for decades. And as the historical record shows, many leaders have guided their organizations through difficult periods of Value Migration to reemerge even stronger after the transition (see Figure 12-1). One of their most valuable skills has been the ability to detect the first signals of Value Migration and anticipate its trajectory.

The Challenge: Perspective

Value Migration is hard to detect; day-to-day tactical activities consume all of an organization's energy and make it difficult to see long-

FIGURE 12-1   THE "MOVE BEFORE YOU HAVE TO"
HALL OF FAME

Company	Leader	Transition
• Sears	• Wood	• From catalogs to counters
• Sears	• Wood	• From urban to suburban
• NBC	• Sarnoff	• From radio to television
• IBM	• Watson, Jr.	• From tabulating to computing
• GE	• Welch	• From bureaucracy to competition
• Merck	• Vagelos	• From average-resourced R&D to blockbuster development process
		• From traditional sales force to account management and low-cost distribution
• Blockbuster	• Huizenga	• From video rentals to broad-based entertainment
• Intel	• Grove	• From DRAMs to processor chips
• Turner	• Turner	• From program recycling to original programming
• AT&T	• Allen	• From monopoly to marketing

By attacking their own business designs before competitors did, aggressive CEOs moved maturing companies back into rapid value inflow.

term changes. In the value inflow phase, keeping up with demand makes it hard to even consider the need to change. For those organizations in the stability phase, past success clouds clarity of vision. The more successful the organization, the less likely that the beginnings of Value Migration will be perceived. In value outflow, stemming losses supersedes all other activities.

Exacerbating an organization's natural tendency to focus inward is the fact that Value Migration is a complex process whose early stages are silent, subtle, and typically asymptomatic. The identity and priorities of customers can shift in ways that may not be immediately apparent to the incumbents in an industry. For instance, within many corporate computing customers, the locus of decision making shifted gradually from the corporate MIS group, to company departments, to individuals. From Folgers corporate offices, it did not seem obvious that fringe movements in the South and the Pacific Northwest were important precursors to a massive shift in the priorities and behavior of coffee consumers.

Equally difficult to detect is the emergence of new competitors. Detection is particularly hard when a new business design emerges, as it often does, from beyond the circle of traditional competitors. Long periods of industry stability only exacerbate the problem. Traditional competitors are used to focusing on each other, not on new and nontraditional entrants at the edge of the competitive field of vision. These new competitors are also hard to identify given such industry mind-sets as: We make steel, they make plastic. We produce gross rating points, they install coaxial cable. We sell high-end merchandise, they discount.

Early detection, however, is a prerequisite to sharing in the next cycle of value growth. The shape of the aggregate profit curve illustrates the reward for early detection (see Figure 12-2). Late detection and late response raise the cost of participation and reduce the opportunity for profit and value growth. The management teams of U.S. integrated steel companies accurately perceived the migration of value to minimills—10 years too late. LTV's newly announced minimill project (in 1995) will yield only a fraction of the profit and value growth that it would have in 1985.

Although the early stages of Value Migration are extremely difficult to detect, there is an early warning system that can greatly improve your ability to pick up key signals and anticipate the future of your industry. Its first component is a thorough, strategic understanding of your customers. The second is a hypersensitive competitive radar screen. It is the interaction of shifting customer priorities and the new options for meeting them that initiates Value Migration. The final component of this early warning system is a rich vocabulary of Value Migration patterns from other industries. Familiarity with the way in which customer priorities, competing business designs, and external shocks have triggered Value Migration in other indus-

FIGURE 12-2   THE PROFIT CURVE

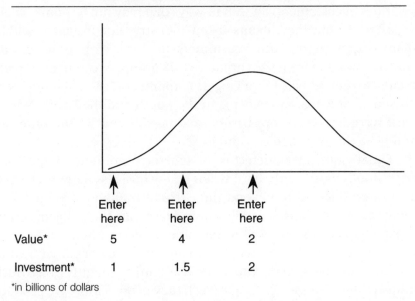

	Enter here	Enter here	Enter here
Value*	5	4	2
Investment*	1	1.5	2

*in billions of dollars

tries can help you gain a clearer perspective on the dynamics at work in your own environment.

Understanding the Customer

As the evolution of the steel, airlines, coffee, pharmaceuticals, and computing industries have shown, the customer is the fundamental driver of the Value Migration process. To gain an early indication of the way in which your customers' priorities will shift, it is essential to examine your customers along three dimensions: wealth, power, and needs maturity.

1. *Customer wealth.* Changes in customer wealth create new priorities and new opportunities for value growth. Although increasing customer wealth can increase the amount of total revenue and profit available, it is dangerous to assume that a rising tide of customer wealth will lift the boats of all business designs evenly or predictably. In the 1920s, the incomes of U.S. consumers rose. While GM responded with a business model built around a product line matched to different wealth levels, Ford did not. Value flowed dramatically to GM. It is equally dangerous to assume that falling customer wealth

will translate into value outflow for the supplying industry. By tailoring its business design to the emerging priorities of price and time sensitivity, Wal-Mart capitalized on the stagnating real incomes of many Americans in the 1980s to generate more than $60 billion in market value.

2. *Customer power.* Customers gain power when their concentration increases relative to suppliers and when differentiation among suppliers declines. The movement of power from supplier to customer is occurring simultaneously across industries as varied as pharmaceuticals, business forms, office equipment, and consumer products. Measuring customer power is not yet a precise science. However, even a crude supplier power index is better than none (see Figure 12-3). Unless suppliers develop an antidote to customer power (such as a new cycle of innovation, or a movement from products to services and solutions), value will continue to flow away

FIGURE 12-3   SUPPLIER POWER INDEX

Product	Customers	Distribution of Power Suppliers/Customers
• Unique	• Highly fragmented	• 90/10
• Highly differentiated	• Fragmented	• 70/30
• Differentiated	• Moderately concentrated	• 50/50
• Weakly differentiated	• Concentrated	• 30/70
• Pure commodity	• Highly concentrated	• 10/90

The relative power of customers influences the direction in which value will flow.

from suppliers. Without preemptive action, the outflow can be significant and irreversible.

3. *Customer needs maturity.* The mapping of changing customer needs yields the greatest predictive power for Value Migration. As noted in Chapter 1, customer needs are met by the benefits and features of products or services. Customer needs, wealth, and power are all filtered through the customer's decision-making system to form priorities. While needs indicate what products or services customers want to purchase, it is their priorities that provide insight into what business design will serve them and earn a profit.

As customers evolve, they begin to say, "I don't care about your historical abilities to _____ (fill in any item on a long list of obsolete skills). My business has changed, my needs have changed. What I really care about is _____. What I will pay a premium for is _____."

CAD/CAM. The computer-aided design/computer-aided manufacturing (CAD/CAM) market provides an excellent illustration of how a strategic understanding of maturing customer needs allowed a series of new entrants to create massive and rapid Value Migration during the 1980s and early 1990s.

The CAD/CAM market began as drafting automation for large auto and aerospace firms. By the 1980s, the needs of the market were expanded to include all five steps of the CAD/CAM process: concept, design, analysis, drafting, and numerically controlled manufacturing. The industry was led by IBM, Computervision, and Intergraph, whose products integrated all the steps but were best of breed in none. Their business designs bundled hardware, software, and service into a complete package.

In the mid-1980s, customer needs began to change. Drafting technology was becoming mature, and customers were comfortable with it. They were no longer looking for higher drafting performance, but a more cost-effective drafting solution.

Autodesk, a new entrant, invested in a PC-based product that delivered most of the functionality of traditional drafting solutions at a fraction of the cost. It not only cherry-picked the drafting functions at big accounts, it also opened the market to tens of thousands of small and medium enterprises. It correctly identified that customers' drafting needs had changed and developed its offering accordingly. Its business design, characterized by product line focus (drafting) and a software-only offering, was well matched to emerging customer priorities. In seven years, its market value expanded from $200 million to $1.2 billion.

As drafting matured, analysis and testing were becoming economically more important. In this area, the customer was looking for higher performance, not lower software cost. The capability to perfect computerized structural testing could reduce other process costs and shorten cycle times. Again, customer priorities had shifted. A new business design that responded to this shift could create and capture significant value. Another new entrant, SDRC, emerged as the leading provider of technologically sophisticated analysis software. The market value of its software-only business design increased by $400 million from 1988 to 1993.

The third high-value need in the market was also performance related. Engineers, a new segment of customers, needed three-dimensional modeling capability at the concept stage. Parametric Technology Corporation invested to meet this need, and like SDRC, invested early enough and well enough to emerge as the undisputed technology and performance leader. The market value of its product-focused, software-only business design expanded by $1 billion from 1989 to 1993.

In each case, changes in the relative importance of customer needs and in the customer's decision-making system created opportunity for a new business design. As often happens, each time it was a single element of that decision system—e.g., sophistication in concept modeling and cost effectiveness in drafting—that drove the change. The traditional incumbents in the market failed to detect these shifts and to forge a new strategic understanding of the customer. As a result, the newcomers created and captured an enormous amount of market value in the CAD/CAM business (see Figure 12-4).

Understanding how customer needs mature is a simple concept; nevertheless, it can be an extraordinarily powerful mechanism. It determines the types of business designs that will be most effective and profitable. Diagnosing the way that needs have matured in the past can help anticipate the pace and characteristics of future needs maturity. The CAD/CAM example illustrates the predictive power of needs maturity (see Figure 12-5). The pattern is clear: When needs are emerging, the customer looks for performance. When needs are mature, the customer looks for lower cost. This systematic

FIGURE 12-4   VALUE CREATION

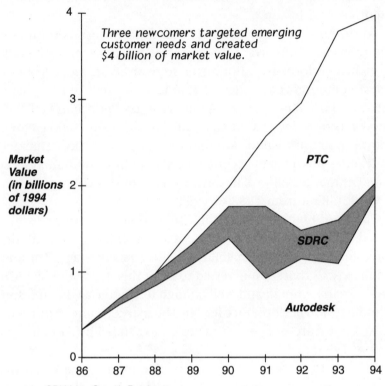

SOURCE: CDI Value Growth Database.

transformation of customer needs and priorities applies across most industries.

The pattern has significant implications for investment behavior. Investments in improved performance for mature needs provide no returns. The customer doesn't care. A dollar invested gets little in return. Investment in improved cost-effectiveness for mature needs, however, can yield extraordinary returns. One dollar invested can yield 10 (Autodesk). Investments in improved performance for emerging needs can also yield enormous profit. One dollar invested can yield 10 or 20 in return (SDRC and PTC).

Expanding the Competitive Field of Vision

Customers drive Value Migration. However, customers and their priorities do not exist in a vacuum. The evolution of customer priori-

FIGURE 12-5   NEEDS MATURITY CURVE

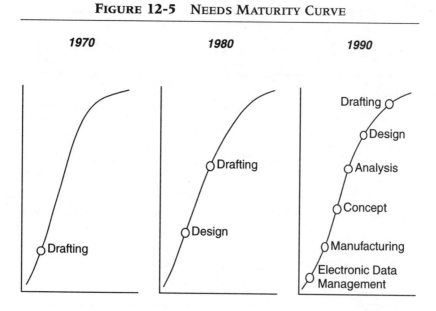

As needs matured in each customer function, a new business design was required to capture value.

ties is affected by the range of new product/service options available. The second component of the early warning system is a systematic, disciplined approach to identifying and evaluating competing business designs.

Most companies have a well-defined set of competitors that they monitor and benchmark. Often, this set is too narrow. For most companies, value erosion is often triggered not by the traditional players, but by outsiders with new, more effective business designs (see Figure 12-6). To anticipate migration, companies are best served by moving from the narrow perspective of competitive tunnel vision to the 360-degree view of a competitive radar screen. A broader competitive field of vision enables you to identify direct, indirect, and peripheral competitors that trigger the Value Migration process by providing the customer new options.

Although extremely challenging, the process of moving from tunnel vision to radar screen can be facilitated by recognizing the impact of two major trends that are responsible for the proliferation of new business designs across many industries. Understanding the

Figure 12-6 The Competitive Field of Vision

Industry	Traditional Competitors...	and Those That Really Mattered
• Retailing	• Sears, Montgomery Ward, JC Penney	• Kmart, Wal-Mart, Target, Toys "R" Us, Circuit City, The Limited, The Gap
• Automotive	• GM, Ford, Chrysler	• Toyota, Honda, Nissan, Hyundai, Volvo
• Media	• ABC, CBS, NBC	• Turner, Diller, TCI, Blockbuster Video
• Computing	• IBM, DEC, Wang, Apple	• Microsoft, Novell, Intel
• Advertising	• Ogilvy, Y&R, Burnett, McCann Erickson	• CAA, Morris, Chiat/Day
• Steel	• U.S. Steel, Bethlehem, Inland	• Nippon Steel, Nippon Kokan
		• Dow, GE Plastics
		• Alcoa
		• Nucor, Chaparral

While the incumbents battled each other, *unconventional players captured the new value.*

globalization of competition and the rise of entrepreneurism will dramatically enhance your view of the competitive field.

1. *Globalization.* "Global competition" used to mean Japan and Germany. Today it means Japan, Germany, Taiwan, Korea, India, Mexico, Singapore, Brazil, Spain, Eastern Europe, and, in an increasing number of sectors, China. This difference signals not only vulnerability (as more companies volunteer to serve your customers) but opportunity as well. In 1970, the market capitalization of the world's companies was $929 billion and 66 percent of that was in the United States. In 1993, the market capitalization of the world's companies was $12.6 trillion, with 64 percent of that *outside* the United States.

That's a great deal of market value creation. Those with a regional perspective cannot see it. Only those with a global perspective have a larger field in which to compete and create value growth.

2. *Entrepreneurism.* In 1948, there was one venture capital organization in the United States; in 1994, there were 628 venture and investment firms. The infrastructure supporting ventures has moved from nonexistent to fully developed, along every dimension: legal, accounting, recruiting, and so forth.

The number of viable entrepreneurial attacks on traditional industry leaders has exploded. They are effective for a host of reasons:

a. Infrastructure support.

b. Financial attractiveness to investors (the hope for value growth weighed against the certainty of value stagnation for many blue chips).

c. The ability to energize and motivate employees to outperform their counterparts in large, bureaucratic organizations.

d. Investment in business designs appropriate to the next cycle of value creation rather than in modifying designs that are no longer effective.

The fact that the attacks are indirect serves only to heighten their effectiveness. P&G, Nestlé, and General Foods have yet to realize that Starbucks is attacking the center of their grocery store coffee business. For years they thought of Starbucks as "cafes," not "coffee." For years, IBM, DEC, and HP thought of Microsoft as "software," not "computing." For years, JC Penney, Sears, and department stores thought of Wal-Mart as "discounting," not "retailing." For years, the networks thought of TCI as "cable," not "home video entertainment."

An important new design that is emerging is the alliance of active ingredient and scale, entrepreneur and industry leader. Iris–Lotus, Lotus–AT&T, and JetForm–Moore are just a few examples of this phenomenon. In these instances, a critical business design element is value recapture. One party (the active ingredient) can't charge enough for the value it creates. The other party (the scale owner) doesn't have the differentiation necessary to move its bulk product. The combination has the potential to create aggregate revenue and profit growth that is not achievable by either partner alone.

But perhaps the most significant implication of the entrepreneur-ial explosion is the redefinition of R&D. Value-creating R&D, value-creating innovation, used to be centered on new products and new process technology. This is no longer true. Most of the resources spent by large organizations pursuing new products and process technology do not produce returns in excess of the cost of capital. There is less yield available from the numerous R&D fields that were once extraordinarily productive. There is a depletion of blockbuster technical opportunity.

The size of the R&D "laboratory" hasn't changed, the definition has. It has shifted from beakers, molecules, and hardware architec-tures to new combinations of existing capabilities that better create customer utility and profit. The nation's top 500 laboratories are being replaced by the nation's 628 investment firms as the source of innovation that matters most, the value-creating kind. Monitoring these laboratories for emerging new business designs will be critical to early detection of Value Migration in many industries.

3. *Industry value maps.* Once you have identified the full cast of competing business designs on your radar screen, the next step is to understand their economic power and momentum. A fully functional radar screen not only indicates the presence of an intruder but also gives some indication of its size, strength, and momentum relative to your own.

First, characterize your own business design in terms of its funda-mental assumptions and its basic elements, as articulated in Chapter 2. These elements include customer selection, scope, differentiation, value recapture, purchasing, manufacturing/operations, capital intensity, organizational configuration, and go-to-market mecha-nism. Then compare your approach to that of competitors: tradi-tional, newcomers, and nontraditionals. Whose economic logic is more compelling? How significant are the differences between your design and those of the most effective new approaches, both in terms of economics and in the ability to create customer utility? The greater the differences, the more rapid the Value Migration will be.

To test your hypotheses about the relative economic power of the competing business designs, map the market value of your indus-try using the metrics described in Chapter 3. Although its judgment is hardly error free, Wall Street can help you identify those companies whose superior ability to meet future customer needs is not yet fully measured by revenue or market share. Measuring share of market value can greatly widen your field of vision and improve your ability to anticipate value shifts.

Mapping Value Migration should be done early enough so that your organization can capitalize on opportunities. The market value/revenue measure can be used to create a first approximation of relative position, and to explore the reasons behind the ratios (your own and those of your most dynamic competitors). It is also important to assign approximate market value/revenue indices to major business units within your company, allowing you to understand their relative health and profit vitality.

The basic questions to answer in the mapping process include: Where is the company (and its major business units) positioned on the market value/revenue slope? Why? How is the ability to earn a profit changing in the industry? Where is it moving from? Where is it moving to? What factors are driving the movement? Is the migration of value complete and irreversible, or partial? How rapidly is value migrating?

Once you have mapped Value Migration in your industry, see if the resulting pattern matches that in another industry. Anticipating migration is easier when managers can capitalize on the experience of others.

Applying Strategic Pattern Recognition

Together, a full understanding of the customer and a wide competitive field of vision permit managers to detect Value Migration. However, learning to anticipate Value Migration is an inductive process. Speed and skill are immeasurably enhanced by familiarity with a wide range of examples and elements of examples. As in chess, the more patterns you've mastered, the faster you are. The more cases that are understood and internalized, the easier it is for an organization to come up with an honest and accurate assessment of its true situation.

Prior examples of how value has migrated can be extremely helpful in building the patterns relevant to your industry. There is no need to repeat the strategic errors already made by others. There is, however, great value in repeating the astute moves that were made by others to capitalize on Value Migration in their industries.

When examining patterns, it is important to consider not only what happened, but how fast it happened and to what degree. Past examples can help create a framework for estimating the rate and magnitude of market value shifts for your industry (DEC declined $16 billion in six years; Bethlehem Steel, $5 billion in 16 years). Knowing rate and magnitude is essential to obtain an accurate reading of your situation, to gain a clear sense of how quickly your organization needs to move, and to assess the level of risk it should be prepared to assume.

1. *The collapse of the middle.* Across many industries there has been a shift from routine product sales to a more customer-specific bundling of price, distribution, support, and information. Movement is in one of two directions: low-cost distribution of the same products, or the conversion of products and services to value-added business solutions. Chapter 10 discussed a broad cross-section of low-cost distribution opportunities. Chapter 11 examined two examples of high-end solutions.

There are numerous other areas of opportunity for the application of these models. The arena of business forms provides an excellent example. For every $1 that customers spend on business forms, they spend $20 on the system for using the forms (labor for filling out and routing the forms, storage, revisions). What matters to the customer is not the physical product (which is abundantly available at high quality, low cost, and quick delivery), but the system that uses it. Services and solutions to rationalize the system are more complex and difficult to deliver, but that is where the future value is. The ability to outsource the entire process is more valuable still.

The same phenomenon is true in the auto industry, where the leading-edge practice is to outsource completely as many component and subassemblies as possible. This enables the car maker to focus on the handful of issues that matter the most: the design, the engine, the power train, chassis, and styling. The value is shifting from components to systems.

The pharmaceuticals industry is witnessing both sides of the collapse of the middle. At the low end, cost-effective mail-order distribution is attracting the attention of price-sensitive managed care organizations. In the two years following the Merck–Medco merger, every major pharmacy benefit manager in the country has been courted by a pharmaceutical manufacturer seeking to capitalize on this pattern of Value Migration.

At the high end, there is a shift from manufacturing pills to delivering complete disease management. The cost of pharmaceutical therapy for a patient may be $1,000–$2,000 per year. However, the overall cost of treating the disease can be as high as $30,000–$100,000 per year. The leverage is not in reducing the cost of the pill, but in reducing the cost of the disease. Payers are looking for solutions (pills plus testing plus monitoring plus management) that reduce the one number that matters: the total cost of the disease.

Across a broad spectrum of industries, low-cost distributors like Wal-Mart, The Home Depot, Dell, Grainger, and Charles Schwab have already created more than $100 billion of market value. Similarly, the shift from products to solutions is creating enormous value-creation opportunities for those willing to see them. Ultimately it leads to the outsourcing business design as a major, perhaps *the* major, engine of value growth in the future. It is a shift that has fueled EDS' growth to $19 billion in value in the past decade, and EDS is just a symbol of a process that is providing value growth to companies as diverse as Johnson Controls, Honeywell, Federal Express, Ryder, UPS, and others. Again, it is a carefully crafted business design, rather than superior technology alone, that is the value driver.

2. *The emergence of new customer sets.* For entrenched competitors, the entry of new types of customers can be disorienting and difficult to respond to effectively. In the airline industry, deregulation created a large base of price-sensitive leisure travelers. In pharmaceuticals, concern about rising health-care costs created a group of powerful organized buyers. In both industries, emergence of these groups forced suppliers to develop low-cost business designs.

Perhaps the most dramatic example of a newly emerging customer base was in computing, where the rise of the individual user drove a massive migration of value from integrated to specialized business designs. The common lesson of these diverse industry examples is the necessity to have a wide customer field of vision. Identifying emerging customer sets and evaluating their wealth, power, and basic needs can be a critical first step in creating the next wave of value growth in your industry.

3. *Migration within the value chain.* Many corporations define their mission as creating products or services. The product or service that the value chain generates is more important than any one step in the chain itself. However the most successful competitors are acutely aware of the differential strategic importance of individual steps of the value chain. They thrive by concentrating on the particular activities that allow them to capture maximum value.

In the pharmaceutical industry, Merck keenly perceived that value was shifting from basic research to blockbuster-focused development. Its business design concentrated on mastering this activity. In the early 1990s, CEO Roy Vagelos defied industry conventional wisdom and predicted that value would shift farther downstream to distribution. His conviction was borne out by the lofty multiples that Merck, SmithKline Beecham, and Eli Lilly paid to acquire some of their biggest customers, the pharmacy benefit managers.

In the computing industry, the migration within the value chain was more complex. When computer end-users were less sophisticated and proprietary architecture defined the marketplace, IBM's strategy of being an integrated provider allowed it to capture enormous value. But the open-architecture world enabled sophisticated users to break up the value chain and pay a premium for only the most scarce and critical activities. IBM realized belatedly that the key activities in the computing value chain had been taken over by its suppliers, Microsoft and Intel. While significant value has migrated upstream to suppliers, companies such as EDS and Hewlett-Packard initiated Value Migration downstream in the delivery of computing solutions to the end-user.

4. *Redefinition of the product/service offering.* Often a dramatic change in customer priorities drives Value Migration. In other cases, customer priorities evolve much more slowly. In these instances, it is new business designs that trigger Value Migration by redefining the product/service offering in the eyes of the customer.

In the coffee industry, Starbucks and the gourmet roasters capitalized on the opportunity to change the way customers thought about coffee. By using high-quality Arabica beans, they transformed the product from the daily grind into an affordable luxury. The go-to-market mechanism of European-style cafes further redefined coffee, transforming it from a beverage into an experience.

FIGURE 12-7   VALUE MIGRATION

Customers

1. Who is the customer? Are decision makers and influencers changing? If so, how do their buying criteria differ?

2. What are the customers' economics and process flow?

3. Which customers' needs are mature and require a more cost-effective solution? Which needs are emerging and require a performance solution?

4. Given the customers' economics and needs profile, how are their priorities changing?

5. What do you think will be the customers' most important future needs?

New Business Designs

6. How many distinct new business designs have been introduced in your industry in the past five years?

7. What is their customer and economic rationale?

8. How do their economics compare to yours?

9. How do their customer ratings compare to yours?

Value Movement

10. Map the Value Migration that enabled you to gain your present position. Who was the vanquished incumbent? Why?

11. What is the total market value of your industry? What is your share of that value? Who is gaining share of value most rapidly?

12. Which industries are economic neighbors of your own (e.g., steel, aluminum, plastics)? Is your industry losing value to them? Why? How rapidly?

A similar repositioning in the eyes of the customer triggered Value Migration away from the U.S. integrated steel manufacturers. In this case, aluminum producers focused on developing beer and soda cans with pop-tops, adding considerable functionality to the end product. Making cans from tin-plated steel was still possible, but no longer as attractive after the entrance of the aluminum-based business design. The new entrant fundamentally changed canners' expectations of their materials suppliers.

This pattern of Value Migration emphasizes the importance of a broad competitive field of vision. Even when customer priorities change slowly, new business designs can initiate significant value flows.

From Early Detection to Shifting the Mental Model

Measuring customer change, expanding the competitive field of vision, and seeing your industry evolution in the context of established patterns are several of the tools used to detect and anticipate Value Migration (see Figure 12-7). In the next decade, the methodology for anticipating Value Migration will become increasingly sophisticated and effective. The bottleneck, however, will lie not in method, but in mind-set. No amount of methodology can overcome the power of denial, the power of institutional memory. No amount of comparative business-design analysis will overcome the powerful psychology of disparagement that greets radically new approaches to the customer. When institutional memory is stronger than the diligent search for profit, value erosion will inevitably follow. How can institutional memory be defeated?

Chapter **13**

How to Defeat Institutional Memory

- How can I increase the likelihood that my organization will recognize the early warning signals of Value Migration?

- Is my organization capable of responding to Value Migration? How can I make it more capable?

STEEL EXECUTIVES AT THE DUQUESNE CLUB in Pittsburgh dismiss minimills and the Japanese steelmakers as marginal players. IBM cannot conceive of selling computers through the mail. Procter & Gamble insists that whole-bean coffee vendors do not compete in its market. All these are examples of institutional memory, the progressive mental narrowing that eventually leaves individuals and organizations unable to think outside the bounds of their past experience. It is the number-one cause of stagnation or demise among successful corporations.

But if symptoms and diagnoses of institutional memory seem so familiar, why do cures and preventative medicine remain so elusive? This chapter examines a sample of the corporations that have developed effective means of coping with institutional memory. First, it considers the critical role that a visionary and strong-willed leader can play in helping an organization resist the gravitational pull of conventional wisdom and industry-think. Second, it explores how several companies have woven techniques for thwarting institutional memory into the fabric of their daily operations. Finally, it proposes several specific actions for breaking the grip of institutional memory on your organization.

The Strong Leader

As chief strategist, the CEO assumes primary responsibility for setting the corporation's long-term course. In a world characterized by rapidly changing customers and competitors, globalizing markets, and chronic uncertainty, merely formulating a winning strategy is a huge challenge. But setting the course may be the easiest part of the CEO's job. Having identified where he or she wants to go, the CEO is then responsible for propelling the organization toward the desired end. An absence of memory can help.

Jack Welch—The CEO Without a Memory

There are many characteristics that have made Jack Welch famous, notorious, feared, respected, and admired. He is hard-driving and focused. He creates a simple and consistent strategic message that is communicated clearly to the organization. He is a consummate high-level marketer. And an extraordinary creator of value and value growth.

One of Welch's least noted characteristics (and perhaps the most useful in a world marked by rapid shifts in customer priorities and rapid business-design obsolescence) is the absence of strong allegiance to the past. Welch has zero institutional memory. He has no loyalty to what went before. The phrase, "We've always done it this way" is meaningless to him.

The phrase "This is what the customer wants" gets his attention. It also gets a question: "How can we make money at it?" Welch keeps his focus on the future, on the customer, and on how to create profit growth.

Perhaps this mind-set is easier for Welch because he is a GE insider who is really an outsider. He came from the plastics business in Pittsfield, Massachusetts, hardly a part of GE's historic mainstream. His formative experience there was largely one of creating a future that didn't exist, of teaching customers about Lexan, and helping customers get utility from GE's plastics product line. Success in that business hinged on creating the future rather than being a caretaker of the past.

The fact that Welch has no institutional memory and doesn't allow others to nurture their own is one of GE's most valuable assets. It also illustrates why so many outsiders have been brought in to save large, previously successful organizations. A newcomer is unencumbered by the organizational rules that created past success. A newcomer has zero mental space devoted to maintenance of an historical business design.

Like successive generations of chip architecture, business design architecture carries baggage from the past that ultimately renders it uncompetitive. At some point in the business design cycle, the mental overhead occupies so much of the available memory and processing power that the right thing to do is to write it off, and start with a new mentality.

Andy Grove—Leaping over the Chasm

Often, the CEO is so tied to the foundations of past success that he or she is incapable of vigorously embracing the new customer realities and reformulating the company's business design to meet them. To make a major change in strategic course, many companies have found it necessary to make a change in CEO.

Andy Grove is a rare exception. Twelve years after fleeing his native Hungary with $20 in his pocket, Grove helped establish Intel, a memory chip manufacturer based in California. As a founder, he had deeper roots than anyone in the memory chip production that had been the company's raison d'être since its inception. Nevertheless, he was able to see that the only profitable future for Intel lay elsewhere, and dedicated himself to destroying the old organization and building a new one.

In the 1990s, Intel has become one of the most powerful forces in computing. But the path from a Berkeley basement to Intel's current $27 billion in market value was far from linear. As recently as 1985, Intel was a money-losing manufacturer of rapidly commoditizing DRAM chips. Faced with ferocious Asian competition, Intel had fallen from first to third in global market share and was sinking fast.

The key move that reversed Intel's fortunes was Grove's decision to abandon memory chips, which store data, in favor of processor chips, which do the PC's thinking. Walking away from its expertise and corporate heritage traumatized Intel. It also saved the company.

Grove's recasting of Intel is a powerful lesson in breaking free of institutional memory. By 1985, memory chips were pure commodities. Growing buyer power and large competitors with substantial fixed assets threatened to doom Intel to an unprofitable and ultimately futile struggle to reduce costs and gain share. "There is at least one point in the history of any company when you have to change dramatically to rise to the next performance level," said Grove. "Miss that moment and you start to decline."[1]

The industry context that enabled Intel to change its business design was a shift from proprietary technology and vertical integration to open architecture. This shift meant that different firms could play in different horizontal niches, designing architecture, producing chips, assembling machines, and manufacturing peripherals. "I wouldn't say categorically that companies structured the old way cannot survive," Grove explained, "but it's hard to see them thriving. Anything that can be done in the vertical way can be done more cheaply by collections of specialist companies organized horizontally."

Grove discovered that major changes in strategic trajectory must be driven by the highest levels of the organization. "We came to realize that the formulation and articulation of strategy is the job of top management," he said. If the impetus for change comes from only one functional area, the difficult execution process becomes impossible. "Until top management recognized the shift from DRAMS to microprocessors and articulated it as a strategy, Intel suffered from what I call strategic dissonance," he continued. "While we were shifting our capacity to microprocessors, we still had our best development people working on memory projects. That made no sense."

Intel's financial picture catalyzed the difficult resource reallocation process. "Our rate of change got accelerated by the fact that we were losing a lot of money. Emotionally, it's easier to change when you're hemorrhaging." Intel has since become the world's largest semiconductor company and pace-setter in leading-edge microprocessors. "A corporation is a living organism, and it has to continue to shed its skin," Grove said. "Methods have to change. Focus has to change. Values have to change."

One key lesson from Intel's transformation, according to Grove, is that "Technology can make you lose but it can't make you a winner." To create and capture persistent value, technologies and products must be linked to successful business designs. Focusing on what customers value, then educating them about the superiority of its product and service offerings, are two critical elements of Intel's business design. Before the company's "Intel Inside" ad campaign, few end-users cared much about microprocessors. Now Intel components are a prerequisite for market-savvy hardware assemblers seeking to make their machines attractive to end-users.

Intel's goal in the mid-1990s is to manage the next strategic transition, not as a desperate bid for survival but as a proactive move from a mature strength to an emerging one. "The more successful we are as a microprocessor company, the more difficult it will be to become something else," said Grove. "To take advantage of some of the opportunities I see ahead, we're going to have to transform ourselves again. The time to do it is while our core business is still strong."

With no rising tide of red ink to create a sense of urgency, Intel will rely on distant early warning systems to trigger its next move. The key mechanism is an unremitting focus on what creates utility for computer users. "Today we're a microprocessor company with 100 million customers," said Grove. "Not the people who pay our invoices, but the end-users of PCs whose minds we have to win in order to succeed. We have to figure out what their need will be years from now, what sort of application software they'll be using." To keep its competitive field of vision wide-angled and the crippling effects of institutional memory at a minimum, Intel has also articulated its corporate mission broadly. It defines itself not as a producer of specific products such as microprocessors, but rather as the "preeminent supplier of building blocks to the new computing industry."

Another lesson in the Intel case is to look not only at absolute levels of sales, profit, or market value but also at where future growth will come from. Large, favorable numbers can distract attention from the fundamental question of how much fuel is left in the growth engine. Consider that an automobile on a highway might well attain its highest absolute speed with a tablespoon of gas in the tank.

Grove uses computer hardware assemblers as examples of companies whose institutional memory distracted them from checking the gas gauge often enough. As he puts it, "The only thing preventing the old-line [manufacturers] from exploiting [the opportunity of networking] is mind-set. Systems integration is a service, and these companies grew up bending sheet metal. They like bending sheet metal. These companies should go where the business is. They ought to make this move while the going is good."

Institutionalized Tactics

Chief executive officers who have little of their own institutional memory, and have the skill and stamina to drive that perspective throughout the organization, may be best equipped to defeat institutional memory, but they are rare. Fortunately, strong-minded CEOs are not the only mechanism. In some instances, the defenses against institutional memory rest in the fabric of the organization itself. Some companies and government bodies have been able to develop structures, cultures, or processes that combat institutional memory on an ongoing basis.

The tactics of these organizations for maintaining flexibility and a broad competitive field of vision may not attract the attention that the achievements of a Welch or a Grove do, but because the roots of the tactics extend deeper into an organization than the top spot can, they ultimately may prove more durable.

The Legitimized Contrarian

Perhaps one of the best examples of an internal safeguard against institutional memory comes from the U.S. military. More than two decades ago, the Pentagon modified its structure to ensure that a fresh viewpoint would always be represented in its strongly hierarchical organization.

The Pentagon's secret weapon in the battle against group-think is the Office of Net Assessment, headed by Professor Andrew Marshall, a nuclear strategist who joined the armed forces during the Truman administration. Marshall has been in his current post for the past 20 years. His charter: keeping an eye on the long view. His focus: How will the next war be fought and won?

In empowering Marshall, the Pentagon operated on three basic principles: (1) the power of an extraordinarily talented, farsighted individual who is allowed to dissent from conventional organizational thinking, (2) the importance of top management support and sponsorship, and (3) the value of mechanisms (such as simulation, role playing, or other nonpassive forms of communication) that allow uncomfortable contrarian thinking to seep into the mind-set of those who run the organization today and who make decisions that will determine its ability to be successful 10 years from now.

Marshall's hand guided numerous strategic successes during the Cold War. In the mid-1970s, Marshall and James Roche, now chief strategist for Northrop Grumman, drew attention to the vulnerability of European ports and spearheaded the development of the navy's plan to keep Soviet warships bottled up in the Arctic Sea. While the CIA significantly underestimated the burden of the defense budget on the Soviet state in the late 1970s, Marshall was writing a paper entitled "The Vulnerabilities of the Soviet System," which identified some of the key determinants of the collapse of communism.

Marshall has thrived as an internal outsider because he has been given the liberty to think creatively about the future, even if doing so means being at odds with military canon. At present, Marshall is challenging the received learning and basic assumptions about some of the military establishment's crown jewels: army tanks, navy aircraft carriers, and air force fighters and bombers. For a staffer enmeshed in the organization's internal politics, criticizing these programs would be professional suicide. But being critical does not jeopardize Marshall's job; it *is* his job. The Office of Net Assessment helps the U.S. military avoid being blinded by its own success. It is an institutionalized device to fight institutional memory.

A second essential element in Marshall's success has been high-level support. Every president since Nixon has given Marshall the resources to continue his mission. Other powerful Marshall backers come from within the military itself, such as Admiral William Owens, vice-chairman of the Joint Chiefs of Staff. "No one would ever agree with everything Andy says," remarked Defense Secretary William Perry, "but I always find him worth listening to." Marshall is "truly an original thinker," Perry concluded.[2]

One benefit of this high-level support is protection. If Marshall were not insulated from the major stakeholders in the programs he criticizes, he would probably be ineffective. Another benefit is that ideas actually get translated into action. For example, the army has already reallocated funds away from industrial-age weapons systems such as tanks toward information-age technology that will revolutionize global security.

The third necessary condition for Marshall's success (and that of any legitimite contrarian) is a means to achieve wider organizational buy-in to potentially unpleasant messages. One Marshall-inspired tool for changing some of the defense community's mental models was an extensive, classified war game pitting the United States against China in the year 2020. In this simulation, the United States deployed an updated version of the forces that defeated Iraq in the Gulf War. Despite the skill of military strategists and practitioners, the United States was badly routed by the Chinese, who deployed a low-cost, high-tech, off-the-shelf arsenal. The nontraditional exercise conveyed Marshall's message more effectively than any memo, presentation, or report: If the country is to maintain its global superiority, it must be willing to challenge conventional military wisdom with increased vigor. It will not win the next war the same way it won the last one.

3M: The Virtual Start-Up

The Office of Net Assessment has proved to be a valuable modification to the Pentagon's otherwise hierarchical structure and conformist culture. But the interface between Marshall and all but the most senior members of the military establishment is very indirect. For an example of how the *whole* organization can combat institutional memory, consider the 3M Corporation.

Rolling up her sleeves, a talented, entrepreneurially minded materials scientist begins tests on a synthetic fabric that promises to protect operating room personnel from germs and microbes. Earlier this morning, her business plan presentation had won strong support from her financial backers. Despite the fact that the technology would take at least five years to commercialize, they immediately provided additional funding.

Hundreds of variations of this scene are played out each year by moonlighters in university laboratories and entrepreneurs running small start-up operations. These individuals focus on nothing but the future and its myriad opportunities for value creation.

Hundreds of variations of this scene are also played out each year at one of America's largest and most venerable industrial corporations. Since its founding in 1902, 3M has grown to $15 billion in sales and more than 80,000 employees worldwide. 3M enjoys the size and success that often create debilitating institutional memory. Nevertheless, it has a system for defeating institutional memory within its organization. 3M's approach has enabled the company to undergo constant metamorphosis in tune with the marketplace, transitioning from abrasives to adhesives to chemicals to video tape to computer diskettes and other core product areas. In 1993, *The Financial Times* called 3M "the world's most innovative multinational."[3]

Although it remains a *Fortune* 50 company, 3M makes its employees believe that they work in much smaller, more flexible organizations. Through creative organizational structure and practices, 3M has created "the virtual start-up."

The first element of the virtual start-up is operating units that are kept as small as possible; 3M forces them to split repeatedly as they grow. Within each unit, employees are encouraged to use 15 percent of their time to develop and work on independent projects. Each division maintains an internal capital market to fund these efforts. If the home division fails to see the potential of a project, an individual or team can approach several alternative sources of funding within the corporation. The practice is strongly supported by top management: Each year the corporation aims to generate 25 percent of its revenues from products that did not exist five years ago.

3M has discovered that taking the long view is a key element in the battle against institutional memory. Challenging conventional wisdom requires substantial effort and does not yield immediate returns. If the time line of an organization expires with the close of the quarter, investing in unconventional thinking seems costly. A longer term view amortizes the cost of unconventional thinking over time and permits a focus on future benefits. If products developed through 3M's virtual start-up machine seem out of step with market demand, 3M places them in suspended animation. For example, a 10-year-old method for identifying and counting microbes only took off commercially in 1992, when a food-poisoning epidemic at a chain restaurant created a large, instant demand for the product. "We sold a year's supply in a week," said CEO L. D. DeSimone.[4]

This approach has focused the collective mind of the organization away from the past and toward the future. For instance, 3M's constant stream of new product introductions enables it to challenge effectively industry wisdom that profits in some categories have simply been exhausted. In the building supply area, which many considered depressed, 3M successfully commercialized a mold-resistant roofing material. "If you sit back and [accept industry opinion], you're going to rot," said DeSimone.

Powered and protected by its culture, 3M has been anything but stagnant. It now markets 60,000 products on 30 major technology platforms. Though twenty-eighth on the *Fortune* 500 in terms of sales, it is eleventh in terms of profit generation, and shareholder value has doubled in real terms since the mid-1980s. 3M has been on *Fortune*'s list of America's ten most admired companies for 10 of the past 11 years, and for a sixth consecutive year has been honored by Toyota as a top-ranked supplier.

Will 3M fall asleep on its cushion of success? Not likely. The mechanisms of the virtual start-up are at work in good times as well as bad, serving as preventive medicine against institutional memory rather than emergency surgery for a moribund company. "We are acting to stay healthy," DeSimone explained. "Many students, academics, and professors will write incessantly that you cannot change unless there's a disaster of some kind. We keep telling people that it's not true."

Royal Dutch Shell—The Culture of Questioning

Much like 3M, the Anglo-Dutch petroleum giant Royal Dutch Shell has been successful in weaving defenses against institutional memory into its business processes and corporate culture.

One of the world's greatest industrial enterprises, Shell has been called "an impressive machine for garnering capital and investing it wisely."[5] With sales of more than $100 billion, it is the world's largest petroleum concern. It commands the largest tanker fleet on the planet, pumps out over 3.5 million barrels of oil each day, owns more than 50,000 retail gas stations, and sits on a mountain of cash and marketable securities larger than the reserves of many sovereign nations. Shell's size, performance, and proud heritage might indicate a strong force field of institutional memory. Instead, the organization remains market-oriented and remarkably nimble.

Like the Pentagon, Shell has benefited by taking the long view. Unlike the military, however, Shell encourages critical self-assessment throughout the organization. Shell's culture of questioning is a product of decades of organizational paranoia. The company did not always dominate the oil industry. For much of its existence, it lived in the threatening shadow of Exxon (formerly John D. Rockefeller's Standard Oil Trust and then Standard Oil of New Jersey). In the early decades, Shell had to live by its wits as Rockefeller launched repeated price wars in different markets in an attempt to crush competition abroad as he had already done in the United States. At one point, the hostile American giant's takeover threats forced Shell to create a special class of nonvoting stock.

Shell's longstanding sense of insecurity was exacerbated by a constant shortage of crude oil. A sudden drought of crude would render useless huge downstream investments in refineries, distribution, and retailing. Ensuring a steady supply was crucial. But Shell lacked the preferential access to Middle Eastern sources that the American majors enjoyed, thanks to the backing of the U.S. government. As late as 1979, Shell bought as much as 60 percent of its crude on the open market, a much higher proportion than any of the other majors. Former Shell Managing Director Dirk de Bruyne said, "I didn't sleep for 10 years because I didn't have it [privileged access to crude oil.]"[6]

Shell's lack of secure supply forced it to develop sharp trading skills, keep downstream operations profitable, and remain hypersensitive to even remote or improbable competitive threats. This obsession with the long term resulted in the development of "scenario planning" by Pierre Wack and the strategic planning department of Shell in the late 1960s. Much studied in management circles, the process forces managers to identify their basic assumptions, expose them to the harsh light of known and knowable facts, ferret out internal contradictions, create new assumptions, and develop investment plans based on those.

Scenario planning is not gazing into a crystal ball. The process forces decision makers to reevaluate rigorously their most fundamental convictions about their businesses. The critical first step in the process is identifying predetermined events: developments that are 90 percent certain to unfold based on what has already happened, taking into account the vested interests of the key parties involved.

When Shell planners considered the vested interests of the largest oil-producing states in the early 1970s, they found that none had both the ability and the incentive to produce more oil. In an environment of rapidly increasing demand, a shortage was a foregone conclusion; the oil embargo was a predetermined event. One lesson of this brilliant and highly profitable application of scenario planning is that much of the future is actually knowable to a high degree of certainty, given a rigorous examination of the facts. To highlight the importance of exploiting already available information, Wack cites a French proverb: "A poorly examined fact is more dangerous than wrong reasoning."[7]

After defining predetermined events, the scenario-planning process turns to critical uncertainties. Some elements of the future, of course, remain unknowable. When confronted with a range of uncertainties, however, it is possible to identify the relatively small number of uncertainties most critical to the future profitability and growth of a business. These revolve around how key players—competitors, customers, suppliers, and developers of key technology—will respond to the predetermined events. In Shell's case, the critical uncertainties were the reactions of Western governments and the rest of the Seven Sisters to the impending oil shortage.

Armed with a list of predetermined events and critical uncertainties, managers can revisit the "trouble-free" projections of the future that they held coming into the scenario planning. The key question becomes, "What would be necessary for the 'trouble-free' outcome to unfold?" Often, the predetermined events and critical uncertainties totally undermine management's incoming assumptions. Achieving management buy-in to the new findings rarely poses a problem. Unlike a memo or report, the scenario-planning process has tremendous power to jar management out of its comfortable conception of the future as a linear projection of the past. The key advantage of scenario planning is that it is the management team itself which generates the predetermined events and critical uncertainties that expose the flaws in its prior thinking. It effectively communicates a critical but uncomfortable message.

While scenario planning shatters old visions, it also generates a series of alternative, different "future worlds" that extend far beyond management's conventional thinking. The common foundation of all the future worlds is the list of predetermined events. Different critical uncertainties give each world its distinctive characteristics. Two worlds being pondered by Shell planners in the early 1990s were dubbed "Sustainable World" and "Global Mercantilism." In the first, the United States, Japan, and the EC avoid a trade war. The ensuing pattern of stable economic growth allows governments to focus on a wide range of environmental concerns, shifting energy consumption from oil to cleaner burning natural gas. "Global Mercantilism" describes a world of hostile trading blocs and economic instability. In this scenario, environmental issues become a prisoner's dilemma, no lasting international agreements on emissions reductions are reached, and oil consumption keeps rising.

If future worlds are to expand management's mental models, they must meet several conditions. First, they must describe fundamentally different worlds, not simply different outcomes in the same world. Each world must also be internally consistent. Finally, the worlds must push management to address something other than that indicated by past experience. The point of generating these worlds is not to determine which is more probable, but to broaden the field of vision to include a full range of threats and opportunities.

During the first oil crisis, Shell turned scenario planning into a key source of competitive advantage. In early 1973, Shell distributed a pink book to government leaders, warning that the supply-and-demand dynamics of oil were dangerously unbalanced and that a scramble for limited supplies could happen at any time. When the eventual crisis came, the organization's prior planning enabled it to respond far more effectively than its American rivals. The other majors went into crisis mode, centralized all control, and sought favor with OPEC members. In contrast, Shell decentralized decision-making power to the operating units, which faced very different local situations, and directed resources away from the Middle East to more reliable sources of crude. According to one industry expert, "In 1970, Shell had been considered the weakest of the seven largest oil companies. By 1979, it was perhaps the strongest."[8]

Clearly, Shell's investment in scenario planning paid off. But in the early 1980s, Shell realized that it was not fully capitalizing on all its potential benefits. The impediments to realizing the full benefits were twofold. First, scenario planning was used in an irregular,

episodic fashion. Second, its use was restricted to the strategic planning group. To remedy these problems, Shell began integrating the
first principles of scenario planning—articulating expectations, identifying underlying assumptions, subjecting those assumptions to
close scrutiny—to the annual group-planning process performed
throughout the corporation at the business unit level.

The new system enables line managers in all of Shell's 260 SBUs
to "think together in a systematic and disciplined way."[9] Managers
integrate the principles of scenario planning into their annual business plan development in four phases:

- Generation of multiple scenarios
- Assessment of competitive positioning
- Refinement of strategic vision
- Management of options

As a result, a higher degree of questioning assumptions and
challenging conventional wisdom is now woven into the fabric of
Shell's corporate culture. Scenario planning is now a companywide
antidote to institutional memory.

Since 1980, Shell has overtaken Exxon to become the largest
and most profitable petroleum company in the world. Between 1980
and 1994, shareholder value increased from $22 billion to $58 billion.

The First Steps in the Battle

The mechanisms employed by the Department of Defense, 3M, and
Shell to maintain organizational flexibility and stimulate "out of the
box" thinking required years, in some cases decades, to develop.
Their evolution has absorbed substantial resources and has been
catalyzed by the unique circumstances of those organizations.
Clearly, it would be difficult, if not impossible, simply to graft these
solutions onto another organization and expect the same high-
quality results.

However, some aspects or versions of these tools are readily
transferable. For example, organizations of virtually any size can use
scenario planning to expand their competitive fields of vision, gain
an early reading on emerging customer priorities, and shake off old
assumptions that do not match reality.

HOW TO DEFEAT INSTITUTIONAL MEMORY

At one printing company, the management team's scenario-planning exercise generated two very different future worlds. One centered on a vastly expanded information superhighway, which would enable consumers of printed material to read, shop, and entertain themselves electronically. Another focused on rapid advances in software technology and a changing regulatory regime. Each world had very different implications concerning what customers would be willing to pay for and which competitors would try to meet those priorities. Based on its analysis of predetermined events and critical uncertainties, the management team was able to focus its strategic thinking and prioritize future investments.

Successful scenario planning demands preparation. Perhaps the most important prerequisite to a fruitful session is a well-developed, objective fact base covering the key parties and their vested interests. Whether employees or consultants, the individuals preparing the information must have objectivity, ample time to absorb the information, and most important, the skill to avoid examining the facts poorly. Depending on the rate of change in a particular industry, companies may benefit from a full scenario-planning session every one to three years.

In addition to strong CEO leadership and institutionalized processes, there are several specific techniques and practices that an organization can use to keep institutional memory in check.

1. *Visit your customers' conventions, not your own.* Every company invests considerable resources to keep up with developments in its industry. Industry conventions reinforce industry-think. They are not the place to be. The place to be is at your customers' conventions. They are an opportunity to learn customer language, concerns, and frustrations. They let you learn customer-think, which provides a constant challenge to the hidden assumptions that your organization holds dear.

2. *Change your company's informational diet.* Every company is inundated with data on its financials and its primary, traditional competitors. Change the blend. Introduce a flow of information about customers' financials, buying criteria, systems costs, and so forth. Also start a flow of information about new, "small," apparently remote competitors (the kind that history has shown can achieve value leadership within five to seven years). Maintain a database of IPOs in any area that could be remotely construed as a part of your

industry. Again, this change in information flow will challenge your organization's most strongly held assumptions.

3. *Aggressively recruit talent from industries other than your own.* Hiring primarily from within your industry leads to the in-breeding of ideas that makes it difficult to see how the customer has changed. Deliberately hiring talent from outside will generate different perspectives. The debate engendered by a flow of new ideas can be irritating and uncomfortable, but may save the company.

4. *Determine a date when your present business design will be obsolete and articulate why.* The ultimate forcing function. Not a pleasant exercise, but potentially a company-saving move.

5. *Have lunch once a quarter with a venture capitalist or money manager active in your industry.* The opinions you hear will be radically different from your industry's and your company's. Unfettered by industry-think and more intently focused on maximizing investment returns, an investor's views can help sharpen your own as to where future value opportunities lie and what changes in your business design are necessary to capitalize on them.

Institutional memory is a funny sort of malady. The more successful the company, the stronger the effect of the disease. It's almost as if the fundamental nature of success is self-limiting.

A company can certainly rely on an exceptional CEO to defeat institutional memory. But an organization need not bet its future on the extraordinary action of an extraordinary individual. Legitimizing a contrarian (or a team of them), aspiring to a certain rate of change (as in the case of 3M), diffusing a method for constant rechallenge of assumptions, and utilizing the less formal but powerful tools listed above are all effective and more enduring methods.

The rising rate of unprofitability in large companies shows that customer priorities change more rapidly than business designs do. Institutional memory slows (or even prevents) the introduction of new business designs. Every organization can use the methods described above to defeat institutional memory, allowing it to achieve sustained success with its customers and its shareholders alike.

Chapter 14

How to Profit from Value Migration

- How can I protect the value of my existing business design?
- How can I take advantage of Value Migration by creating a new, more powerful business design?

ANTICIPATING VALUE MIGRATION arms you with the impetus to change. It allows you to see threats to your business, to recognize the need to adjust to changing customer priorities and new competitive business designs. It also allows you to see new opportunities that can be the source of future value growth, if you can develop the appropriate business design. Overcoming institutional memory creates organizational momentum and alignment around those opportunities and threats.

These efforts will create no value for your organization, however, if you are not able to develop the capabilities to profit from Value Migration. Profiting comes down to two tasks—creating new business designs while extending the useful economic life of old ones.

Developing strategic business designs is a critical new corporate skill. Developing that skill systematically is difficult. There is no organizational box labeled "Business Design" or "New Business Design Development" or "Business Design R&D." There are no individuals with formal training in "business design." There is no specific budget for business design either. Creating an effective business design is the task that matters most (to customers and shareholders), and yet it is the one for which the company is least prepared. It does not require enormous resources, but it does require great skill. In a way, business design creation is as leveraged today as R&D used to be, when R&D was the primary generator of new value growth.

Future Value Growth: Building the Next-Generation Business Design

The fundamental goal of top executives is to grow the value of their companies. With the steady compression of the business design lifecycle, it is critical that management invest time today to develop the business design of tomorrow. For small companies headed by visionary entrepreneurs, being forward-looking comes naturally; it is necessary for mere survival. For established global giants cushioned by large revenue streams, embracing the future is often more difficult. As the rapid migration of value away from IBM and other large competitors illustrates, an established position is no guarantee of long-term security. It is only by focusing on crafting new business designs that a company can hope to participate in the next cycle of value growth.

Although the task of developing a business design is challenging, a systematic approach can make that task substantially more manageable (see Figure 14-1). It makes certain that all the right questions are asked in an effective sequence. The critical creative part of the sequence is Step 5, which challenges management to generate the broadest range of options before narrowing the focus to the two or three leading candidates. The process is painstaking, but with so much future profit at stake, it deserves at least as much thought as is devoted to administrative matters (which routinely consume several times more senior professional hours than business design).

It is the combination of multiple dimensions that determines the value creation power of a given business design. Success is defined by the integration of the complete package. Incomplete business designs fail (for example, differentiated technology that does not have an effective go-to-market mechanism). Inherently inconsistent designs fail (everyday low-price retailing without a low-cost infrastructure). Overinflated business designs may do a great job of satis-

FIGURE 14-1   BUSINESS DESIGN PROCESS

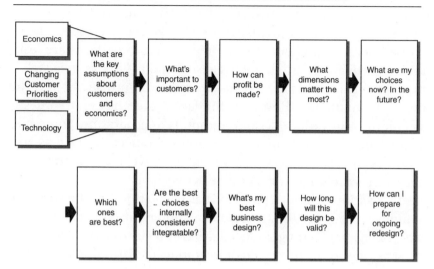

fying customer priorities, but they do not capture value in a sustainable way (witness the rapid rise—and fall—of People Express).

Analysis of how strategic business design has been applied in the examples used throughout this book provides a set of guidelines that will make your first attempts more productive, effective, and powerful.

1. *Bring the customer directly into the design process.* Although business designs can benefit from close customer contact in every phase of their lifecycles, perhaps nowhere can the customer be as great a source of value as in the initial development of the business design. Conventional market research and focus groups are standard vehicles for testing the viability of a new business concept. But only by investigating decision-making processes and changing priorities will you gain a complete strategic understanding of the customer. The process is uncomfortable, ego-bruising, and extremely valuable.

2. *Use models and precedents from other industries.* Business design is both a rigorous and creative process. You can save significant time and other resources by borrowing elements from companies within and outside your industry. A business design's economic power depends on how it functions as a total system. Familiar, borrowed, or seemingly unremarkable business design elements can generate tremendous value when combined in an original way.

Perhaps the most critical element in most business designs is value recapture. It is the mechanism that allows the provider to create utility *while making a profit*. This issue has become especially important because traditional value recapture mechanisms are losing their effectiveness. In chemicals distribution, for example, falling margins mean that service can no longer be provided "free" but must be unbundled. However, the last decade has also witnessed significant innovation in value-recapture mechanisms. Some have created great revenue stability, or "annuity power," as well as great profit. Astute business design architects have realized that these approaches are often transferrable across industries.

Innovation in value recapture has been critical to the success of a number of business designs. EDS and other outsourcers (once they have built a very strong knowledge base on customers) have moved value recapture from systems integration fees to multiyear, fixed-price outsourcing contracts—an application of the "annuity power" principle for revenue stability and high profit levels. GE has moved to recapture value by shifting its emphasis from manufacturing equipment to the financing of it. Arrowhead and Ionics (water treatment companies) have shifted from selling water treatment units to selling "water." They deliver water of a specified purity. As in the case of GE's financing business, this shift responds to customer priorities by providing what the customer requires without the customer having to add capital expenditures onto its balance sheet.

Other cases of innovative value recapture are not intentional, but gifts. For the movie studios, the invention of the VCR and the establishment of the video store (and then the video store chain) created a powerful new value-recapture mechanism, without the studios having to lift a finger. All they had to do was negotiate the contracts.

Among the studios, Disney has gone the furthest to develop new value-recapture approaches. The company sought to harness the full potential value of its creative output with theme parks, books, tapes, apparel, new product lines (watches and the like), licensing, developing a retail store chain, and so forth. Disney is perhaps the best single example of maximizing value through the purposeful creation of a dozen different vehicles to recapture the full value of the original creative output of a firm, in a way that no amount of high pricing would have made possible.

Many companies are failing to follow Disney's lead, failing to recapture the value of their brand names and the power of their creative and technical capabilities. These organizations are sitting on underutilized assets that could create significant market value if linked to creative value-recapture mechanisms.

The emerging market for disease management in the U.S. health-care market is another example of creative value recapture. As pharmaceutical companies experiment with actually managing patients for a fee (capitation), they are being paid by the market for the expertise that they have built up. This extension of the value-recapture mechanism will allow pharmaceutical companies to protect the value that they have created in building a knowledge base about a disease in the face of dramatically reduced margins on their traditional products.

Effective value recapture is often closely dependent on scope (the dimensions of a business design are rarely independent). For Coca-Cola, its multibusiness system consisting of grocery (where its share is 1 to 1 versus Pepsi), restaurants (where it wins 2:1), vending machines (3:1), and international markets (4:1) is as important to value generation as the quality of Coke's advertising. Margins in grocery are good, in restaurants they're excellent, and in vending machines and international markets they're extraordinary. Coca-Cola couldn't recapture the profits in the restaurant, vending, and international sectors without the strong brand position in grocery. The company's scope allows it to capture value in the most profitable segments.

Microsoft's operating-system-plus-applications business design represents a similar link between scope and value recapture. Microsoft gains control through the operating system, and earns additional profits on the applications. That business design is more important to Microsoft's value growth than the quality of its technology.

3. *Acquire the relevant new core competences.* The art of business design is more than building on existing core competences. When developing fundamental assumptions and bringing the customer into the business design process, you may learn that your core competences are simply not valued by the customer.

Though painful, this realization should not be allowed to dull the imperative to develop new business designs. Broadcast networks need to develop cable programming positions and expertise. Mechanical equipment makers need to acquire electronic and electromechanical capabilities.

Powerful precedents indicate that daring to step beyond existing core competences can yield extraordinary returns. Acquisitions and p>shrewd internal capital and talent allocation permitted Kansas City Southern to transform itself from a railroad into a financial services company, dramatically increasing shareholder value. Iron ore producer M.A. Hanna bought into the plastics business and vaulted back into the value inflow stage within the materials industry.

4. *Protect your new business design from the traditional organization.* Many successful organizations are averse to new business designs that look different, reflect different norms and values, and succeed in different ways. If a new business design is commingled with the existing structure, it will be drawn by the gravitational pull of the old ways of doing business and be crushed.

Astute CEOs have gone out of their way to protect new business designs, separating them from the base organization until they reach critical mass and can then be integrated into the company's overall structure. One pharmaceutical firm kept its nascent biotech unit outside its traditional R&D organization's boundaries so it could move at the rapid pace set by leading biotech rivals. IBM developed the PC in Boca Raton, not at Armonk headquarters. In a printing company, the CEO kept a new service delivery unit separate until it was strong enough to be a partner, rather than a servant, of the base organization. In each case, the company's overall position with customers improved dramatically because of the company's broadened repertoire of skills for solving customer problems.

In the past decade, it has become increasingly acceptable to start new business designs outside the existing organizational framework. When Honda introduced the Acura, it used a completely separate dealer organization. Toyota and Nissan did the same with Lexus and Infiniti, respectively. At Toyota, this separation enabled the company to achieve extraordinary levels of customer service, advancing the frontiers of business design even for a company as innovative in the field as Toyota.

Maximize the Value of Your Existing Business Design

Entrepreneurs and venture capitalists create business designs from blank sheets of paper. As noted, executives in large corporations must be able to do the same within their organizations: recognizing, incubating, and developing the value-generating business designs of tomorrow. However, executives in large enterprises are also charged with maximizing the value resident in existing business designs. The first step in this process is introspection.

1. *Critically examine your existing design.* Marketing managers have learned that the only way to preserve a leadership position is to attack their own products before competitors do. Similarly, strategists must recognize that the first step toward maximizing the value of an existing business design is to expose it to brutally honest scrutiny.

At the outset, the most important step is evaluating fundamental assumptions. These assumptions support and shape the other elements of the business design. No process is more difficult because so many of the assumptions have never been made explicit. But no process is more valuable, since assumptions are the genetic code that determines long-term success or failure. As a reminder of the importance of assumptions, consider Toyota, as described in Chapter 2. Ohno and Shingo reversed five key assumptions and set the genetic code for a business design that created three decades of value growth.

If the existing fundamental assumptions are still valid, then the business design retains substantial value-generating power. The task of management must focus on value protection. If the assumptions have become obsolete and invalid, the business design's stream of future earnings will be weak and decline over time. In this case, the priority becomes efficiently managing the decline. In either instance, maximizing the business design's existing value requires early and decisive action.

2. *Protect your value.* If your fundamental assumptions still match your customers' priorities and the economic logic of your industry, your value position is still viable. In this case, you should focus on modifying your business design in order to prolong the value stability phase and avoid slipping into value outflow.

The basis of successful value protection is optimizing the economics of the existing business design. Complexity reduction, reengineering, and other initiatives to lower cost structure are value-protecting actions. On the revenue side, mature businesses can protect value by reinforcing their franchises with their most important customers. When companies successfully execute these and other value protection initiatives, they create a stable financial platform from which to look for new value growth opportunities. When they fail, they quickly slip through stability into value outflow.

One example of a preventable migration was the flow from the steel to the plastics industry for automotive and machinery applications. This value outflow was preventable because the customer was looking for higher performance and functionality, not just lower price. The customer placed a premium on such characteristics as lighter weight, corrosion resistance, and greater formability. Timely investment by the steel companies in product performance R&D would have moderated the incursions of GE, Dow, and Borg-Warner.

Improvement in the properties of steel in the past five years have made it much more competitive against other materials across many applications. But the improvement came too late. First, the steel industry is a shadow of its former self. Second, it is too late to deter continued investment by the plastics makers. A determined counterattack a decade ago would have reduced the growth rate of plastic, reduced plastics' funds for investment in R&D and manufacturing, reduced the prospect for future growth, and therefore reduced management's appetite for investment. Today, however, the plastics business is very important to GE, Dow, and the other players. They will not withdraw without a fight. In fact, they are looking for more growth. The migration that was preventable 10 years ago has become irreversible.

In the United States, consumer packaged goods and automobiles are two sectors in which migration has been self-inflicted. In consumer packaged goods, unrelenting price increases have fundamentally broken the integrity of the value equation for the customer. In automobiles, poor quality and lackluster design have driven customers to competitors. In both industries these trends continue to threaten some competitors. But each industry has players that effectively protect value: P&G in consumer packaged goods, and Ford in automotive.

CONSUMER PACKAGED GOODS. Unlike technology-intensive categories, consumer packaged goods historically have enjoyed extremely long lifecycles. Cycles were measured in decades (Ivory and Coke are 100 years old; Tide is 50). Important pillars of this stability included the relative price insensitivity of customers, the importance of brand in communicating quality, and the positive impact of cumulative marketing investment. The best consumer franchises became extremely durable. Only sustained neglect could erode and undermine them.

However, this is precisely what unfolded in the 1980s. During this decade, the packaged goods manufacturers increased customer utility very little. What they did increase—dramatically—was price, which rose relentlessly at twice the rate of inflation. Brands began the decade 20–30 percent more expensive than their generic alternatives. By the early 1990s, brands were often 100 percent more expensive than generics.

Management's pricing behavior pumped value toward the consumer goods companies in a dramatic—and unsustainable—way. The collapse in value that followed (1991–1993) was inevitable. Aggressive pricing drove the consumer to search aggressively for other options.

Yet even the mass exodus of customers failed to create a sense of urgency in most packaged goods companies. In contrast, P&G spared no effort to arrest this outflow, and, in fact, arrested it through exemplary value protection measures. P&G realized that scale and point-of-sale information technology were causing power to flow from manufacturers to retailers. Furthermore, the packaged goods companies' primary marketing vehicle, network TV advertising, was becoming less effective and less cost-effective every year. In this environment, industry price increases, unaccompanied by increases in quality or improvements in customer utility, were eroding the brand loyalty of many consumers.

As early as 1987, P&G and Wal-Mart jointly developed an innovative business design for the management of large-scale manufacturer-retailer relationships. Interface and systems costs were cut significantly, creating enormous economic benefit. Inventory turns increased dramatically as well. P&G moderated the rate at which value and power flowed to Wal-Mart.

P&G also shut down marginal plants and discontinued marginal products. Furthermore, it understood that the only counterbalance to retailer power was innovation, and it increased its rate of new product launches significantly. Also, because of the deteriorating economics of the old business design, P&G had to perform product development differently. Development could no longer be regional—it had to be global. P&G moved quickly in that direction.

Today, every development project is geared toward global launch within several months of introduction in the product's first regional market.

P&G also moved to reduce the industry's irrational price dance, which went as follows: raise list price, issue coupons, conduct many sales. Then, do it all over again. All this activity served to confuse and annoy the consumer. P&G developed an everyday low-pricing program that, although only partially successful, dampened the swings in price irrationality in the supermarket and began a movement toward greater integrity in the pricing process.

Despite all these efforts, there is no question that the genie has been let out of the lamp. Credible, high-quality, generic alternatives have been established; store brands continue to gain force. Without the actions P&G took, value migration would have accelerated. Because of vigorous and timely changes in its business design, P&G has at least arrested the migration process in its base businesses. This effort, coupled with aggressive value growth initiatives, has enabled P&G to buck the trend of its peers. From 1991 to 1994, P&G's market value grew $9 billion. Meanwhile, the market values of many of its competitors have dropped.

AUTOMOTIVE. As in the case of packaged goods, the U.S. auto industry possessed a viable profit position in the stability zone. In the late 1970s, however, the industry seemed to want to drive customers and profits away. Costs grew, quality deteriorated, and design stagnated. As a result, the 1980–1983 recession was far deeper for the Big Three than it had to be.

Since the early 1980s, Chrysler and Ford have succeeded in preventing terminal migration away from their position (GM is still struggling). Ford's value protection initiatives are most instructive. Management took dramatic action to reduce costs, improve quality, and introduce a customer-driven product development process. Collectively, these measures effectively protected the value of a company faced with preventable, rather than irreversible, migration.

When a business design's fundamental assumptions are still valid, value protection initiatives can optimize profit generation. P&G and Ford illustrate ways in which astute and tenacious companies can fine-tune elements of their business designs to prolong their economic lives. However, the logic of Value Migration eventually pushes business designs from stability to value outflow, where a new set of initiatives is required.

3. *Limit value outflow.* When evolving customer priorities, competition from new business designs, external shocks, or an industry's changing economics invalidate a business model's most basic assumptions, the best course is to withdraw investment in a value-maximizing way.

CREATIVELY UNDERINVEST IN THE OLD BUSINESS DESIGN. Radically cutting off investment funds to current sources of cash flow is always a dangerous strategy. If you begin underinvesting early enough, however, it is unnecessary. The key is to focus on capacity maintenance (and improvement of cost position) and to fight actively against the inevitable tendency to overshoot investment in the old design. Thus, it becomes critically important to use capital budgeting to ask, for example: Do we need another blast furnace or mainframe factory? Or are we better off reducing our capacity and investing to improve its cost and quality position?

Creative underinvestment aggressively questions the logic of capacity additions. It causes less to be invested in the old business design, redirecting investment from capacity expansion toward cost improvement and demand generation.

The key concept in this underinvestment process is not value abandonment, but value protection—management in a way that extends the useful economic life of the old design. Value protection is critical to providing funding for the new design and for the acquisition of new capabilities.

Frequently the issue is not money, but mind-set. "We stick to our knitting," the philosophy goes. Fair enough, unless knitting is becoming irrelevant and customers are no longer permitting you to profit from it.

COMPRESS THE COST-REDUCTION CYCLE. When Value Migration occurs, radically changing the cost structure of the old business design is imperative. But *how* it is changed makes all the difference.

Typically, cost reductions are delayed and then made across-the-board (e.g., eliminate 10 percent from every department). They are not oriented toward what the business design should look like at the end of the reduction process. Consequently, the effort usually fails. In fact, cost reduction and internal reengineering more often than not misconstrue the fundamental nature of the problem. The point is not to become more efficient at activities that are losing customer and economic relevance, but rather to alter the business design in a way that matches customer demands and is consistent with the new economic order in your industry.

Changing your business design to anticipate Value Migration requires that you ask which capabilities, functions, and competences are no longer relevant. Which ones still have value (from a customer perspective)? Which new functions and capabilities must we develop or acquire to be successful in the future?

The difference in mind-set and outcomes between a delayed, across-the-board cost reduction approach and a Value Migration–driven business design approach is illustrated by two companies, both experiencing the flight of value away from traditional proprietary minicomputer design and manufacturing (see Figure 14-2). The first competitor, A, moved quickly to reduce cost and protect its resource-generating ability despite rapid revenue decline. The second competitor, B, continued to hope that its business would be viable, and moved much more slowly. It thus generated *no* resources for reinvestment in a new business design.

Competitor B's mind-set was reflected in the mix of its cost reduction. It cut selling cost by 30 percent, R&D by 30 percent, overhead by 40 percent, and manufacturing by 40 percent—a classic

FIGURE 14-2   COST REDUCTION TIMING

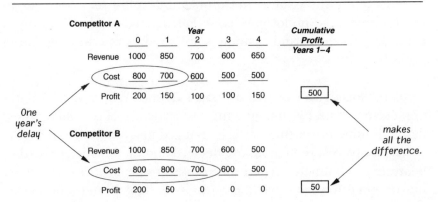

across-the-board approach. In contrast, Competitor A reduced selling expense by 70 percent, making a traumatic but necessary shift from a direct sales approach to lower-cost distribution channels. It cut overhead by 60 percent, manufacturing by 30 percent, and R&D by 20 percent. Within R&D, the mix of expenditure shifted from hardware to software, and within hardware from proprietary to open systems. By year four, its strategy was generating strong new revenue and profit growth, while Competitor B slid toward bankruptcy.

Major, painful cost reductions are inevitable when business designs lose their economic relevance. The best defense is to ask at the time the strategy is set and the business design is developed: How long will this strategy and this business design be good for? History shows that this crucial question must always be asked, and in today's business landscape, it must be asked frequently and insistently.

Profit Principles: Managing Value Migration on an Ongoing Basis

This chapter has focused on strategies and tactics that allow managers to profit from Value Migration in their industries. Most have been situation-specific, related to the protection of a stable business design, the efficient movement away from an obsolete design, or the building of a new one. But there are overarching guidelines that can help maximize the total value of a corporation on an ongoing basis.

1. *Keep 10–30 percent of your investment and revenue in the value inflow phase.* Value Migration has significant portfolio implications. If 100 percent of the organization's revenue is in the outflow phase, value growth is impossible. If a critical mass of revenue is in the inflow phase, significant value growth can be achieved even by very large organizations. Maintaining at least 10–30 percent of revenue in the inflow phase is a powerful forcing function. It energizes the search for new business designs, and it limits the amount of investment in obsolete ones.

2. *Be more demanding of the business plans you examine.* If you aren't reading a lot of new business plans, that's a warning signal in itself. Most business plans today do not pass muster in terms of realistic prospects for value growth. If page 1 of the plan does not state

a. The unique value proposition, and how long it will be unique (any duration more than 6–8 quarters is suspect),

b. Which customers will be served (and which will not) and why,

c. What the scope of activities will be (in terms of products and services and value chain steps) and why, and

d. What the value recapture approach will be,

the rest of it does not deserve your time. It simply won't matter unless these four issues hold out some hope for profitability and value creation.

Being brutally demanding of a business plan either will bring it into the zone of potential profitability or make it clear that it cannot be profitable. Most business designs fail for predictable customer, economic, or competitive reasons. Better to spot these defects at the business plan stage, when they can be rethought, than at the market stage, when the cost of repair and redirection is enormous.

3. *At transition time, move quickly.* The transition from stability to value outflow can be very rapid. Although traditional organizational approaches may argue for gradualism, at the transition points between Value Migration phases the external rate of change is so discontinuous that gradualism can be fatal. Better to say "the game has changed, perhaps abruptly, and we must change with it," than to debate and incrementalize your way into stagnation.

Rapid action is necessary for several reasons. First, there is usually not enough room in the new "value space" to accommodate all the traditional players and the new competitors. The first mover gets the lion's share of profit and value growth. Furthermore, the odds of implementing a successful new business design are far higher for a company if it starts its transformation as Value Migration is just beginning to accelerate. With a large market capitalization, companies can ensure the financing required to move in new directions and to acquire the resources and capabilities needed to thrive in the new environment. After customers start leaving, however, market value shrinks, financing is more difficult and expensive to obtain, and competitors are likely to have already staked out strong positions in the new value space. Eventually, a company crosses the point of no return; it is unable to create a new business design that can achieve profitability and heads either for bankruptcy or long-term stagnation.

Can Giants Grow Their Market Value?

Value creation is always difficult. It is the most difficult at the two extremes of the spectrum. For very small companies, failure rates are extremely high. For the very largest companies, the sheer quantity of value to be protected is daunting.

Although size is certainly a challenge to future value growth, it is not an insurmountable one. It can be met by anticipating how Value Migration will occur in your industry and by developing the business designs that will enable your organization to be its beneficiary rather than its victim. Very large companies can achieve and sustain value growth, despite (or perhaps because of) the significant Value Migration in their industries (see Figure 14-3).

For the ambitious company, competitive stability is a curse. The intensity of Value Migration has increased in the 1990s, and it is

FIGURE 14-3   CAN GIANTS GROW THEIR MARKET VALUE?

| | Market Value* | |
	1984	1994
AT&T	40	89
GE	37	123
HP	12	26
Motorola	6	34
Disney	4	26
EDS	5	20
Intel	5	27

The big can be nimble in the game of business chess.

SOURCE: CDI Value Growth Database.
*in billions of 1994 dollars.

likely to remain high for the foreseeable future. The ambitious will be blessed. Understanding how the migration process works, anticipating its major movements, and making the right strategic moves will enable even the largest companies to create value growth for their customers, shareholders, and employees. Profiting from Value Migration requires the invention of new business designs and the smart management of old ones—strategic moves in the game of business chess. As we will see in the last chapter, how these few key moves are made—and when—will determine which companies will succeed in creating sustained value growth.

Chapter 15

Five Moves . . . or Fewer

- ■ What five moves will capture most of the value growth in my industry?

ACHIEVING SUSTAINED VALUE GROWTH has become an increasingly high-risk, high-stakes activity. The critical importance of understanding and making the right value creation moves has never been more urgent.

Remember IBM. There were five key Value Migration moves to be made by a leader who had been accustomed to parrying competitors' moves for decades:

1. Take back the processor chip from Intel.
2. Take back the operating system from Microsoft.
3. Cover the EDS move in systems integration.
4. Cover the Novell move in network software and distribution.
5. Cover the Dell move in low-cost distribution.

The combined effect of all these actions would have not only protected IBM's value, but enabled modest value growth—an extraordinary accomplishment for so large a mass of value (IBM was worth $111 billion in 1983).

It was, in fact, five key moves that created that enormous value in the first place:

1. 1953—shift from tabulating to computing.
2. 1950s—use every corporate resource to achieve unquestioned leadership in computing by 1959.
3. 1964—introduce the IBM 360 mainframe, the new computing paradigm, and the new business design for the industry.
4. 1960s—force entry into the Japanese market.
5. 1981—launch the PC.

For Intel, it was two moves that determined most of its value growth:

1. 1985—shift from DRAMs to microprocessor chips.
2. 1980s—streamline the product development cycle to maintain six quarters of uniqueness.

There is no question that IBM opened the door for Intel by designing the Intel processor into the PC. There is also no question that Intel walked through the door, closed it, and bolted it against all others.

In 1995, Intel is at another critical juncture. Again, two moves will make all the difference:

1. Defeat the IBM-Motorola RISC chip.
2. Become the standard chip in video communications.

For Merck's Vagelos, there were two key moves a decade apart that were responsible for most of the company's $33 billion value growth:

1. 1978—rework the company's business design to focus exclusively on projects with blockbuster potential.
2. 1990—pull resources out of the traditional business design (reduce the sales force, overhead, and other nonessential costs), and build a sophisticated key-account management program while acquiring Medco to ensure control of distribution.

In each case, some of Merck's competitors followed with similar moves. Glaxo's brilliant success in the 1980s resulted in large part from its blockbuster focus. SmithKline Beecham followed Merck into the distribution business. This rapid following suggests that these competitors understand the urgency of preempting the markets of tomorrow to gain large returns.

For Nucor's Iverson, there were two key moves in the mid-1980s that transformed the modest minimill into a steel powerhouse:

1. Find an alternative to scrap (iron carbide).
2. Develop a way to make narrow, strip flat-rolled steel.

Iverson has moved several years ahead of the other minimills. It will be interesting to observe what competitors' catch-up moves will be.

A High-Stakes World

These kinds of major, strategic moves—Value Migration moves—are the critical choices that a company makes to capture and control most of the value in its industry's next cycle of value growth. They are moves that preempt markets. They may involve technology choices, creation of required scale at certain parts of the value chain, or the development of an entirely new offering that gives added utility to customers. As in chess, they are the critical initiatives that define how the rest of the game can be played. They create a position, a configuration of forces that all competitors will have to respond to. Value Migration moves are the ones that have the highest risks and the highest returns. They define a company's direction.

It takes no more than five moves to capture most of the value in your industry's next value growth cycle. That's a sobering thought. You really have to be good at business chess to win the new Value Migration game. You have to sharpen your intuition to detect when the next critical juncture will occur and what major moves will be in play, and then concentrate on choosing the right business design. As in chess, when you take your hand off the piece you just moved, you are committed. As in chess, one false move can spell the end of the game, or mean years of fighting a rear-guard action to recover.

It's uncomfortable to come to terms with the high-stakes nature of value growth. It's a fundamentally different game than TQM or reengineering, where making hundreds of small right decisions are critical to success. The nature of the Value Migration game and how it is played has changed the tactics from "many small" right actions to "a few big" right ones. It will be a challenge for many leaders who succeeded with "many small" right decisions to become equally effective in the "few big" decisions world.

It's important to see, however, that this transition is an integral part of the underlying shift in the business landscape. Several parallel developments symbolize this transition.

Twenty years ago, for example, the vast majority of trades on the New York Stock Exchange (more than 80 percent) were small transactions. Block trades (more than 10,000 shares) were the exception. Today, block trades account for more than 55 percent of NYSE activity, and the proportion is rising rapidly.

In the world of materials purchasing, success used to be a function of many small decisions. Auto companies, equipment makers, or packaged goods companies made thousands of decisions as they bought materials from hundreds of companies. In the past decade, however, materials purchasers have consolidated suppliers, moved toward multiregional or global purchasing, and sought long-term partnerships. The number of decisions has moved from thousands to hundreds, the number of suppliers from hundreds to dozens, the length of contracts from single-year to multiyear, the scope from regional to global. Fewer decisions, higher stakes, higher rewards, and much higher risks.

The Ford Mondeo program is an example. The winning suppliers were awarded not 200,000 units, but 700,000 (because of global purchasing). Great performance by the successful suppliers gives them an inside track on converting an annual contract into a multi-year (initially three-year) relationship. A 200,000-unit decision has evolved into a 2-million unit decision.

The same phenomenon is evident in the consumer packaged-goods industry. The rule used to be: 20 percent of your customers account for 80 percent of your volume. With the emergence of Wal-Mart, Target, and other distribution giants, the rule has shifted toward even greater concentration. Today, for companies as diverse as Kodak, P&G, and Campbell, the rule is: Your top *20 customers* (not 20 percent) account for 80 percent of your volume.[1] Getting the relationship right with these top 20 accounts means more to future value growth than doing everything perfectly for the other thousands of accounts in the system.

Responding to the pressure to make a few big moves may be uncomfortable, but it is not without precedent. The concentration of success and failure has been a basic fact of life in the aircraft industry for more than a decade. There are three producers of jet engines—GE, Pratt & Whitney, and Rolls-Royce. They deal with a small number of decision makers, a few aircraft assemblers and 20–30 major airlines. Each decision, each move, affects enormous amounts of value and must be made with great care. This industry is a microcosm of the kinds of stakes involved in the new Value Migration game.

The more right moves you make, the more margin for error. Sam Walton acknowledged the blunders that he made at Wal-Mart. Like any aggressive chess player (like Bobby Fisher or Gary Kasparov), Walton's style led to many errors, but reaped enormous gains.

Walton's is not the only style that works. Merck's Vagelos was more circumspect, much less freewheeling. But he saw with absolute clarity when major transitions required major moves. And he made them happen with thorough preparation and absolute conviction.

Gates at Microsoft and John Malone at TCI embody yet another style. Few people have spent as much time thinking about the future shape of the chessboard as they have. In a curious blend of attack and thoughtfulness, they've created industry patterns that have forced everybody else to react to their initiatives.

Grove's Intel is a classic example of the old IBM: great gamble for great gain.[2] On its face, Grove's shift from memory chips to microprocessors, and his initiative to cut development cycles in half were "bet the company" moves. However, a careful look underneath the surface (analysis of customer priorities, customer power, and ease of business design imitation) reveals that they were the only moves Intel could have made.

Can Good Moves Be Learned?

The best way to understand Value Migration moves is empirically. Look at patterns of extraordinary value growth, and track back to the moves that mattered. Fortunately, the history of Value Migration in the past decade has many examples of moves made by one competitor versus those *not* made by others with the same information. With the identical information, starting position, and well-defined and successful business design, radically different moves were made by highly talented companies. Analyzing the key moves made in past games makes it possible to explore why and how HP moved to low-cost distribution and Global Account Management while IBM and DEC did not (until four years later), why Ford shifted to a customer-driven development process while GM and Chrysler did not, why Merck focused on blockbuster development while the other pharmaceutical firms did not, why Nucor moved to flat-rolled steel and new raw materials while other minimills did not.

The critical lesson of these examples is that one player had the foresight and guts to make a more customer-grounded, economically on-target move, and was rewarded with enormous value growth.

There is a growing library of Value Migration games and moves from which to learn. Developing a strategic move is often a new skill for many business leaders. There are four ways to acquire it: trial and error, studying the grand masters' games, learning from errors, and performing low-cost, controlled experiments.

Trial and Error

Trial and error works in any field of learning. However, it takes a long time, and almost always involves losing a lot of value along the way. You can run out of value before mastering the skill. Today, trial and error is unnecessary. There is enough cumulative experience to learn from to make effective, value-creating moves.

Study Grand Masters' Games

There is a small cadre of individuals who have created more than $200 billion in value growth over the past two decades (see Figure 15-1). One can reverse-engineer their styles (attacking, cautious, and circumspect). More important, one can reverse-engineer their mind-sets that led, in each case, to a few key moves.

Several principles are revealed with reverse-engineering. The most important is customer-grounded thinking. Each of these players developed and was guided by a strategic perspective on the

..

FIGURE 15-1   THE GRAND MASTERS OF VALUE GROWTH

Player	Key Moves	Value Created 1980–1994 (in billions of dollars)
• Welch (GE)	• Divestitures • GECC • GE Plastics	$97
• Walton (Wal-Mart)	• Build low-cost model • Market selection	$56
• Vagelos (Merck)	• Blockbuster process • Account management • Medco	$38
• Gates (Microsoft)	• Own the standard • OS *and* applications • Developer marketing	$34[a]
• Petersen (Ford)	• Quality • Customer-driven process • Outsourcing	$24[b]
• Grove (Intel)	• DRAM to microprocessor • Six Quarter development lead	$24
• Malone (TCI)	• 16% share • Multisource revenue model • Partial ownership leverage • Foreign investment	$22

• Platt (HP)	• Quality leadership
	• PC laser printer
	• Workstations
	• New go-to-market mechanisms
	  - Low-cost channels
	  - Global account management
		$17

• Noorda (Novell)	• Distributors • Alliances	$6[c]
• Iverson (Nucor)	• Hot strip • Iron carbide	$4
• Kelleher (SWAir)	• Build low-cost model • Market selection	$2
Visionary leaders	*focused on making the right moves and*	*created enormous value.*

SOURCE: CDI Value Growth Database.
[a]1986 IPO
[b]Shareholder value
[c]1985 IPO

customer. Each had a strong sense of the customer's "I care about" and "I don't care about" zones.

So, for example, Vagelos understood that in the 1970s and 1980s the customer (at that time, the physician) cared about innovation and would switch to the first entrant in a new category. As a result, the late entrants would be rewarded with much lower market shares. Merck designed its business design to be first. It went so far as to withdraw resources from its own late entrants so it could better fund its early ones.

Welch understood that many of GE's manufactured products had long ago entered the customer's "I don't care" zone and that customers had too many product options. In contrast, the customer cared deeply about financing, the ability to acquire equipment without having to put the capital on its balance sheet. The options for meeting this need were fewer. Welch divested billions of dollars of manufacturing businesses and invested aggressively in GE Capital, escaping value decline on one hand and enjoying vigorous value growth on the other.

For Gates, there were two essential issues customers cared about. The first was ease of use, so Gates brought Apple-like ease of use to tens of millions of PC users. The second was applications, so Gates adopted a unique single-minded focus on marketing to software applications developers. Microsoft invested tens of millions of dollars on communications, marketing, and support of this extremely large (several thousand individuals and companies) and fragmented group because it was the volume and value of applications that created utility for the customer and therefore defined the value of the operating system in which they were written.

At Novell, Noorda's defining customer insight was simple (and missed or unimitated by the others). Network software is useless unless properly installed, tested, debugged, and serviced (exactly the same concept that defined IBM's mainframe business in the 1960s). Noorda developed a group of several thousand certified network installers who provided customers with the critical hassle-free component of their Novell Netware purchase.

The most extreme example of the customer-grounded principle was Donald Petersen at Ford. His oft repeated injunction was: "Unless we're customer-driven, our cars won't be either." Petersen applied this maxim literally. Starting with the breakthrough Taurus development effort in the early 1980s, he captured directly from customers the key information needed to make the car succeed. By the early 1990s, Ford had five of the ten best-selling cars in America.

Several characteristics of this group of grand masters are important to note. Clearly, they think harder and longer than their opponents. Clearly, they play a lot of games, and make a lot of moves in their heads, before committing their organizations to the real move. Clearly, their mind-set is to question constantly industry assumptions and institutional memory. Clearly, they have a great deal of experience in applying this critical skill.

To get a sense of the experience factor, and how it can be built, consider the following questions:

- How many value growth moves have I made (personally or as part of a team) in the past decade? (Imagine the whole process—picking up the piece, moving it across the board to the square you want, then raising your hand from the piece with a finality that implies "I am committed.")
- Write them down.
- What was the customer and economic rationale underlying the moves?
- Did the moves create value growth? How much? Why?
- How many value growth moves did I not think of?
- How many moves will I *need* to make in the next five years?
- What five moves will capture most of the value growth in my industry?

Learn from Errors

While studying the grand masters of value growth, there is a powerful tendency to focus on their winning moves and to overlook their errors. Sam Walton was refreshingly candid about his numerous mistakes:

> I don't know how the folks around our executive office see me, and I know they get frustrated with the way I make everything go back and forth on so many issues that come up. But I see myself as being a little more inclined than most of them to take

chances. Sometimes, of course, that leads me into mistakes. . . .

Our Hypermarts weren't disasters, but they were disappointments. They were marginally profitable stores, and they taught us what our next step should be in combining grocery and general merchandising. But I was mistaken in my vision of the potential the Hypermart held in this country. . . .

We conducted other similar, but less publicized, experiments that didn't work out so well either. Our dot Discount Drug concept grew to 25 stores before we decided it wasn't going to be profitable enough. And we tried one home improvement center called Save Mor which was also not a success. . . .

But when one of our experiments works, watch out. Take Sam's Clubs, for example. It was an experiment when we started it up in 1983, and now nine years later it's a $10 billion business with more than 217 stores and terrific growth potential.[3]

Gates has also had his share of errors. Despite the fundamental importance of networking software, Microsoft has not been able to make a dent in Novell's leading network position. Despite the enormous utility created by Notes for workgroups, Microsoft has been unable to match Lotus' success.

In studying past games, like those described in Part II, think about the major errors made. Understanding the wrong moves can be as helpful as internalizing the right ones. Major errors include wrong-direction moves (such as moving upscale when customers want low price), timing errors (making the right move four years late), and fail-to-cover moves (not imitating a competitor as soon as it discovers the right way to go).

Practice Applications Thinking

Even when the moves of others are well understood, there's another critical step in the learning process: applications thinking. To improve your strategic skills, ask: *Can* I use this move? If so, how can I translate it successfully to my own predicament?

For example, you can apply the logic of the Merck blockbuster process to other arenas. Consider publishing, entertainment, R&D, or other portfolio situations, where a small number of large successes far outweigh dozens of minor victories or mediocre product entries. Similarly, you can apply the Merck–Medco move to industrial situations characterized by declining product differentiation and the increasing importance of direct customer contact and control.

By applying the past moves to other industries, you learn how to apply their logic to your own. For example, you can frame the Iverson move to alternative raw materials by asking yourself: Did I have an obsolete business design five years ago? Or in the case of Grove's DRAM move: Do I have a dead business design? In the case of Petersen: Do I have a product design process that is customer informed, let alone customer driven? In the case of Gates ask: Can I create and control a standard? Where's the real value to the customer (the 3,000 applications)? Do I need a related business (operating system and applications) to recapture some of the value I've created for the customer?

Covering moves are among the most interesting to think about because they provide opportunities to look for relatively low-cost, low-risk moves. The following questions can help focus the learning process on potential value protection through covering moves, that is, fast imitation to avoid leaving an uncontested value space to a competitor. Should

- GM have covered Ford's Taurus move?
- Big Steel have covered the minimill move with a minimill network?
- Folgers have covered the Brothers' whole-bean and Starbucks' cafe moves?
- Apple have covered the Microsoft move (in applications developer marketing)?
- IBM have covered the Dell move?

And finally, ask yourself, "What move should I be covering today?"

Applications thinking translates successful designs into key questions and principles that can work for you. Without it, the precedents are merely interesting. With it, the precedents can play a direct role in helping your company achieve its next phase of value growth.

Begin the Game

It is a little frightening to play chess after a successful career of football and basketball. Business chess is a game that is as demanding as the others, but in very different ways. It is not physical stamina, but stamina of thought. It is not just transactional concentration, but constant shuttling between a focus on the current move and imagining the next several moves out. It is an unrelenting exercise of matching patterns on the current game board to the countless patterns in your mind.

Although it is frightening, business chess is also exhilarating, fun to learn, and fun to play. And it is easily learned, more so today than 10 or 20 years ago. The games the grand masters have played, the moves they have made, the errors they have committed (and avoided) are the new curriculum, the new syllabus for business strategy. Learning what they have done, and how, and why, is the highest-return investment you can make.

Begin by asking: What five moves will capture most of my industry's value growth? Give yourself a couple of months to analyze and assimilate the grand masters' key moves. Then come back and determine the five (or fewer) critical moves for your company.

Once the moves have been designed, the next step is to develop a business design and fast-track its implementation, so you can capture the value of the moves before the next cycle of Value Migration begins.

This focus will require all the tools described in this book. It will test the limits of your organization's fact and knowledge bases, and its ability to imagine the scenarios that will confront it.

Playing business chess is an acquired skill. Your proficiency will improve with time and practice. But rest assured, it is *the* skill that will help your organization get ahead of the Value Migration curve, and enjoy the considerable benefits of industry leadership (even as you worry about when value will migrate again).

Notes

Chapter 1

1. Market value and most other financial data used throughout this book are derived from Corporate Decisions, Inc.'s Value Growth Database. This proprietary database is based on information compiled by Compustat, a service provided by Standard & Poor's, a division of McGraw-Hill, and supplied to Corporate Decisions, Inc., on a contractual basis. Information from Compustat is supplemented and adjusted to reflect variations in financial reporting that could distort the financial performance of a company. The data used throughout the text and exhibits are expressed in real (inflation adjusted) dollars unless otherwise noted.

2. In large companies there is often a predominant business design that drives the value of the entire company. In companies with many large-scale business designs, isolating the financial measures associated with each business design is important. In many of the examples used in this book, we have isolated the relevant business design to make the most relevant comparison. For example, the market value of USX has been disaggregated into U.S. Steel and Marathon Oil.

3. Revenue is used to measure the scale of a business. In some industries (financial services, for example), other measures of scale, such as assets or capital employed, have proved more appropriate. For most industries, however, revenue is the most useful approximation of a company's scale. For that reason, we will use it throughout.

4. IBM was ranked number one in *Fortune* magazine's annual poll of America's most admired companies in 1983, 1984, 1985, and 1986.

5. Author's interview with senior pharmaceutical executive, summer 1994.

6. A study by W. G. Chase and H. A. Simon demonstrated the power of pattern recognition in chess. They created two chess boards, one of a game in progress and one with the pieces arranged at random. They showed the boards to two groups, novices and chess masters. The novices could see no difference between the boards, but the masters recognized the patterns of the "in-progress" board and the chaos of the random board. Recognizing the in-progress board

allowed them to recount how the game had unfolded and how it would progress. (W. G. Chase and H. A. Simon, "Perception in Chess," *Cognitive Psychology* 17 [1973]: 391–416.)

Chapter 2

1. MIT Commission on Industrial Productivity working paper, "The Transformation of the U.S. Chemicals Industry," vol. 1 (Cambridge, Mass.: MIT, 1989). The data came from Michael J. Bennett, "Chemicals: An industry sheds its smokestack image," *Technology Review* (July 1987): 36.
2. Neil Gross and Peter Coy, "The Technology Paradox," *Business Week,* March 6, 1995, 76–81.
3. Ratio as of December 1994. For the years 1992 and 1993, Southwest's market value/revenue ratio exceeded 2.0. Even with recent price wars that have driven down Southwest's market value, its business design remains considerably more powerful than United's. See Chapter 6 for a more thorough discussion of Value Migration in the airline industry.
4. Shigeo Shingo, *Study of Toyota Production System* (Tokyo: Japan Management Association, 1981).
5. Ibid.
6. John F. Love, *McDonald's: Behind the Arches* (New York: Bantam Books, 1986).
7. Ibid., 20.

Chapter 3

1. The ratio of market value to revenue is a simple estimation of the power of a business design. The exact values that define the three phases will vary, based on the economic structure of an industry. The values that we use as examples (1.0 and 2.0) have proven to be useful thresholds in numerous industries. In some industries with structurally low margins (e.g., grocery), the normative values for inflow, stability, and outflow may differ.
2. For example, EDS has been separable from General Motors because stockholders have been able to purchase shares of this "subsidiary" company independently.

Chapter 5

1. Total estimated market value is based on revenues and average value multiples for integrated mills.
2. Dow Chemical USA President David Rooke as quoted in "Materials 1982: A Modern Plastics Special Report," *Modern Plastics,* January 1982, 61.

3. Peter Nulty, "Quanex: The Less-Is-More Strategy," *Fortune,* December 2, 1991, 102, 106.

4. Peter Marcus, steel industry analyst, PaineWebber & Co.

Chapter 6

1. Elizabeth Bailey, David Graham, and Daniel Kaplan, *Deregulating the Airlines* (Cambridge, Mass.: MIT Press, 1985).

2. Scott McShan and Robert Windle, "The Implications of Hub and Spoke Routing for Airline Costs and Competitiveness," *Logistics and Transportation Review,* vol 25. no. 3, 1990: 209.

3. Barbara Pederson and James Glab, *Rapid Descent: Deregulation and the Shakeout in the Airlines* (New York: Simon & Schuster, 1994).

4. Stephen Solomon, "The Bully of the Skies Cries Uncle," *New York Times Magazine,* September 5, 1993.

5. Ibid.

Chapter 8

1. Jane Harvey, "Gourmet Coffees Perk Up in Popularity," *USA Today,* July 6, 1992, 4D.

2. Total market value estimated using revenues and industry average market value multiples.

3. Dori Jones Yang, "The Starbucks Enterprise Shifts into Warp Speed," *Business Week,* October 24, 1994, 76.

Chapter 9

1. Stratford Sherman, "How Intel Makes Spending Pay Off," *Fortune,* February 22, 1993, 58–60.

2. Andrew S. Rappaport and Shmuel Halevi, "The Computerless Computer Company," *Harvard Business Review* (July–August 1991): 69–80.

Chapter 10

1. B. Shapiro, S. Doyle, and A. Slywotzky, "Strategic Sales Management: A Boardroom Issue," #9-595-018 (Boston: Harvard Business School, 1994).

2. "Store Wars" (Food Industry Survey), *The Economist,* December 4, 1993, 5–7.

3. "The Schwab Revolution," *Business Week,* December 19, 1994, 89.

4. Leslie Wayne, "The Next Giant in Mutual Funds?" *New York Times,* March 20, 1994, Section 3.

5. Ibid.

6. Ibid.

7. Ibid.
8. AgrEvo press conference, Frankfurt, December 1994.

Chapter 11

1. J. B. Quinn and F. G. Hilmer, "Strategic Outsourcing," *Sloan Management Review* (June 1994): 43
2. D. M. Togut, "Data Processing Outsourcing Market: Industry Report" (New York: The First Boston Corporation, April 29, 1992).
3. Ibid., 4.
4. Ibid., 11.

Chapter 13

1. All Grove quotes are from Stratford Sherman, "How Intel Makes Spending Pay Off," *Fortune*, February 22, 1993, 56–61.
2. Thomas E. Ricks, "Warning Shot: How Wars Are Fought Will Change Radically, Pentagon Planner Says," *The Wall Street Journal*, July 15, 1994, 1.
3. Christopher Lorenz, "No Less Than Rebirth—Companies Must Do More Than Restructure," *The Financial Times*, October 4, 1993, 10.
4. All DeSimone quotes are from Mike Meyers, "3M Ups Ante for New Products, Sales, Productivity," *Star Tribune*, April 15, 1993, 1D.
5. Lawrence Minard and Carol E. Curtis, "Exxon, Move Over," *Forbes*, November 24, 1980, 129.
6. Ibid.
7. Pierre Wack, "Scenario Planning: Uncharted Waters Ahead," *Harvard Business Review* (September–October 1985): 73–89.
8. Milton Moscovitz, *The Global Marketplace*, quoted in Peter Senge, *The Fifth Discipline* (New York: Doubleday, 1990).
9. Paul J. H. Shoemaker and Cornelius A. J. M. van der Heijden, "Integrating Scenarios into Strategic Planning at Royal Dutch Shell," *Planning Review*, May 1992, 41.

Chapter 15

1. B. Shapiro, S. Doyle, and A. Slywotzky, "Strategic Sales Management: A Boardroom Issue," #9-595-018 (Boston: Harvard Business School, 1994), 5.
2. B. Shapiro, R. Tedlow, and A. Slywotzky, "Why Great Companies Go Wrong," *New York Times*, November 6, 1994.
3. Sam Walton with John Huey, *Made in America, My Story* (New York: Doubleday, 1992), 253–255.

Index

About the Author

Adrian J. Slywotzky is a founding partner of Corporate Decisions, Inc. of Boston, Massachusetts, a strategy consulting firm that focuses on value growth. Since 1979, he has consulted in a broad range of industries, including information services, financial services, consumer products, health care, pharmaceuticals, computer hardware and software, specialty chemicals, electronic materials, steel, broadcasting, and retailing.

Mr. Slywotzky is a frequent speaker on Value Migration and Strategic Customer Investment, two methodologies for achieving maximum returns on investment through a superior understanding of changing customer priorities and values. He is the co-author of "Leveraging to Beat the Odds: The New Marketing Mindset," published in the *Harvard Business Review.* He holds degrees from Harvard College, Harvard Law School, and Harvard Business School.